KENMORE MICROWAVE COOKING

SPACEMASTER

A Benjamin Company Book

Associate Publishers: Robert C. Dougherty, Beth Politi
Editor: Julie Hogan
Production Assistants: Virginia Schomp, Susan Jablonski, Pat Drew, Greta Ebel
Chief Home Economists: Betty Sullivan, Thelma Pressman
Consulting Home Economists: Dora Jonassen, Lynn Haven, Marie Schmidt, Alice Stoltzner, Roxanne McCall
Project Manager: Jim Wilson
Art & Design: Thomas C. Brecklin
Typography: A-Line, Milwaukee
Photography: Walter Storck
Cover Photography: Teri Sandison; also pages 69, 87, 100, 120, 130, 164, 167, 169, 171, 189

USER INSTRUCTIONS

PRECAUTIONS TO AVOID POSSIBLE EXPOSURE TO EXCESSIVE MICROWAVE ENERGY

(a) DO NOT ATTEMPT to operate this oven with the door open since open-door operation can result in harmful exposure to microwave energy. It is important not to defeat or tamper with the safety interlocks.

(b) DO NOT PLACE any object between the oven front face and the door or allow soil or cleaner residue to accumulate on sealing surfaces.

(c) DO NOT OPERATE the oven if it is damaged. It is particularly important that the oven door closes properly and that there is no damage to the:
  (1) DOOR (bent)
  (2) HINGES AND LATCHES (broken or loosened)
  (3) DOOR SEALS AND SEALING SURFACES

(d) THE OVEN SHOULD NOT BE ADJUSTED OR REPAIRED BY ANYONE EXCEPT PROPERLY QUALIFIED SERVICE PERSONNEL.

Library of Congress Catalog Card Number: 78-71995
ISBN: 0-87502-119-0
Published by The Benjamin Company, Inc.
One Westchester Plaza
Elmsford, New York 10523
Printed in Japan
0 9 8 7 6 5 4 3 2 1

CONTENTS

What's It All About?

Welcome to the exciting world of *automatic* microwave cooking! You are joining the countless thousands of people who have discovered the joys of the microwave oven and have delighted in this fast, easy, and efficient method of cooking. In addition, you have an important plus: here, for the first time, is a microwave oven that has an entire cookbook preset in its computer memory for you. You do not need to calculate the cooking times for any of the 300 recipes in this cookbook.

But, as with any new appliance, before you start using it you should take time to read the instructions carefully. The illustrated introductory chapters present an intensive cooking school in book form. Like any comprehensive conventional cookbook, this book tries to leave nothing to chance, so that cooking in the microwave oven will be as easy as it looks, and is. Take a few minutes to familiarize yourself with the principles and techniques of the oven and of microwave cooking. Then try the wonderful recipes in the chapters that follow. You'll soon find you will want to use the microwave oven for just about all of your cooking needs.

To install your oven, follow the instructions in your Use & Care Manual. The oven operates on standard 110-120v household current and does not require an expert to ready it for regular use.

The Kenmore Spacemaster Auto Recipe 300 Microwave Oven requires little maintenance. Unlike a conventional oven which generates heat in the oven cavity, there is no heat in the microwave cavity. As a result, food and grease do not become baked onto the oven's surfaces. Just a simple wiping is all you need to keep the oven clean. Again, follow your Use & Care Manual's directions for the few simple cleaning steps.

Keep the door and gasket free of food buildup to maintain a tight seal. Now, let's find out how the microwave oven works.

How Does It Work?

In conventional cooking with gas or electricity, food on top of the stove cooks by heat applied to the bottom of the pan, and in the oven by hot air which surrounds the food. In microwave cooking, microwaves travel directly to the food, without heating the oven. Inside the top of the microwave oven is a magnetron vacuum tube, which converts ordinary electrical energy into high-frequency microwaves, just like radio and television waves. A fan-like device called a stirrer helps to distribute the microwaves evenly throughout the oven. Microwaves are waves of energy, not heat. They are either reflected, passed through, or absorbed, depending upon the material contacted. For example, metal reflects microwaves; glass, pottery, paper, and most plastics allow the waves to pass through; and, finally, food absorbs microwaves. Very simply then, the absorbed microwave energy causes the food molecules to vibrate rapidly against each other, inducing friction, which in turn produces the heat that cooks the food. This is somewhat similar to the way heat is generated when you rub your hands together. The waves penetrate the food, and cooking begins from the exterior. The interior then cooks by conduction. The prime rib photo on page 7 illustrates this principle. This process produces the much-appreciated cooking speed of the microwave oven. Because the cooking containers used in the microwave oven do not absorb microwave energy, they do not become hot. The microwaves pass through the containers directly into the food. However, the containers may absorb heat from the food itself, so you will occasionally need to use potholders. The see-through panel in the microwave oven door is made of a specially-prepared material that contains a metal screen. The metal screen reflects the microwaves, yet enables you to observe the food as it cooks. The waves cannot penetrate this screen. Opening the microwave oven door turns the unit off automatically, so you can stir, turn, or check doneness with ease. And you don't have to face that blast of hot air you expect when opening a conventional oven.

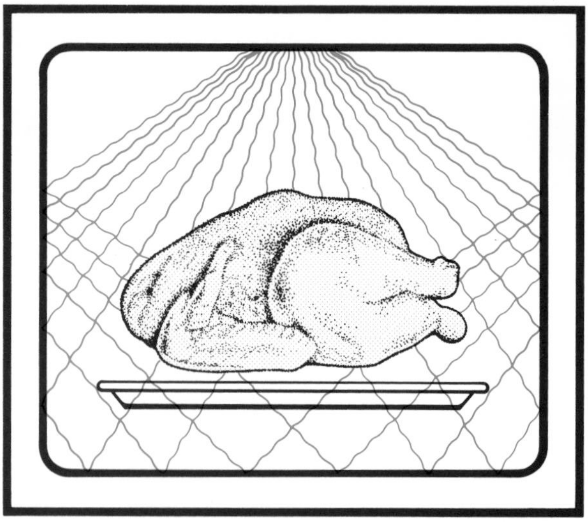

Microwaves bounce off oven walls and are absorbed by food. The air in the oven remains cool.

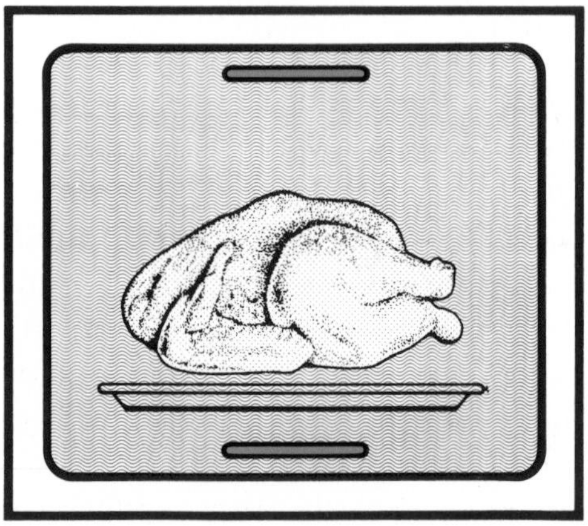

Conventional ovens cook by hot air.

Now that you've learned something about how the microwave oven works, let's take a look at all the wonderful things you can do with it.

Look What You Can Do!

You can cook just about anything in the microwave oven, but some foods are so especially good done this way that we want to show several of them to you. The recipes for all the dishes illustrated here are included in the book. You'll find that the microwave oven not only cooks food superbly from scratch, but also reheats and defrosts with excellent results. Let's take a look.

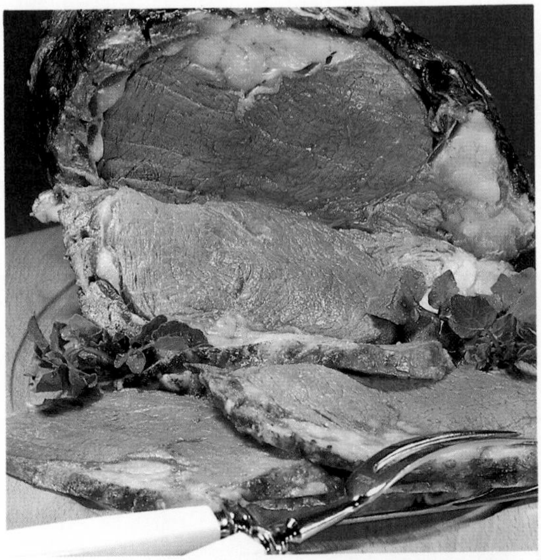

□ *Roast beef* is juicy and rare, with less shrinkage than in the conventional oven. □ You can enjoy all kinds of *vegetables* at their wholesome best. Their true flavor and color are preserved. Potatoes are fluffy, cauliflower crisp, and broccoli the beautiful green it was born with. □ You'll want *scrambled eggs* for breakfast, lunch, and supper when you've tried them microwave-style. They're fluffier than in conventional cooking, and more pleasing to the eye as well as the palate. □ You'll think positively about *leftovers* after you try them reheated in the microwave. Food will have that just-cooked taste and look.

□ Cook luscious *chocolate cakes,* so tantalizingly moist, rich, and high. □ *Fruit,* such as this baked apple, can be prepared without water. Like vegetables, fruit retains that just-picked color and flavor. □ *Sauces* are a blessing to cook in the microwave oven making constant stirring a thing of the past. Just imagine the convenience of mixing, cooking, and serving all in the same container. Hollandaise sauce is smooth with just a few stirrings. □ The microwave can't be beaten for *heating rolls and bread* so quickly they don't have a chance to be anything but perfect. And you can cook them right in the serving basket as long as there are no metal fasteners or trim. □ *Bacon* cooked in the microwave is incomparable — flat and crisp — and one slice takes less than a minute to

cook. It can be placed on a micro-proof bacon rack or between paper toweling. □ *Candy* is a particular favorite with microwave cooks because it's as easy as pie. Chocolate and caramelized mixtures won't require constant stirring. Try this white chocolate Almond Bark or the party mints and see for yourself. □ *Hot appetizers* are ready as needed, cooking quickly, with no mess and no pan to clean. Just cook them directly on paper plates or in your serving dish. Rumaki (bacon-wrapped chicken livers and water chestnuts) and mushrooms make delectable hors d'oeuvres. □ All kinds of *casseroles* cook without sticking to the dish in the microwave oven and they are still at their flavorful best later, thanks to just a few minutes of microwave reheating.

☐ Explore the pleasures of cooking *seafood* in your microwave oven. Fish fillets and steaks are moist and tender, their natural juices enhancing their delicate flavor. ☐ And for a pick-me-up that's really quick, there's no equal to a *bowl of soup,* a cup of coffee, or a mug of cocoa served directly from the oven. ☐ *Melt chocolate* and *soften butter or cream cheese* in seconds and save the time and the mess of double boilers and burned pans.

Now that you've had a sampling of what this appliance can do, let's take a look at what you need to know in order to start cooking.

Here's What You Need to Know

In this chapter you will find everything you need to know to make microwave cooking easy, efficient, and pleasurable. Once you know the principles, the techniques will become second nature. Read this basic information with its accompanying illustrations carefully. As you begin to use the oven, you can always refer back to this handy guide whenever a question arises about a cooking term or method. Here you will learn why some foods cook faster than others, what you should know about timing and temperature, which cooking utensils are appropriate, how to cook most efficiently, and much more.

Because of the unique qualities of microwave energy, microwave cooking uses certain terms and methods that are different from those of conventional cooking. For example, in microwave cooking, many foods complete cooking during *standing time,* either in the oven or after being removed from the oven.

You may wonder why you need to know this information when 300 recipes have been preset for you. Fair question. If you follow the preset recipes *exactly,* you will be pleased with the results. But chances are you will frequently find that your available ingredients vary somewhat from the preset recipe. Just a few ounces difference in a piece of meat, for example, can significantly change microwave cooking time. Of course, you'll also need to know this data to use recipes from magazines and to adapt for personal tastes (do any two people like their scrambled eggs exactly alike?). In any event, study now can eliminate frustration later. Let's go to school.

ABOUT TIMING

Time is an important element in microwave cooking. But isn't that statement true for all cooking? You, the cook, have to be the judge as you consider your family's preferences and use your own instincts. Chances are, you can tell if a chicken is done simply by looking at it. You might even scoff at the timing chart given on a package because you know that a particular food always seems to need more or less time. It is important to know that even though the microwave oven is a superb product of computer technology, it is no more or less precise than any other cooking system. Nevertheless, because of the speed with which most foods are cooked, timing is more crucial in microwave cooking than in conventional cooking. One minute can cause a significant difference. When you consider that a cooking task requiring one hour in a conventional oven generally needs only one-quarter of that time in a microwave oven, you can understand why microwave cooking requires a somewhat different approach to timing. Where an extra minute in conventional cooking is seldom critical, in microwave cooking one minute can be the difference between overcooked or undercooked food. Cooking times for preset recipes are precise, of course. If you have altered the ingredients or have a personal doneness preference, be sure to check the food as it cooks. As you become familiar with your oven, you will recognize when to begin to check for doneness. Remember that it is better to undercook and add more cooking time than to overcook — then it's too late.

Cooking times could always be precise if a way could be found to guarantee that all foods would be exactly the same each time we cook them, and if the electric company would guarantee not to alter our power (there are frequent changes in the voltage levels reaching our homes). The fact is that one potato or one steak varies from another in density, moisture or fat content, shape, weight, and temperature. This is true of all food. The cook must be ready to adjust to the changes, to be flexible and observant. This discussion really comes down to the fact that you, not the microwave oven, are the cook. The oven can't make judgments, so you must. This applies even when you are using one of the 300 preset recipes. They have all been meticulously kitchen tested by expert home economists. You will find that the timing will very rarely need to be altered. As in all fine cooking, however, microwave cooking needs and benefits from your personal touch. The preset timing is presented in italics with each recipe.

CHARACTERISTICS THAT AFFECT TIMING

Many characteristics of food, such as quantity, shape, density, and starting temperature affect timing. Understanding them will help you become a skilled and successful microwave cook.

Quantity

The larger the volume of food there is, the more time is needed to cook it. One ear of corn in the husk cooks in about 3 minutes; 3 ears may cook in 8 minutes. Therefore, if the quantity in a recipe is changed, an adjustment in timing is necessary. Many of the preset recipes have such timing changes automatically calculated for you. They are identified with this symbol ⊞ throughout the book. Consult the Use & Care Manual for details.

When changing the quantity of a recipe on your own, follow this general rule: When doubling a recipe, increase the cooking time approximately 50 percent. When cutting a recipe in half, reduce the time by approximately 40 percent.

Shape and Size

Thin food cooks faster than thick food; thin sections faster than thick. Small pieces also cook faster than large pieces. For even cooking, place thick pieces toward the outside of the dish, since the outside areas cook faster than the inside areas. For best results, try to cook pieces of similar size and shape together.

Height

As in conventional cooking, areas that are closer to the energy source cook faster. In most microwave ovens, the energy source is at the top of the oven. Food close to the top may require shielding with pieces of aluminum foil or turning for even cooking.

Density

Dense foods, like potatoes, roast beef, and carrots, take longer to cook than porous foods, such as cakes, ground beef, and apples, because it takes the microwaves longer to penetrate the denser texture. For example, a 2-pound roast will take longer than a 2-pound meat loaf.

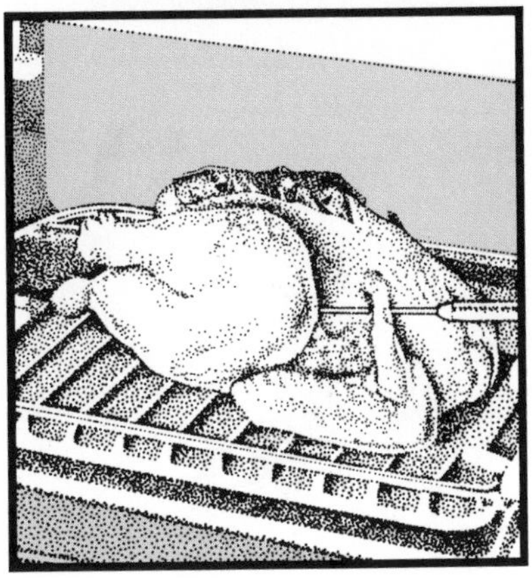

The density of food affects cooking time (above). Irregularly-shaped food requires special arrangement (above left). Food areas close to the energy source are turned or shielded during cooking (left).

Moisture Content

Moist food cooks faster than dry food because microwave energy is easily absorbed by the moisture within the food. For example, 1 cup of sliced zucchini will cook faster than 1 cup of carrots because of the high water content in the zucchini. In fact, the amount of free moisture within a food helps determine how rapidly it cooks.

Sugar and Fat Content

Food high in sugar and fat heats quicker than items low in these ingredients, because microwave energy is attracted by sugar and fat. For example, the fruit or cheese filling of a sweet roll will heat faster than the roll itself and will be hotter, since sugar and fat reach higher temperatures than food low in sugar or fat content.

Moist food cooks faster than dry (left). Frozen food takes longer to cook than canned (center). A sweet roll heats a bit faster than a dininer roll (right).

Delicate Ingredients

This term is used to refer to food that cooks so quickly in the microwave oven that it can overcook — toughening, separating, or curdling. For example, mayonnaise, cheese, eggs, cream, dairy sour cream, etc. Other food may "pop," such as snails, oysters, and chicken livers. For this reason, a lower power setting is often recommended for proper cooking. However, when these ingredients are mixed with other food, as in a casserole, stew, or soup, you may use a higher power setting, because volume automatically slows down the cooking.

Starting Temperature

As in conventional cooking, the temperature at which food is placed in the microwave oven affects the length of cooking time. More time is needed to cook food just out of the refrigerator than food at room temperature. For example, it takes longer to heat frozen green beans than canned green beans. Also, hot tap water will start boiling sooner than cold. Recipes in this book assume that food is at its normal storage temperature.

ABOUT UTENSILS

A wide variety of cookware and cooking implements can be used in the microwave oven. In order to indicate an item made of material that is safe and recommended for microwave cooking, we have created a new term, *microproof.* The Materials Checklist and Microproof Utensils Chart on the following pages will aid you in selecting the appropriate microproof utensil. Except for metal, most materials are microproof for at least a limited amount of cooking time. But unless specifically approved, items made of metal, even partially, are never to be used in the microwave oven, because they reflect microwaves, preventing them from passing through the cooking utensil into the food. In addition, metal that touches the oven sides will cause sparks, a static charge, known as arcing. Arcing is not harmful to you, though it will deface the oven. Metal twist ties or dishes or cups with gold or silver trim should not be used. See the Materials Checklist for those approved types of metal, such as pieces of aluminum foil, used as a shield over certain areas of food to prevent overcooking, or metal clips attached to frozen turkey.

When selecting a new piece of cookware, first check the manufacturer's directions. Also review the Materials Checklist and the Guide to Microproof Cookware. If you are still in doubt, try this test: Pour a cup of water into an ovenproof glass measure and place in the oven next to the container or dish to be tested. Cook on HI for 1 minute. If the new dish feels hot, don't use it — it is absorbing microwave energy. If it feels warm, the dish may only be used for warming food. If it remains at room temperature, it is *microproof.*

The rapid growth of microwave cooking has created many new products for use in the microwave oven. Among these are microproof replacements for cookware formerly available only in metal. You'll find a wide variety at your store — cake, bundt, and muffin pans, roasting racks, etc. When you add these to traditional microproof cookware and the incredible array of microproof plastic and paper products, you'll find that microwave cooking enables you to select from many more kinds of cookware than available for conventional cooking.

Selecting Containers

Containers should accommodate the food being cooked. Whenever possible use round or oval dishes, so that the microwaves are absorbed evenly into the food. Square corners in cookware receive more concentration of energy than the rest of the dish, so the food in the corners tends to overcook. Some cake and loaf recipes call for ring molds or bundt pans to facilitate more even cooking. This is because the center area in a round or oval dish generally cooks more slowly than the outside. Round cookware with a small glass inserted open end up in the center works just as well to eliminate undercooked centers. When a particular size or

Unique roasting racks, browning dishes, and other cookware have been developed for microwave use (top left). Familiar items, such as molds and muffin pans, are now available in microproof materials (top right). A wide variety of glass, ceramic, and wood items are perfect for microwave use (above right). All kinds of paper products make microwave cooking especially easy (above left). Many plastics are safe for microwave use (left).

shape of container is specified in a recipe, it should be used. Varying the container size or shape may change cooking time. A 2-quart casserole called for in a recipe refers to a bowl-shaped cooking utensil. A 12×8-inch or a 9-inch round baking dish refers to a shallow cooking dish. In the case of puddings, sauces, and candies, large containers are specified to prevent the liquids, especially milk-based ones, from boiling over. For best results, try to use the dish cited in the recipe.

Materials Checklist

☐ CHINA, POTTERY: Ideal for microwave use. However, if they have metallic trim or glaze, they are not microproof and should not be used.

☐ GLASS: An excellent microwave cooking material. Especially useful for baking pies to check doneness of pie shells through the bottom. Since ovenproof glass is always safe, "microproof" is not mentioned in any recipe where a glass item is specified.

☐ METALS: *Not* suitable except as follows:

Small strips of aluminum foil can be used to cover areas on large pieces of meat or poultry that defrost or cook more rapidly than the rest of the piece — for example, a roast with jagged areas or thin ends, or the wing or breast bone of poultry. This method is known as shielding in microwave cooking.

Shallow aluminum frozen TV dinner trays with foil covers removed can be heated, provided that the trays do not exceed 3/4-inch depth. (However, TV dinners heat much faster if you "pop" the blocks of food out and arrange them on microproof dinner plates.)

Frozen poultry containing metal clamps may be defrosted in the microwave oven without removing the clamps. Remove the clamps after defrosting.

Trays or any foil or metal item must be at least 1 inch from oven walls.

☐ PAPER: Approved for short-term cooking and for reheating at low settings. These must not be foil-lined. Extended use may cause the paper to burn. Waxed paper is a suitable covering.

☐ PLASTICS: A wide variety of plastic cookware is available for microwave use. Use only if labeled for microwave use by the manufacturer. Select plastic wrap that is specifically recommended for use in the microwave oven.

☐ PLASTIC COOKING POUCHES: Can be used. Slit the pouch so steam can escape.

☐ STRAW AND WOOD: Can be used for quick warming. Be certain no metal is used on the straw or wood items.

Browning Dish

A browning dish is used to sear, grill, fry, or brown food. It is made to absorb microwave energy when the dish is preheated empty. A special coating on the bottom of the dish becomes very hot when preheated in the microwave oven. There are a variety of dishes available. Follow the manufacturer's instructions for care and use and for the length of time to preheat the dish.

After the dish is preheated, vegetable oil or butter may be added to enhance the browning and prevent food from sticking. After the food is placed on the preheated browning dish, the dish is returned to the oven, where the microwaves cook the interior of the food while the hot surface of the dish browns the exterior. The food is then turned over to brown the other side. When cooking hamburger or moist foods, you may wish to pour off accumulated juices before turning the food over. The longer you wait to turn the food the less browning occurs, since the dish cools off rapidly. You may need to drain the dish, wipe it out, and preheat it again. In doubling a recipe, such as fried chicken, wipe out the browning dish after the first batch, reheat the empty dish, and repeat the procedure. Since the browning dish becomes very hot, be sure to use potholders when you are handling it.

Used as a grill, the browning dish speeds cooking time. However, if you wish to use the dish to brown certain foods prior to adding them to a recipe, your recipe time will remain about the same. Some foods, such as eggs or sandwiches, require less heat for browning than other foods, such as chicken or meats.

Bottom Glass Tray

The bottom glass tray in the microwave oven is the primary cooking level. It is made of glass because microwaves penetrate glass to cook the bottom of the food. Glass is also easy to clean. Never operate the oven without the bottom tray in place.

Middle Metal Rack

The removable middle metal rack of your oven is used mainly in whole-meal cooking or when certain double quantities are cooked. The rack is made of specially-engineered metal and is safe for the microwave oven. The microwaves bounce off the rack and are absorbed by the food. Generally, for more even and faster cooking, it is best to cook a few batches one after another rather than on two levels at the same time. The rack should be removed from the oven when not in use.

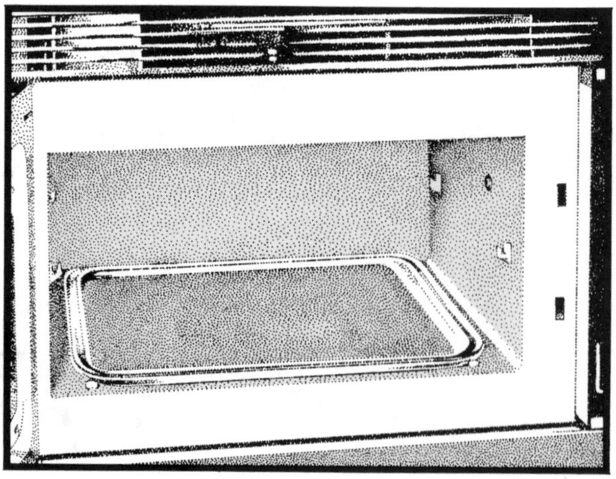

The bottom glass tray is the primary cooking level. The middle metal rack is used for whole meal cooking.

A GUIDE TO MICROPROOF COOKWARE

ITEM	GOOD USE	GENERAL NOTES
China plates, cups	Heating dinners and drinks.	No metal trim.
Cooking pouches (plastic)	Cooking meat, vegetables, rice, other frozen food.	Slit pouch so steam can escape.
Corelle®	Heating dinners, soups, drinks.	Closed-handle cups should not be used.
Corning Ware® or Pyrex casseroles	Cooking main dishes, vegetables, desserts.	No metal trim.
Microwave browning dishes or grills	Searing, grilling, and frying small meat items; grilling sandwiches; frying eggs.	These utensils are specially made to absorb microwaves and preheat to high temperatures. They brown food that otherwise would not brown in a microwave oven.
Microwave roasting racks	Cooking roasts and chickens, squash and potatoes.	Special racks are available for cooking bacon.
Oven film and cooking bags	Cooking roasts or stews.	Substitute string for metal twist ties. Bag itself will not cause tenderizing. Do not use film with foil edges.
Paper plates, cups, napkins	Heating hot dogs, drinks, rolls, appetizers, sandwiches.	Absorbs moisture from baked goods and freshens them. Paper plates and cups with wax coatings should not be used.
Plastic wrap	Covering dishes.	Fold back edge to ventilate, allowing steam to escape.
Pottery and earthenware plates, mugs, etc.	Heating dinners, soups, drinks.	Some pottery has a metallic glaze. To check, use dish test (page 15).
Soft plastics, sherbet cartons	Reheating leftovers.	Used for very short reheating periods.
Thermometers	Measuring temperature of meat, poultry, and candy.	Use only approved microproof meat or candy thermometer in microwave oven. Microwave temperature probe is available with oven (page 26).
TV dinner trays (aluminum)	Frozen dinners or homemade dinners.	No deeper than ¾ inch. Food will receive heat from top surface only. Foil covering food must be removed.
Waxed paper	Covering casseroles. Use as a tent.	Prevents splattering. Helps contain heat where a tight seal is not required. Food temperature may cause some melting.
Wooden spoons, wooden skewers, straw baskets	Stirring puddings and sauces; for shish kabobs, appetizers, warming breads.	Can withstand microwaves for short cooking periods. Be sure no metal fittings on wood or straw.

ABOUT METHODS

The evenness and speed of microwave cooking are affected not only by the characteristics of the food itself, but also by certain methods, described below. Some of these techniques are used in conventional cooking as well, but they have a particular application in microwave cooking because of the special qualities of microwave energy. Many other important variables that influence cooking, defrosting, and reheating in the microwave oven are included here. Becoming familiar with these terms and methods will make microwave cooking easy and successful.

Arrangement

The way food is arranged in the oven and in the dish enhances even cooking and speeds in defrosting, heating, and cooking foods. The microwaves penetrate the outer portion of food first; therefore, foods should be arranged so that the denser, thicker areas are near the edge, and the thinner, more porous areas are near the center. For example, when cooking broccoli, split the heavy stalks to expose more area, then overlap with flowerets; or you can alternate flowerets of cauliflower with broccoli for an attractive dish. This gives even density to the food and provides even cooking.

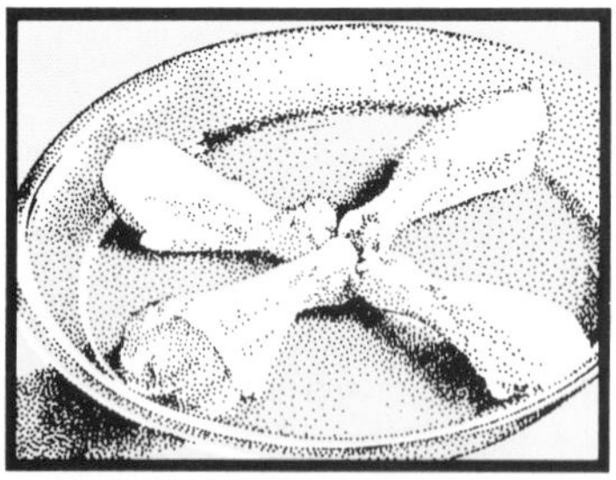

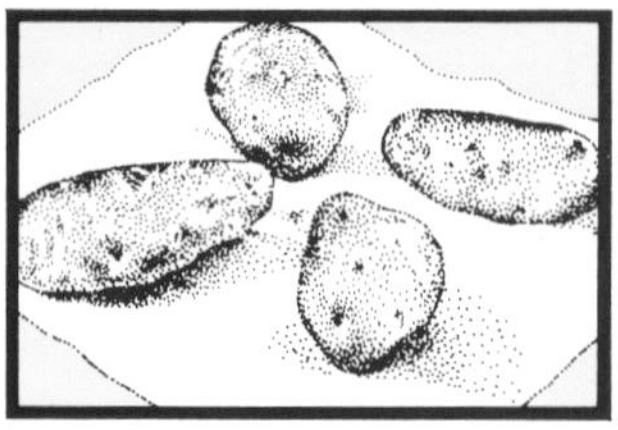

Microwave arrangement methods create unique cook-and-serve opportunities. The cauliflower and broccoli dish, for example, is cooked, covered, for 9 minutes on HI with ¼ cup water.

Place shrimp in a ring with the tails toward the center. Chicken legs should be arranged like the spokes of a wheel, with the bony end toward the center. Items like cupcakes and potatoes should be arranged in a circle, rather than in rows.

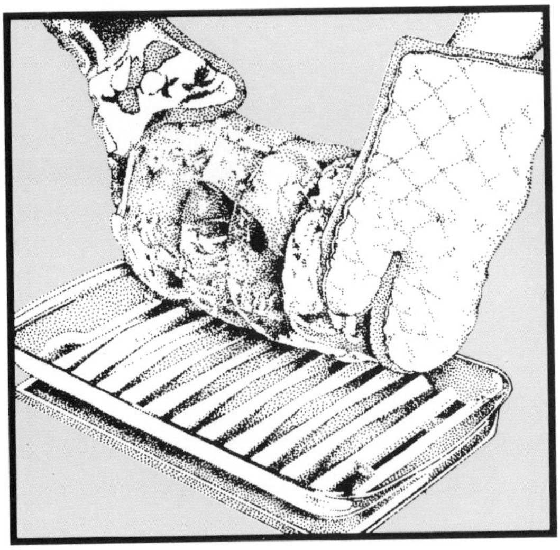

Turning Over

As in conventional cooking, some foods, such as large roasts, whole poultry, a ham, or hamburgers, may require turning over to brown each side and to promote even heating. Any food seared on the browning dish should be turned over. During the defrosting process in the microwave oven, it is often necessary to turn the food.

Rearranging

Sometimes food that cannot be stirred needs repositioning in the cooking utensil to allow even heating throughout. When rearranging food, move the center food to the outside of the dish and the outer food toward the center. Some poultry and beef recipes profit from rearranging halfway through the cooking time.

Stirring

Less stirring is required in microwave cooking than in conventional cooking. When necessary, stir from the outside to the center, since the outside heats faster than the center portion. Stirring blends the flavors and promotes even heating. Stir only as directed in the recipes. Constant stirring is never required in microwave cooking.

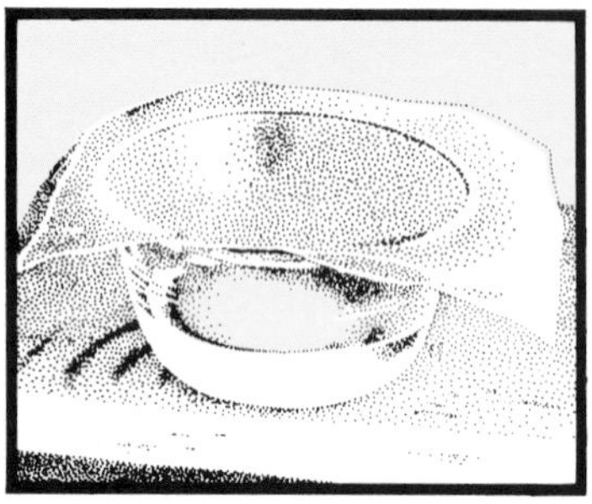

A one-quarter rotation is used for some muffins and cakes (above left). Covers are as important in microwave cooking as in conventional (left and above).

Rotating

A few foods, such as pies and cakes, that cannot be stirred, turned over, or rearranged, call for repositioning the cooking dish one-quarter turn to allow for even distribution of the microwave energy. Rotate only if the baked food is not cooking or rising evenly. Most foods do not need to be rotated.

Covering

Covers are used to trap steam, prevent dehydration, speed cooking time, and help food retain its natural moisture. Suitable tight coverings are microproof casserole tops, glass covers, plastic wraps, oven bags, and microproof plates and saucers. Boilable freezer bags may be used as containers for the frozen food inside. Pierce top with a knife to ventilate before cooking. Remove coverings away from your face to prevent steam burns. Paper toweling is especially useful as a light covering to prevent splatter and absorb moisture. Waxed paper helps to retain heat and moisture.

Shielding

Certain thin or bony areas, such as the wing tips of poultry, the head and tail of fish, or the breastbone of a turkey, cook faster than thicker areas. Covering these parts with small pieces of aluminum foil shields these areas from overcooking, since aluminum foil reflects the microwaves. Besides preventing thin parts of food from cooking more rapidly than thicker ones, shielding may be used during defrosting to cover those portions that defrost more quickly than others. Use aluminum foil only when recommended in recipes. Be careful not to allow the foil to touch the oven walls.

Standing Time

This term refers to the time food needs to complete cooking and thawing after microwave time is over. During standing time, heat continues to be conducted from the outside to the center of the food. Food may remain in the oven for standing time (as it does with many of the preset recipes), or may be placed on a heat-proof counter. This procedure is an essential part of food preparation with the microwave oven. Some foods, such as roasts, require standing time to attain proper internal temperature for rare, medium, or well-done levels. Casseroles need standing time to allow the heat to spread evenly and to complete reheating or cooking. With cakes, pies, and quiches, standing time permits the center to finish cooking. During the standing time outside the oven, place food on a flat surface, such as a heat-resistant bread board or counter top, not on a cooling rack as you would conventionally.

Piercing

It is necessary to break the skin or membrane of certain foods, such as egg yolks, potatoes, liver, chicken giblets, eggplant and squash. Because the skins or membranes retain moisture during cooking, they must be pierced before cooking to prevent bursting and to allow steam to escape. For example, pierce sausage casing in several places before cooking. A toothpick may be used for egg yolks; a fork is best for potatoes and squash; a knife is best to slit plastic cooking bags.

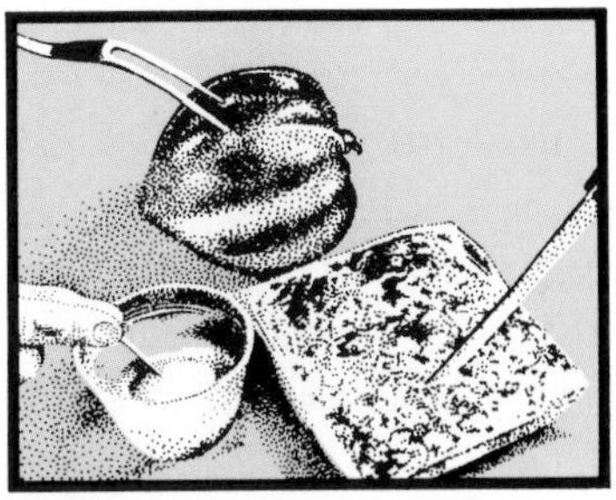

Piercing (above right). The effect of standing time on roast beef (right). Use a flat surface for standing time (above).

Browning

Many foods do not brown in the microwave oven as much as they do in the conventional oven. Depending upon the fat content, most food will brown in 8 to 10 minutes in the microwave oven. For example, bacon browns in minutes because of its high fat content, but poultry will not brown even after 10 minutes. For food that cooks too quickly to brown, such as hamburgers, fried eggs, steak or cutlets, a special browning dish is available (page 17). The longer the cooking time, or the higher the fat content, the more browning will be achieved. You can also create a browned look on roasts, poultry, steaks, and other foods by brushing on a browning agent, such as gravy mix, soy sauce, dehydrated onion soup mix, paprika, etc. Cakes, bread, and pie shells do not brown as they do in conventional cooking. Using chocolate, spices, or whole wheat flour helps attain the dark color. Otherwise, you can create appealing color by adding frostings, toppings, glazes, or dark spices such as cinnamon.

Adjusting for High Altitudes

As in conventional cooking, microwave cooking at high altitudes requires adjustments in cooking time for leavened products like breads and cakes. Other foods may require a slightly longer cooking time to become tender, since water boils at a lower temperature. Usually, for every 3 minutes of microwave cooking time you add 1 minute for the higher altitude. Therefore, a recipe calling for 3 minutes needs 4 minutes and a recipe requiring 6 minutes needs 8 minutes. The wisest procedure is to start with the time given in the recipe and then check for doneness before adding additional time. Adding time is easy, but overcooking can be a real problem. Here again your judgment is vital.

Getting to Know Your Oven

Your microwave oven gives you the ability to select from many power settings, from zero to 100 percent — HI (max. power). Just as in a conventional oven, these settings give you flexibility and control. Selection of the appropriate power setting is automatic, as is the timing, for the 300 preset recipes. For other recipes and for items identified in the *Cooking Guides* (see recipe chapters), you set the power to suit the food being cooked. In addition to HI, there are 99 settings. The *Guide* (below) identifies the main settings and gives them some familiar cooking terms and their most frequent uses. You may find, however, that other settings work best for you. You may want to do some defrosting on 25 or 33, for example.

Touch Pad

The touch pads on the oven control panel need only be touched to activate the oven. The beep tone sounds to assure you that the setting is being entered.

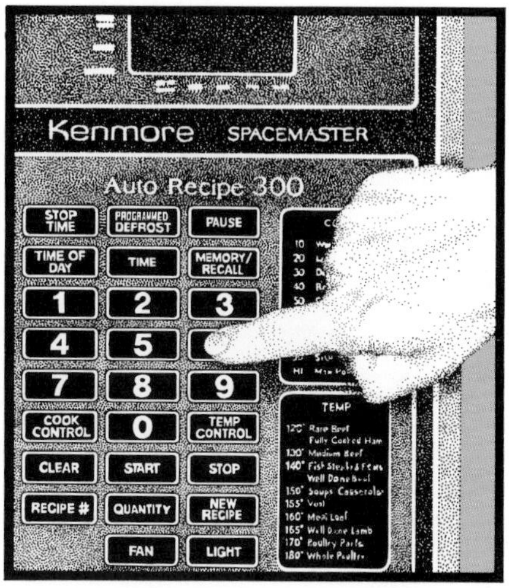

Guide for Cook Control Settings

Main Setting	***Suggested Cooking Uses***
1	Raising bread dough.
10 (warm)	Softening cream cheese; keeping casseroles and main dishes warm.
20 (low)	Softening chocolate; heating breads, rolls, pancakes, tacos, tortillas, and French toast; clarifying butter; taking chill out of fruit; heating small amounts of food.
30 (defrost)	Thawing meats, poultry, and seafood; finish cooking casseroles, stews, and some sauces; cooking small quantities of most foods.
40 (braise)	Cooking less tender cuts of meat in liquid and slow-cooking dishes; finish cooking less tender roasts.
50 (simmer)	Cooking stews and soups after bringing to a boil; cooking baked custards and pasta.
60 (bake)	Cooking scrambled eggs, cakes.
70 (roast)	Cooking rump roast, ham, veal, and lamb; cooking cheese dishes; cooking eggs, meatloaf, and milk; cooking quick breads and cereal products.
80 (reheat)	Quickly reheating precooked or prepared foods; heating sandwiches.
90 (sauté)	Quickly cooking onions, celery, and green peppers; reheating meat slices quickly.
HI (max. power)	Cooking tender cuts of meat; cooking poultry, fish, vegetables, and most casseroles; preheating the browning dish; boiling water; thickening some sauces; cooking muffins. Cooking whole meal, i.e. two or three dishes at once (see pages 206-218).

Temperature Probe

When inserted into the food, the temperature probe enables you to cook food to a preselected internal temperature. When the desired temperature is reached, the oven automatically holds food warm up to one hour. Instead of setting the oven to a certain number of minutes, you set the probe at the exact temperature you want the food to reach prior to standing time to attain desired doneness. The oven must also be set at the power level at which the food is to be cooked. If a power setting is not selected, the oven cooks at HI. Probe temperature and power setting are automatically determined for the preset recipes that use the probe. The probe provides accuracy in cooking almost any food, from instant coffee and sauces to beef casseroles and roast chicken. You can even watch the display window as the food reaches the selected temperature.

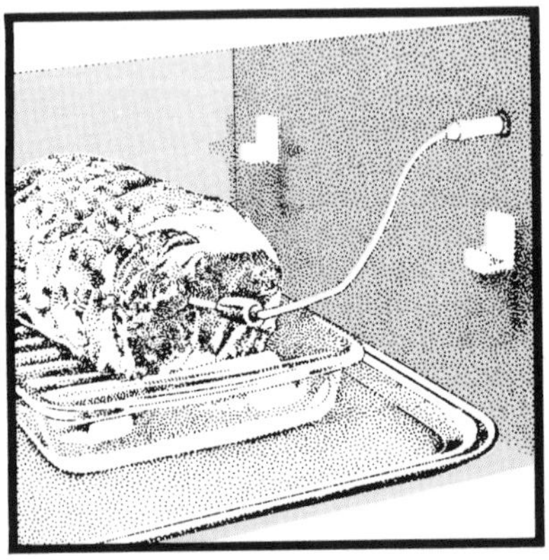

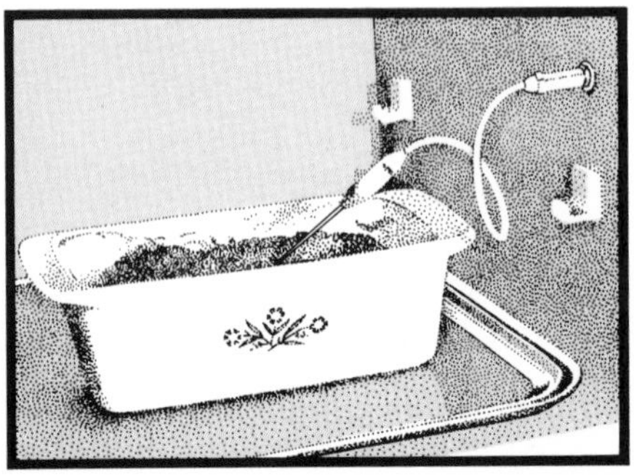

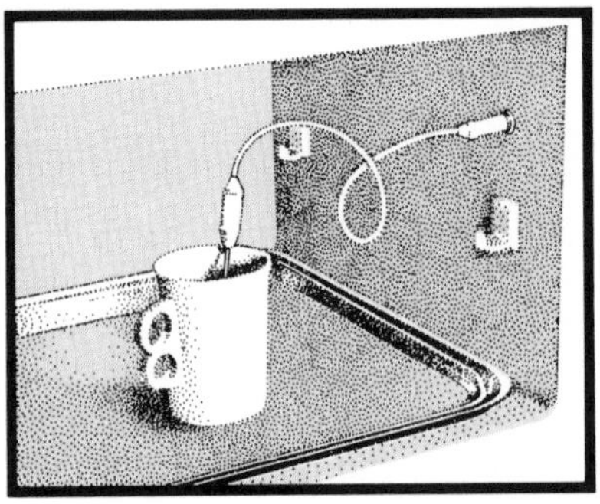

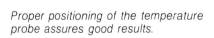

Proper positioning of the temperature probe assures good results.

Meatloaf is easiest when the temperature probe is used.

The probe must be carefully and properly inserted in the food to obtain the best results. As a rule, the probe tip should be in the center of the dish, cup, or casserole or in the thickest portion of the meat. Do not allow the probe to touch bone, fat, or any metal foil if it is being used as a shield. After using the probe, remove from oven, use warm soapy water to wash the part that contacted the food, rinse, and dry. Do not immerse the entire unit in water or wash it in the dishwasher.

The "Guide to the Temperature Probe" provides a range from 120°F to 200°F. Follow the directions in the recipes for placement of the probe, temperature, and covering of the dish, if specified, and consult the tips below for step-by-step directions for using the probe.

Standing time is essential for most foods to reach their optimum serving temperature. Because of the nature of microwave energy, during standing time the temperature of most food rises about 5°F to 15°F. For example, after 10 minutes of standing time, the temperature of rare beef will reach 135°F; well done lamb will reach its proper 170°F to 180°F. The temperature of beverages, however, drops in 10 minutes from 150°F to 136°F.

Guide to the Temperature Probe*

Suggested Temperature Probe Settings	
120°	Rare Beef, Fully Cooked Ham
130°	Medium Beef
140°	Fish Steaks and Fillets, Well Done Beef
150°	Vegetables, Hot Drinks, Soups, Casseroles
155°	Veal
165°	Well Done Lamb, Well Done Pork
170°	Poultry Parts
180°	Well Done Whole Poultry
200°	Cake Frosting

** Refer to individual Cooking Guides (see Index) for specific instructions.*

Tips for Probe Use

1. Place food in container, as recipe directs.
2. Place temperature probe in the food with the first inch of probe secured in the center of the food. Probe should not touch bone or a fat pocket. Probe should be inserted from the side or the front, not from the top of the food, except when inserting into casseroles, a cup of soup, etc. In general, try to insert probe as close to a horizontal position as possible.

3. Plug temperature probe into the receptacle on side wall of oven cavity.
4. Make sure the end of the temperature probe, inserted in the food, does not touch the cooking container, or sides of oven.
5. Touch "Clear."
6. Touch "Temp Control." Set temperature.
7. If a power setting other than HI is desired, touch "Cook Control." Set power level.
8. Touch "Start."
9. Never operate the oven with the temperature probe in the cavity unless the probe is plugged in and inserted into the food.
10. Use potholders to remove temperature probe. It may be hot.
11. Do not use temperature probe with a browning dish or aluminum TV trays.

Reheating

One of the major assets of the microwave oven is its efficiency in reheating cooked food. Not only does most food reheat quickly, but it also retains moisture and its just-cooked flavor when properly arranged and covered. If someone is late for dinner, there's no need to fret. Just place a microproof plate containing the cooked food in your oven; in moments, dinner is ready once again. Reheat food in serving dishes or on paper plates and save extra clean-up time. Take-out food, which usually arrives at your home cooled off, can be easily reheated in seconds to its original state in your microwave oven. No more cold pizzas! Or lukewarm hamburgers. Follow these tips to help get excellent results:

- ☐ Use 80 (reheat) except when otherwise specified. You can use the temperature probe for reheating casseroles, beverages, and other appropriate food. Insert probe into the largest or most dense piece of food and set temperature control at 150°F to 160°F.
- ☐ To arrange a combination of different foods on a plate, place the dense food, like meat, at the outer edges and the more porous food, like breads, toward the center.
- ☐ Dense food, such as mashed potatoes and casseroles, cooks more quickly and evenly if a depression is made in the center, or if the food is shaped in a ring.
- ☐ To retain moisture during reheating, cover food with plastic wrap or a microproof lid.
- ☐ Spread food out in a shallow container rather than piling it high, for quicker and more even heating.
- ☐ As a general guide to reheating a plate of food start with 1½ to 2 minutes, then check for doneness. If the plate on which the food is cooked feels warm, the food is probably heated through, since its warmth has heated the plate.

Let's Use the Oven

Now it's time for some practical experience using all the features of your Kenmore Spacemaster Auto Recipe 300 Microwave Oven. First, a quick hot drink, then a simple breakfast, and an easy lunch. Finally, you'll be introduced to the special convenience of preset recipes with a first course soup. You have read through the preceding introductory material and have checked your Use & Care Manual. Your oven is ready for use, so let's begin by making a cup of instant coffee, tea, or instant soup to enjoy right now!

Lesson One

A quick pick-me-up

Take your favorite mug or cup; be sure there is no gold or silver trim or metallic glaze. If you are not certain that your mug is microproof, test it as directed on page 15. Then follow these step-by-step directions:

1. Fill mug or cup with water and place in the center of the oven on the bottom glass tray. Close the oven door.

CLEAR

2. Touch the "clear" pad to clear any previous information.

TIME **2** **0** **0**

3. Touch the "time" pad and then touch pads 2-0-0. Your oven is now set to heat 2 minutes on HI. It is not necessary to touch "cook control" because your oven is automatically on HI unless changed to another setting.

START

4. Now touch the "start" pad.
5. The timer will beep when 2 minutes are up. The oven turns off automatically. Open the door.
6. Remove the mug. The handle will be cool enough to hold and the cup itself will be warm from the heated water.
7. Stir in instant coffee, tea, or instant soup.
8. Relax and have a nice "cuppa". (Next time, you may want to use the preset recipe on page 59.)

Lesson Two

Practice Breakfast

Frozen Orange Juice (5-ounce can)
Sweet Roll
Instant Coffee

1. Spoon frozen juice into a 4-cup glass measure or microproof serving pitcher, and place in oven. Close door.

2. Touch "clear" pad; touch "time" pad; then touch pads 2 and 0. The oven is set for 20 seconds at HI.

3. Touch "start."
4. When the timer beeps, open door and remove container. Let stand 5 minutes before adding water.
5. Meanwhile, prepare coffee as directed on page 29.
6. Set sweet roll on paper plate or paper napkin.
7. Place in oven and close door.

8. Touch "clear" pad; touch "time" pad; then touch pads 3 and 0. Touch "cook control" pad, then pads 2 and 0. The oven is set to cook for 30 seconds on 20.

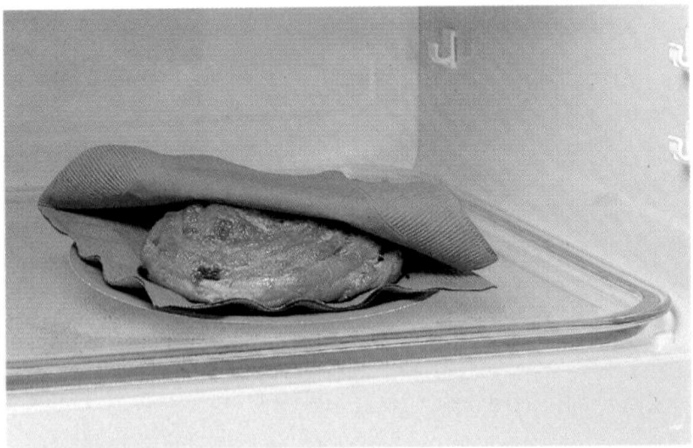

9. Touch "start" pad. Bakery products should be only warm to the touch, since they will be hotter just below the surface. Because microwaves are attracted to sugar, the frosting or jelly may be very hot.
10. Enjoy your breakfast!

Lesson Three

Soup and Sandwich Lunch

1 cup soup (canned or homemade)
1 hot dog
1 hot dog bun, split

1. Pour soup into microproof serving cup.
2. Place tip of temperature probe in center of cup; plug other end into receptacle on side wall of oven cavity.
3. Close door.

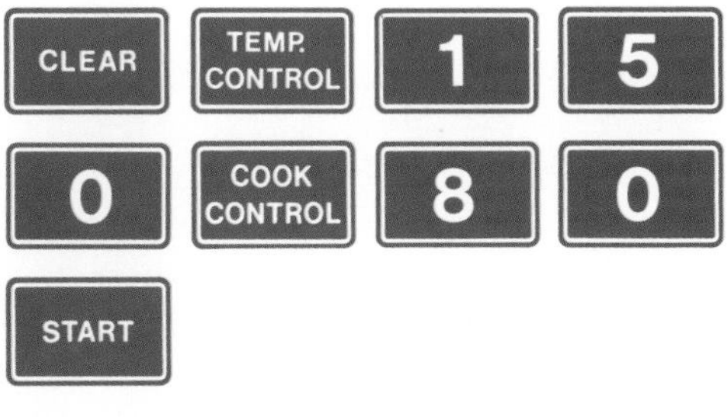

4. Touch "clear," touch "temperature control," touch 1-5-0; touch "cook control," touch 8-0, touch "start." Your oven is now set to heat the soup to 150°F at a cook control setting of 80.

5. Stir once during heating, as follows: when display window shows 100°F, open door; lift probe, stir soup and replace probe. Close door and touch "start" again. The oven will continue to operate on the setting you initially selected and will turn itself off when the soup reaches a temperature of 150°F.
6. Remove temperature probe from oven after use.
7. Set soup aside, covered, while heating sandwich.
8. Place hot dog in bun, wrap in paper toweling. Set in oven and close door.

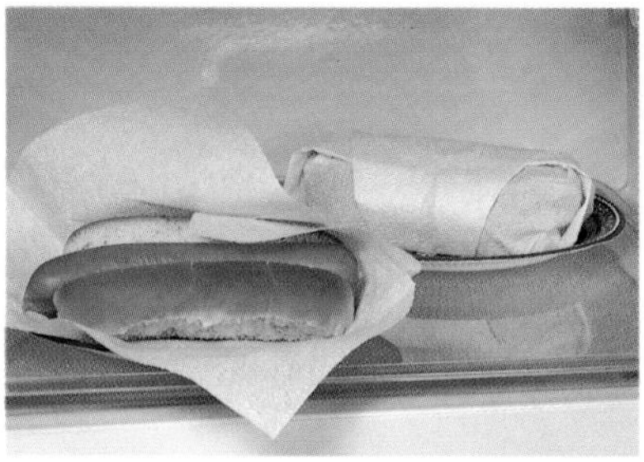

9. Touch "clear," "time," 5-0, "cook control," 8-0, and "start." Oven is set to heat 50 seconds on 80.
10. Bring the mustard; bon appetit!

Lesson Four

First Course Soup

Why not surprise the family with a first course of homemade soup as your first microwave recipe tonight? It's really easy, thanks to the convenience of the preset feature with your Kenmore Spacemaster Auto Recipe 300 oven. We've selected Cream of Corn Soup, Recipe No. 21 (page 51).

Cream of Corn Soup

1 can (17 ounces) cream-style corn
1 can ($13\frac{3}{4}$ ounces) chicken broth
$\frac{2}{3}$ cup water
$\frac{1}{4}$ cup thinly sliced zucchini
2 tablespoons water
1 tablespoon cornstarch
2 large eggs, lightly beaten
1 green onion, finely chopped

1. Combine corn, broth, $\frac{2}{3}$ cup water, and zucchini in 2-quart microproof casserole or soup tureen. Cover and place in oven. (We used one of those handy batter bowls, as pictured. A plate makes a dandy cover!)

2. Touch "clear" pad; touch "recipe #" pad; then touch pads 2 and 1. Oven is ready to cook.

3. Touch "start". (Oven will cook on HI for 13 minutes.)

4. At the end of first cooking sequence, timer will beep and "Pause" will appear in display window. Combine 2 tablespoons water and cornstarch; stir until cornstarch is dissolved. Open door and add cornstarch to soup; blend well. Do not cover.

5. Close door. Touch "Start" pad. (Oven will cook on HI for 5 minutes.)
6. Pour eggs into hot soup in thin stream, stirring briskly. Garnish with green onion — voila! — serve to smiles all around.

On Your Own

You will undoubtedly want to cook some of your favorite conventional recipes in the microwave oven. With a little thought and experimenting you can convert many recipes. Before converting a recipe, study it to determine if it will adapt well to microwave cooking. Look for a recipe in the book that matches your conventional one most closely. For example, find a recipe with the same amount, type, and form of main ingredient, such as 1 pound ground meat or 2 pounds beef cut in 1-inch pieces, etc. Then compare other ingredients, such as pasta or vegetables. The microwave recipe will probably call for less liquid, because there is so little evaporation in microwave cooking.

At the beginning of each recipe chapter, hints on adapting recipes are provided. You will also notice that each preset recipe includes, in italics, the timing and power setting information permanently stored in the computer memory, such as: *(Oven cooks: HI, 10 minutes; 50, 5 minutes.)* You can use that information as a guide in determining timing and power settings for those recipes you wish to adapt. Also use the following guidelines:

- ☐ Candies, bar cookies, meatloaf, and certain baked goods may not need adjustments in ingredients.

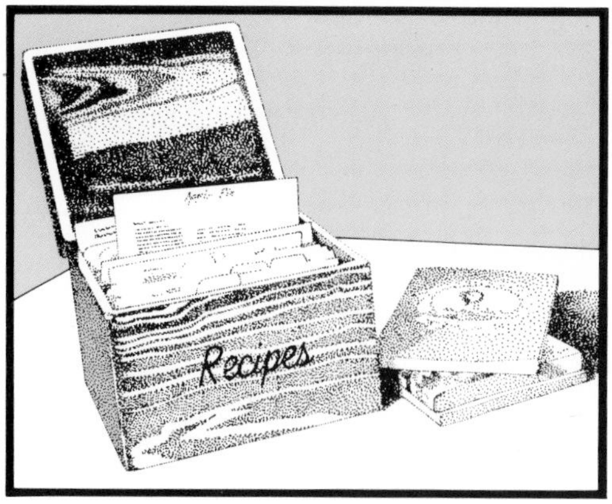

- ☐ In puddings, cakes, sauces, gravies, and some casseroles, liquids should be reduced.

- ☐ Most converted recipes will require adjustments in cooking time. Although a "rule of thumb" always has exceptions, you can generally assume that most microwave recipes are cooked in about one-quarter to one-third of the conventional recipe time. Check for doneness after one-quarter of the time before continuing to cook.

Now let's try converting a conventional recipe to the microwave oven. Suppose you have a favorite recipe for Chicken Marengo that you would like to prepare in your microwave oven. The closest recipe in this book turns out to be Chicken Cacciatore (page 119). Let's see how to convert that Chicken Marengo recipe.

Chicken Marengo
Conventional Style
4 to 6 servings

½ cup flour
1 teaspoon salt
½ teaspoon pepper
1 teaspoon tarragon
1 chicken, 3 pounds, cut up
¼ cup olive oil
¼ cup butter
1 cup dry white wine
2 cups canned tomatoes
1 clove garlic, finely chopped
8 mushrooms (½ pound), sliced
Chopped parsley

Preheat oven to 350°F. Mix flour, salt, pepper, and tarragon, and dredge chicken with seasoned flour. Reserve remaining flour.

In skillet heat oil and butter, and brown chicken. Place chicken in large casserole. Add reserved flour to the fat in skillet and, using a wire whisk, gradually stir in wine. When sauce is thickened and smooth, pour over the chicken and add the tomatoes, garlic, and mushrooms. Cover casserole and bake until chicken is tender, about 45 minutes. Before serving sprinkle with parsley.

Checking the Chicken Cacciatore recipe, you'll notice that the amount of liquid is quite a bit less than in the conventional Chicken Marengo recipe. That's because liquids do not reduce in microwave cooking and we don't want a thin sauce. Notice, too, that the onion is cooked first to be sure it is tender and that the flavor of the dish is fully developed. In converting, the Chicken Marengo recipe has the liquid reduced and the garlic is cooked first. Since the volume of food is about the same, the cooking times and power settings for Chicken Cacciatore are followed for Chicken Marengo Microwave Style. Here's the fully converted recipe:

Chicken Marengo
Microwave Style
4 to 6 servings

1 chicken, 3 pounds, cut up
1 teaspoon salt
½ teaspoon pepper
1 teaspoon tarragon
1 clove garlic, minced
1 tablespoon butter
1 tablespoon olive oil
¼ cup flour
½ cup dry white wine
2 cups canned tomatoes
8 mushrooms (½ pound), sliced
Chopped parsley

Rub chicken with salt, pepper, and tarragon and set aside. Place garlic, butter, and olive oil in 3-quart microproof casserole. Cook, covered, on HI 1 minute. Add flour, stir until smooth, gradually adding wine. Stir in tomatoes and mushrooms. Cook, covered, on HI 5 minutes, stir. Add chicken, immersing pieces in sauce. Cook, covered, on HI 25 to 30 minutes, or until chicken is fork tender. Taste for seasoning, sprinkle with chopped parsley, and allow to stand, covered, 5 minutes before serving.

Butter, olive oil, and flour have been reduced since browning is not part of the microwave recipe. If you wish, however, add more butter and olive oil, dredge chicken in flour, and brown chicken in preheated browning dish. The white wine has been reduced to avoid a too thin sauce.

We've also included a simplified, preset version of Chicken Marengo. See Recipe No. 126 on page 110.

Cooking Casseroles

The microwave oven is exceptionally good for cooking casseroles. Vegetables keep their bright fresh color and crisp texture. Meat is tender and flavorful. Here are some general hints to help you:

- ☐ Most casseroles can be made ahead of time, refrigerated or frozen, then reheated later in the microwave.
- ☐ Casseroles are usually covered with plastic wrap or glass lids during cooking.
- ☐ Allow casseroles to stand 5 to 10 minutes before serving, according to size. Standing time allows the center of the casserole to complete cooking.
- ☐ You will obtain best results if you make ingredients uniform in size, stirring occasionally to distribute heat. If the ingredients are of different sizes, stir more often.
- ☐ Casseroles containing less tender meats need longer simmering on a lower power setting, such as 40 (braise) or 50 (simmer). Casseroles with delicate ingredients such as cream or cheese sauces often need a lower setting like 70 (roast). Cheese toppings added for the last 1 or 2 minutes should cook at a setting no higher than 70 (roast).
- ☐ When used in quick-cooking casseroles, celery, onions, green peppers, and carrots should be sautéed before being added to dish. Rice or noodles should be partially cooked before combining with cooked meats, fish, or poultry. Use higher power settings, such as 80 (reheat) or HI (max. power), for these recipes.

About Low Calories

Scattered through the book are reduced-calorie suggestions and naturally low-calorie recipes. They are listed in the index so you can find them when you need them. In general, you can reduce calories in many recipes by making substitutions such as these:

- ☐ Bouillon or water for butter when sautéing or softening vegetables.
- ☐ Vegetables for potatoes or pasta.
- ☐ Lean meats for fatty ones.
- ☐ Skim milk for whole milk; skim milk cheeses like low-fat cottage, ricotta, and mozzarella for creamy fatty ones.
- ☐ Natural gravy with herbs for cream and butter sauces.
- ☐ Fruits cooked in their natural juices for fruit cooked with sugar added.
- ☐ Skinless chicken breast for regular cut-up chicken.
- ☐ Shellfish and white fish such as sole, halibut, and flounder for mackerel, tuna and other oily fish.

By the Way . . .

To get the greatest pleasure out of your microwave oven, keep in mind that certain food is best done by conventional means of cooking. For the following reasons we don't recommend:

- ☐ Eggs cooked in the shell, because the light membrane surrounding the yolk collects energy, which then causes a steam build-up that could explode the egg. Don't experiment. It's a mess to clean up!

- ☐ Deep-fat frying, because the confined environment of the oven is not suited to the handling of the food or oil and is not safe.

- ☐ Pancakes, because no crust forms. (But the oven is great for reheating pancakes, waffles, and similar items.)

- ☐ Toasting, because it also requires crust development.

- ☐ Popovers, because of the slow steam development necessary to make them rise.

- ☐ Home canning, because it is impossible to judge exact boiling temperatures inside jar and you cannot be sure that the temperature and length of cooking are sufficient to prevent contamination of the food.

- ☐ Chiffon and angel food cakes, because they require steady, dry heat to rise and be tender.

- ☐ Heating bottles with small necks, like those for syrups and toppings, because they are apt to break from the pressure build-up.

- ☐ Large items, such as a 25-pound turkey or a dozen baking potatoes, because the space is not adequate and no time is saved.

Finally, about popcorn:

Do not attempt to pop corn in a paper bag, since the corn may dehydrate and overheat, causing the paper bag to catch on fire. Due to the many variables, such as the age of the corn and its moisture content, popping corn in the microwave oven is not recommended. Microwave popping devices are available. While safe to use, they usually do not give results equal to those of conventional popping methods. If the microwave device is used, *carefully follow the instructions provided with the product.*

Off to a Good Start

Appetizers can be the most creative food of today's entertaining. They can be hot or cold, simple or fancy, light or hearty depending upon the occasion. There are no rules, so you can let your imagination soar. Until now *hot* appetizers were the most troublesome and time-consuming for the host or hostess. But that's no longer true with the microwave oven. Parties are much easier and more enjoyable because the microwave eliminates all that last-minute hassle and lengthy cooking over a hot stove. You can assemble most appetizers and nibbles in advance, and at the right moment, just coolly "heat 'n serve!" This chapter presents many recipes for entertaining your guests, but you'll also be tempted to prepare delicious snacks and munchies just for the family. There's no doubt about it — appetizers cooked in the microwave oven are fun to make, fun to serve, and fun to eat.

Stuffed Mushrooms (page 45), Rumaki (page 44), and Quick Appetizer Pizza (page 44) are ready-to-cook (above and above right). To freshen corn chips and other snacks, just pop the serving bowl or basket in the oven on HI, 15 seconds; let stand 3 minutes (right).

Converting Your Own Recipes

Most of the hot appetizers you've always wanted to make will adapt well to microwave cooking, except for those wrapped in pastry, since the coating does not become crisp. The recipe for Rumaki is an ideal guide for countless skewered appetizers containing seafood, chicken, vegetable, and fruit combinations. And compare your favorite dip recipe with one of the choices here to determine your microwave time and temperature. The enormous variety of finger foods, dippings, and canapés will provide you with continual tasty surprises. Here are some helpful tips:

- ☐ Appetizers and dips that contain cheese, mayonnaise, and other such delicate ingredients are usually heated on 70. A higher setting might cause separation or drying.
- ☐ The temperature probe set at 130°F on 70 provides an excellent alternative for heating hot dips containing seafood, cheese, or food to be served in a chafing dish or fondue pot.
- ☐ Because of its very delicate nature, a sour cream dip should be covered and heated with the temperature probe to 90°F on 50.
- ☐ Toppings for canapés can be made ahead, but do not place on bread or crackers until just before heating to assure a crisp base.
- ☐ Cover appetizers or dips only when the recipe specifies doing so. Use fitted glass lids, waxed paper, plastic wrap, or paper toweling.
- ☐ You can heat two batches of the same or similar appetizers at one time by using both oven levels, the middle metal rack and bottom glass tray, for almost double the time of one batch. Watch closely; those on top may cook more quickly than those on bottom.

COOKING GUIDE — CONVENIENCE APPETIZERS

Food	Amount	Cook Control Setting	Time	or	Temperature Probe Setting	Special Notes
Canned meat spread	4 oz.	80 (reheat)	30 - 45 seconds			Transfer to small microproof bowl.
Canned sausages, cocktail sausages	5 oz.	80 (reheat)	1½ - 2 minutes			Place in covered glass casserole.
Cocktail franks, pizza roll	4 servings	70 (roast)	45 - 60 seconds			Place on paper towels. Roll will not crisp.
Cooked pizza, 10 inches, cut in 8 portions	1 wedge 4 wedges Whole	80 (reheat) 80 (reheat) 70 (roast)	45 - 60 seconds 1½ - 2 minutes 3¼ - 4 minutes			Place on paper towels or paper plate or leave in uncovered cardboard box, points toward center.
Dips, cream	½ cup	10 (warm)	1½ - 2½ minutes	or	130°	Cover with plastic wrap.
Eggrolls, pastry-covered	2 servings	70 (roast)	30 - 45 seconds			Place on paper towels, do not cover.
Swiss fondue, frozen	10 oz.	80 (reheat)	5 - 6 minutes	or	150°	Slit pouch. Place on microproof plate. Stir before serving.

Recipe No. 01

Cheddar Cheese Canapés

Preset Cooking Time: 30 seconds

- 1/4 cup (1 ounce) grated Cheddar cheese
- 2 tablespoons light cream
- 1 tablespoon grated Parmesan cheese
- 1 tablespoon sesame seed
- 1/8 teaspoon Worcestershire sauce
- 1/8 teaspoon hot pepper sauce
- 12 crisp crackers or toast rounds
- Chopped parsley

Combine Cheddar cheese, cream, Parmesan cheese, sesame seed, Worcestershire, and hot pepper sauce; blend until smooth. Spread about 1 teaspoon mixture on each cracker. Arrange canapés on microproof plate. Place in oven. Set recipe number 1. Touch START. *(Oven cooks: 70, 30 seconds.)*

Garnish with parsley, and serve warm.

12 canapés

Recipe No. 02

Crab Supremes

Preset Cooking Time: 1½ minutes

- 1 can (6½ to 7 ounces) crab meat, drained
- 1/2 cup finely minced celery
- 1/2 cup mayonnaise
- 4 teaspoons sweet pickle relish
- 2 teaspoons prepared mustard
- 2 green onions, thinly sliced
- 24 crisp crackers or toast rounds

Place crab meat in bowl; pick over and remove cartilage. Flake with fork. Add celery, mayonnaise, relish, mustard, and green onions; blend well. Spoon about 1 tablespoon mixture onto each cracker. Arrange 12 canapés on microproof plate. Place in oven. Cover with waxed paper. Set recipe number 2. Touch START. *(Oven cooks: 70, 45 seconds.)*

At Pause, remove from oven. Arrange remaining 12 canapés on microproof plate. Place in oven. Cover. Touch START. *(Oven cooks: 70, 45 seconds.)*

Serve warm.

24 canapés

Recipe No. 03

Cold Eggplant Appetizer

Preset Cooking Time: 9 minutes

- 1 eggplant (1 pound)
- 1 small onion, minced
- 1/2 medium green pepper, seeded and minced
- 1 clove garlic, minced
- 1 teaspoon lemon juice
- 1/2 teaspoon salt
- 1/8 teaspoon pepper
- 1 cup plain yogurt

Wash eggplant and pierce skin in several places. Place on microwave roasting rack. Place in oven. Set recipe number 3. Touch START. *(Oven cooks: HI, 7 minutes.)*

At Pause, remove from oven; set aside. Combine onion, green pepper, garlic, and lemon juice in small microproof bowl. Place in oven. Touch START. *(Oven cooks: HI, 2 minutes.)*

Cut eggplant in half lengthwise. Scoop pulp into serving bowl. Add onion mixture, salt, and pepper; blend well. Stir in yogurt. Cover and chill thoroughly before serving. Serve with pumpernickel bread, party rye, or crackers.

2 cups

Cold Eggplant Appetizer is a wonderful low-calorie topping for cut up raw vegetables.

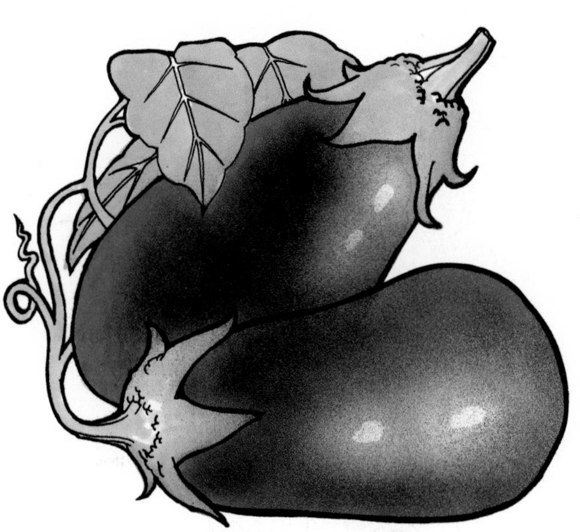

Recipe No. 04

Crunchy Chicken Wings

Preset Cooking Time: 29 minutes

- 14 chicken wings (about 3 pounds)
- 18 buttery crackers
- ½ cup grated Parmesan cheese
- 2 teaspoons parsley flakes
- ½ teaspoon garlic powder
- ½ teaspoon paprika
- Dash pepper
- ¼ cup butter or margarine

Cut chicken wings apart at both joints; discard tips. Pat dry with paper towels; set aside. Break crackers into blender or food processor container. Add remaining ingredients except butter; cover and process until crackers are crumbed. Transfer crumbs to plastic bag; set aside. Place butter in 9-inch microproof pie plate. Place in oven. Set recipe number 4. Touch START. *(Oven cooks: HI, 1 minute.)*

At Pause, remove from oven. Dip chicken in butter, then shake in seasoned crumbs. Arrange half of the chicken over remaining butter in pie plate with thickest parts toward outside of plate. Place in oven. Cover with paper towel. Touch START. *(Oven cooks: HI, 14 minutes.)*

At Pause, remove from oven; set aside and keep warm. Arrange remaining chicken in pie plate as above. Place in oven. Cover. Touch START. *(Oven cooks: HI, 14 minutes.)*

28 pieces

← *Shrimp and Artichokes (page 45), Tiny Meatballs, Toasted Seasoned Pecans (page 45), Nachos (page 42)*

Recipe No. 05

Curry Dipper

Preset Cooking Time: 2 minutes

- 1 can (10¾ ounces) cream of mushroom soup, undiluted
- 1½ tablespoons curry powder
- 1 teaspoon lemon juice
- 1 clove garlic, minced

Combine all ingredients in 4-cup glass measure; blend well. Place in oven. Set recipe number 5. Touch START. *(Oven cooks: HI, 2 minutes.)*

Serve hot with Tiny Meatballs (below), cubed sirloin, shrimp, or scallops.

1¼ cups

Recipe No. 06

Tiny Meatballs

Preset Cooking Time: 12 minutes

- 1 pound lean ground beef
- ½ pound ground pork
- 1 cup dry bread crumbs
- 1 cup milk
- 1 small onion, finely minced
- 1 large egg, lightly beaten
- 2 teaspoons soy sauce
- 1 teaspoon salt
- ¼ teaspoon pepper
- ¼ teaspoon allspice

Combine all ingredients; blend well. Shape into 1-inch balls. Arrange half of the meatballs in single layer on microwave roasting rack. Place in oven. Set recipe number 6. Touch START. *(Oven cooks:* 90, *6 minutes.)*

At Pause, remove meatballs from oven and place in chafing dish to keep warm. Arrange remaining meatballs on rack as above. Place in oven. Touch START. *(Oven cooks:* 90, 6 *minutes.)*

Add to chafing dish. Use toothpicks to spear meatballs. Serve hot with Curry Dipper (above).

60 meatballs

Meatballs can be prepared in advance and reheated on HI 2 to 3 minutes.

Recipe No. 07

Liver and Sausage Pâté

Preset Cooking Time: 12 minutes

- 1 pound chicken livers, rinsed and drained
- ½ pound mild Italian sausages, casings removed
- ⅓ cup cubed onion
- 1 tablespoon bourbon
- ¼ cup heavy cream
- ½ teaspoon salt
- ¼ teaspoon nutmeg
- 2 packages (one 8-ounce and one 3-ounce) cream cheese, softened
- 2 tablespoons butter or margarine, softened
- 1½ tablespoons light cream

Butter 8×4-inch loaf pan. Line bottom and sides with waxed paper or aluminum foil. Cut each chicken liver into 4 pieces; discard membranes; set aside. Break sausages into 4-cup glass measure. Place in oven. Cover with waxed paper. Set recipe number 7. Touch START. *(Oven cooks: HI, 2 minutes.)*

At Pause, stir. Cover. Touch START. *(Oven cooks: HI, 2 minutes.)*

At Pause, remove sausages from glass measure with slotted spoon; set aside. Add chicken livers to drippings in glass measure. Place in oven. Cover with waxed paper. Touch START. *(Oven cooks:* 50, 4 *minutes.)*

At Pause, stir. Cover. Touch START. *(Oven cooks:* 50, 4 *minutes.)*

Place onion and bourbon in blender or food processor container; cover and purée. Add livers, sausages, cream, salt, and nutmeg. Cover and process on high speed, stopping blender and pushing ingredients toward blades if necessary. Pour into prepared loaf pan. Refrigerate at least 12 hours or overnight.

Combine cream cheese, butter, and cream in blender or food processor container. Cover and process on high speed until smooth; set aside.

About 2 hours before serving, loosen paté from pan and unmold onto serving platter. Carefully peel off waxed paper. Spread top and sides generously with cream cheese mixture. Refrigerate 1½ hours, or until topping is firm. Let stand about 30 minutes at room temperature before serving. Garnish with pimiento, capers, watercress, and green onions, if desired. Serve with assorted crackers.

30 servings

Recipe No. 08

Nachos

Preset Cooking Time: 2 minutes

- 1 can (3⅛ ounces) jalapeño bean dip
- 1 bag (8 ounces) tortilla chips
- 1½ cups (6 ounces) grated Cheddar cheese
- 1 can (2¼ ounces) sliced jalapeño peppers

Spread bean dip lightly on chips. Top with cheese and peppers. Arrange 10 chips on microproof plate. Place in oven. Set recipe number 8. Touch START. *(Oven cooks:* 70, 40 *seconds.)*

At Pause, remove from oven. Arrange 10 more chips on microproof plate. Place in oven. Touch START. *(Oven cooks:* 70, 40 *seconds.)*

At Pause, repeat with remaining 10 chips. Touch START. *(Oven cooks:* 70, 40 *seconds.)*

Serve warm.

30 canapés

Stuffed Mushrooms (page 45), Liver and Sausage Pâté →

Recipe No. 09

Party Nibblers

Preset Cooking Time: 6½ minutes

- 2 cups thin pretzel sticks
- 2 cups crispy rice squares cereal
- 2 cups crispy wheat squares cereal
- 2 cups crispy oat circles cereal
- 1½ cups (6 ounces) salted nuts
- 7 tablespoons butter or margarine
- 1 teaspoon Worcestershire sauce
- ½ teaspoon garlic powder
- ½ teaspoon onion powder
- ½ teaspoon celery salt

Combine pretzels, cereals, and nuts in 12×8-inch microproof baking dish; set aside. Place butter in 1-cup glass measure. Place in oven. Set recipe number 9. Touch START. *(Oven cooks: HI, 1½ minutes.)*

At Pause, remove butter from oven. Add Worcestershire and seasonings; blend well. Drizzle over cereal mixture; toss lightly to mix. Place cereal mixture in oven. Touch START. *(Oven cooks: HI, 3 minutes.)*

At Pause, stir. Touch START. *(Oven cooks: HI, 2 minutes.)*

Cool before serving or storing in airtight containers.

2½ quarts

Change combinations or add seasonings according to your taste.

Recipe No. 10

Quick Appetizer Pizza

Preset Cooking Time: 1 minute

- 1 English muffin, split and toasted
- 2 tablespoons pizza sauce
- 6 slices pepperoni
- ¼ cup (1 ounce) shredded mozzarella cheese

Spread each muffin half with 1 tablespoon pizza sauce. Top each with 3 slices pepperoni, then with half of the cheese. Place both halves on microproof plate. Place in oven. Set recipe number 10. Touch START. *(Oven cooks: 70, 1 minute.)*

Let stand 1 minute before serving.

2 servings

Recipe No. 11

Rumaki

Preset Cooking Time: 7 minutes (repeat twice)

- ½ pound chicken livers, rinsed and drained
- ¼ cup soy sauce
- ¼ teaspoon garlic powder
- 12 thin slices bacon, cut into thirds
- 1 can (8 ounces) sliced water chestnuts, drained

Cut chicken livers into thirty-six 1-inch pieces; discard membranes; set aside. Combine soy sauce and garlic powder; blend well. Dip 1 piece liver in soy sauce mixture. Place on 1 piece bacon. Top with 1 slice water chestnut. Roll up and fasten with toothpick; repeat with remaining liver pieces. Place 12 rumaki in circle on microwave roasting rack. Place in oven. Cover with paper towel. Set recipe number 11. Touch START. *(Oven cooks: HI, 4 minutes.)*

At Pause, turn over. Cover. Touch START. *(Oven cooks: HI, 3 minutes.)*

Repeat procedure for remaining rumaki, cooking 12 at a time. Set recipe number for each batch.

36 appetizers

Recipe No. 12

Shrimp and Artichokes

Preset Cooking Time: 5 minutes

- ½ pound small mushrooms
- 1 jar (6 ounces) marinated artichoke hearts, drained
- ¼ cup lemon juice
- 2 tablespoons olive oil
- 2 cloves garlic, minced
- ½ teaspoon salt
- ½ teaspoon oregano
- ½ teaspoon dillweed
- ⅛ teaspoon pepper
- 1 pound small shrimp, in shell

Combine all ingredients except shrimp in microproof bowl; mix lightly; set aside. Arrange shrimp in single layer on round microproof plate, with tails toward center of plate. Place in oven. Cover with waxed paper. Set recipe number 12. Touch START. *(Oven cooks:* 70, 3 *minutes.)*

At Pause, remove from oven. Let stand 5 minutes before shelling and deveining; set aside. Place artichoke mixture in oven. Cover with waxed paper. Touch START. *(Oven cooks:* 70, 2 *minutes.)*

Remove from oven. Carefully stir in shrimp. Place in chafing dish to keep warm.

about 36 appetizers

Recipe No. 13

Stuffed Mushrooms

Preset Cooking Time: 4 minutes

- 24 medium mushrooms, stems removed
- 2 green onions, finely chopped
- ½ cup (2 ounces) shredded Cheddar cheese
- ⅓ cup dry bread crumbs
- ¼ cup butter or margarine, melted
- ½ teaspoon salt
- ½ teaspoon Italian seasoning
- ¼ teaspoon garlic powder
- ⅛ teaspoon pepper
- ½ teaspoon Worcestershire sauce

Chop mushroom stems finely; set caps aside. Combine chopped stems, green onions, and cheese; blend well. Add bread crumbs, butter, seasonings, and Worcestershire; blend well. Spoon mixture into caps, mounding slightly in center. Arrange on 10-inch round microproof plate. Place in oven. Set recipe number 13. Touch START. *(Oven cooks: HI, 4 minutes.)*

24 appetizers

Recipe No. 14

Swiss Fondue

Preset Cooking Time: about 5 minutes

- 1 package (10 ounces) frozen Swiss fondue

Slit pouch and place on microproof plate. Place in oven. Insert temperature probe through slit. Set recipe number 14. Touch START. *(Oven cooks:* 80, *about* 5 *minutes to* 150°*F; holds warm:* 10.*)*

Empty into fondue pot. Stir before serving.

24 servings

Recipe No. 15 ⊞

Toasted Seasoned Pecans

Preset Cooking Time: 5 minutes

- 1 pound pecan halves
- 1 tablespoon seasoned salt
- ¼ cup butter or margarine, cut into eighths

Place pecans in 1½-quart microproof casserole. Sprinkle with seasoned salt. Arrange butter evenly over pecans. Place in oven. Touch START. *(Oven cooks: HI, 3 minutes.)*

At Pause, stir. Touch START. *(Oven cooks: HI, 2 minutes.)*

1 pound

⊞ *Recipe can be increased.* *See "Quantity", page 12.*

From Midday to Midnight

Microwaves perform at their very best with sandwiches, hot drinks, soups, and chowders. For a quick pick-me-up all you need is a minute or two and a mug full of water for a cup of instant soup, or coffee. And, if you like to make soups from scratch without those endless hours of simmering and hovering that are required by conventional cooking, follow these microwave recipes.

Rise and shine with breakfast cocoa and wind down your day with after-dinner coffee swiftly and easily made in your microwave oven. What a convenience for coffee lovers! No more of that bitter mess when coffee is kept warm for more than 15 minutes in the conventional way. Brew your coffee as you normally do and pour what you want to drink now. Refrigerate the rest. Then, throughout the day, pour single cups as you wish from the refrigerated pot. Heat for 1½ to 2 minutes on HI (max. power) and savor the taste of truly fresh coffee.

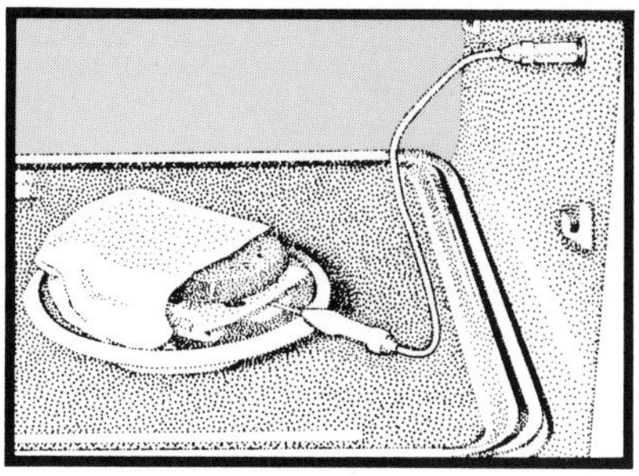

The temperature probe is especially helpful when preparing soup. Note the probe position when a bowl or casserole is covered with plastic wrap: the wrap is not pierced by the probe (above left). The temperature probe can be used when heating 1 to 4 cups of soup: arrange in a circle and insert the probe in one cup (above). Hot Ham and Swiss (page 61) is quickly heated using the probe (left).

← *Country Vegetable Soup (page 50)*

Converting Your Own Soup and Hot Drink Recipes

Soups and hot drinks convert well and easily to the microwave method. Find a recipe here with the approximate density and volume of the family favorite or the new conventional recipe you want to try. You may have to alter an ingredient or two: For example, dried bean soups, such as split pea and navy bean, do not obtain the best results in microwave cooking. However, canned, precooked navy beans, kidney beans, and packaged dry soup mixes are perfect substitutes for dried beans and peas. The tips below will help you obtain excellent results with your own recipes:

- ☐ Be careful with milk-based liquids or 2- or 3-quart quantities, which can boil over quickly. Always select a large enough microproof container to prevent any boiling over, and fill individual cups no more than two-thirds full.
- ☐ Soup is cooked covered. Use microproof casserole lids, waxed paper, or plastic wrap.
- ☐ Soup with uncooked meat and chicken needs slower simmering. Start cooking on HI and finish cooking on 50. Generally, use 80 for soup containing cooked meat and/or vegetables.
- ☐ Cooking time varies with the volume of liquid and density of food in soup.
- ☐ Remember that the microwave's brief cooking time results in less evaporation of liquid than stovetop simmering.
- ☐ Start with one-quarter the time recommended in a conventional recipe and adjust as needed to complete cooking.

Recipe No. 16

Canned Soup

Preset Cooking Time: 2½ to 6 minutes

1 can (10¾ ounces) soup, undiluted

Pour soup into 1½- to 2-quart microproof casserole. Add milk or water as directed on can; blend well. Place in oven. Insert temperature probe. Set recipe number 16. Touch START. *(Oven cooks:* 80, 1 *to* 2½ *minutes to* 120°*F.)*

At Pause, stir. Touch START. *(Oven cooks:* 80, 1½ *to* 3½ *minutes to* 150°*F; holds warm:* 10.)

Cover and let stand 3 minutes before serving.

2 servings

Recipe No. 17

Canadian Green Pea Soup

Preset Cooking Time: 11 minutes

1 can (2 ounces) mushroom stems and pieces
1 tablespoon butter or margarine
2 cans (11½ ounces each) green pea soup, undiluted
1 cup grated carrots
½ teaspoon salt

Drain mushroom liquid into 2-cup measure. Add water to equal 2 cups liquid; set aside. Place butter in 2-quart microproof casserole or soup tureen. Place in oven. Set recipe number 17. Touch START. *(Oven cooks:* 60, 1 *minute.)*

At Pause, add mushrooms, soup, and mushroom-water mixture; stir with fork until blended. Add carrots and salt; blend well. Cover with waxed paper. Touch START. *(Oven cooks:* 80, 10 *minutes.)*

Serve hot with croutons or crackers.

4 to 6 servings

Canadian Green Pea Soup →

Recipe No. 18

Chilled Minted Pea Soup

Preset Cooking Time: 10 minutes

- 1/4 cup coarsely chopped fresh mint leaves
- 1/4 cup chopped parsley
- 1/2 medium head lettuce, cored and chopped
- 2 green onions, chopped
- 2 packages (10 ounces each) frozen peas, thawed
- 1 can (13 3/4 ounces) chicken broth
- 1/2 teaspoon salt
- 1/4 teaspoon white pepper
- 1/2 cup heavy cream
- 4 sprigs fresh mint

Combine chopped mint, parsley, lettuce, green onions, peas, broth, salt, and pepper in 2-quart microproof casserole. Place in oven. Set recipe number 18. Touch START. *(Oven cooks: HI, 10 minutes.)*

Remove from oven. Pour into blender or food processor container. Cover and process on low speed until blended. Increase speed to high; purée. Stir in cream. Cover and chill before serving. Garnish each serving with mint sprig.

4 servings

Recipe No. 19

Cold Fresh Tomato Soup

Preset Cooking Time: 25 minutes

- 2 pounds ripe tomatoes, peeled and cut into eighths
- 2 cups dry white wine
- 1/2 cup chopped onion
- 1 tablespoon sugar
- 2 teaspoons paprika
- 1 teaspoon salt
- 1 strip (2 inches) lemon peel
- 1 sprig parsley
- 1 to 2 teaspoons lemon juice, to taste
- 1/2 cup dairy sour cream or plain yogurt

Combine tomatoes, wine, onion, sugar, paprika, salt, lemon peel, and parsley in 4-quart microproof casserole. Cover and place in oven. Set recipe number 19. Touch START. *(Oven cooks: HI, 10 minutes.)*

At Pause, stir. Cover. Touch START. *(Oven cooks: HI, 15 minutes.)*

At Pause, remove from oven. Discard lemon peel and parsley. Pour soup into blender or food processor container; cover and process on high speed until smooth. Stir in lemon juice. Cover and refrigerate several hours before serving. Top each serving with dollop of sour cream.

4 to 6 servings

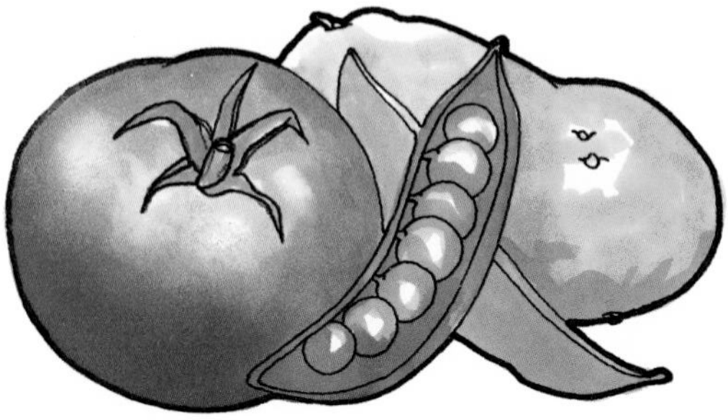

Recipe No. 20

Country Vegetable Soup

Preset Cooking Time: 50 minutes

- 4 cups beef broth
- 2 medium potatoes, peeled and cut into 1/2-inch cubes
- 2 medium carrots, thinly sliced
- 2 small onions, chopped
- 1 can (12 ounces) whole-kernel corn, drained, or 1 1/2 cups fresh corn
- 1 cup shredded cabbage
- 1 can (16 ounces) stewed tomatoes
- 1 teaspoon salt
- 1/2 teaspoon thyme
- 1/8 teaspoon pepper
- 1 bay leaf
- 1/3 cup chopped parsley

Combine all ingredients except parsley in 4-quart microproof casserole. Cover and place in oven. Set recipe number 20. Touch START. *(Oven cooks: HI, 20 minutes.)*

At Pause, stir. Cover. Touch START. *(Oven cooks:* 50, 25 *minutes; stands:* 0, 5 *minutes.)*

Discard bay leaf. Divide parsley among 6 individual soup bowls, and ladle soup over parsley. Serve with crackers or hard rolls.

6 servings

Recipe No. 21 ⊞

Cream of Corn Soup

Preset Cooking Time: 18 minutes

- 1 can (17 ounces) cream-style corn
- 1 can (13¾ ounces) chicken broth
- ⅔ cup water
- ¼ cup thinly sliced zucchini
- 2 tablespoons water
- 1 tablespoon cornstarch
- 2 large eggs, lightly beaten
- 1 green onion, finely chopped

Combine corn, broth, ⅔ cup water, and zucchini in 2-quart microproof casserole or soup tureen. Cover and place in oven. Set recipe number 21. Touch START. *(Oven cooks: HI, 13 minutes.)*

At Pause, combine 2 tablespoons water and cornstarch; stir until cornstarch is dissolved. Add to soup; blend well. Do not cover. Touch START. *(Oven cooks: HI, 5 minutes.)*

Pour eggs into soup in thin stream, stirring briskly. Garnish with green onion, and serve immediately.

4 servings

Recipe No. 22 ⊞

Cream of Mushroom Soup

Preset Cooking Time: 7 minutes

- 3 cups chopped mushrooms
- 2½ cups chicken broth
- ½ teaspoon onion powder
- ¼ teaspoon salt
- ⅛ teaspoon garlic powder
- ⅛ teaspoon white pepper
- 1 cup heavy cream

Combine mushrooms, broth, and seasonings in 2-quart microproof casserole or soup tureen. Place in oven. Set recipe number 22. Touch START. *(Oven cooks: HI, 5 minutes.)*

At Pause, blend in cream. Touch START. *(Oven cooks: 60, 2 minutes.)*

6 servings

You can make a lower-calorie soup by substituting whole milk or undiluted evaporated skim milk for the heavy cream.

Recipe No. 23

Mock Lobster Bisque

Preset Cooking Time: 27 minutes

- 1 pound frozen codfish or haddock fillets
- 1 can (10¾ ounces) tomato soup, undiluted
- 1 can (10¾ ounces) pea soup, undiluted
- 1¼ cups milk
- ½ cup dry sherry

Place fillets in package on paper towels in oven. Set recipe number 23. Touch START. *(Oven defrosts: 30, 8 minutes.)*

At Pause, remove fillets from oven and separate. Arrange on microproof plate. If fillets are of uneven thickness, tuck ends under to make as uniform as possible. Cover with lettuce leaves or well dampened paper towels. Place in oven. Touch START. *(Oven cooks: HI, 4 minutes.)*

At Pause, remove from oven. Flake with fork; discard any bones; reserve drippings, if any. Combine soups, milk, and sherry in 2-quart microproof casserole or soup tureen; blend until smooth. Add fish and drippings. Cover and place in oven. Touch START. *(Oven cooks: 50, 8 minutes.)*

At Pause, stir. Cover. Touch START. *(Oven cooks: 50, 7 minutes.)*

6 servings

⊞ *Recipe can be increased. See "Quantity", page 12.*

Recipe No. 24

Tomato Soup Piquante

Preset Cooking Time: 20 minutes

- ½ cup finely chopped celery
- 1 tablespoon butter or margarine
- 1 quart tomato juice
- 1 can (10½ ounces) beef consommé, undiluted
- 1 tablespoon dry sherry
- 1 teaspoon sugar
- ½ teaspoon thyme
- ½ teaspoon celery salt
- ⅛ teaspoon hot pepper sauce
- 4 to 6 slices lemon

Combine celery and butter in 2-quart microproof casserole or soup tureen. Place in oven. Set recipe number 24. Touch START. *(Oven cooks: HI, 5 minutes.)*

At Pause, add remaining ingredients except lemon. Cover. Touch START. *(Oven cooks: 80, 12 minutes; stands: 0, 3 minutes.)*

Garnish with lemon slices before serving.

4 to 6 servings

Recipe No. 25

French Onion Soup

Preset Cooking Time: 21 minutes

- 3 large onions, quartered and thinly sliced
- ¼ cup butter or margarine
- 2 teaspoons all-purpose flour
- 6 cups beef broth
- ¼ cup dry white wine
- ½ teaspoon salt
- ⅛ teaspoon white pepper
- Garlic powder
- 6 to 8 slices French bread, toasted and buttered
- 1 cup (4 ounces) shredded Swiss cheese

Combine onions and butter in 3-quart microproof casserole. Place in oven. Set recipe number 25. Touch START. *(Oven cooks: HI, 6 minutes.)*

At Pause, stir. Touch START. *(Oven cooks: HI, 6 minutes.)*

At Pause, stir in flour. Touch START. *(Oven cooks: HI, 1 minute.)*

At Pause, stir in broth, wine, salt, and pepper. Cover. Touch START. *(Oven cooks: HI, 8 minutes.)*

To serve, lightly sprinkle garlic powder on hot toast. Nearly fill soup bowls with hot soup; float toast on top. Cover toast generously with cheese and let stand until cheese melts.

6 to 8 servings

You may prefer to prepare this soup early in the day. If so, refrigerate before adding toast. To serve, cover soup and cook on HI 5 minutes, stirring twice during heating. Serve as directed above.

Recipe No. 26

New England Clam Chowder

Preset Cooking Time: 19 minutes

- ¼ cup butter, melted
- ¼ cup all-purpose flour
- 2 cans (7½ ounces each) minced clams
- 2 slices bacon, diced
- 2 medium potatoes, peeled and cut into ½-inch cubes
- 1 medium onion, chopped
- 3 cups milk
- ½ teaspoon salt
- ⅛ teaspoon white pepper

Combine butter and flour; blend well; set aside. Drain clam liquid into 2-cup measure; add water to equal 2 cups liquid; set aside. Place bacon in 3-quart microproof casserole or soup tureen. Place in oven. Set recipe number 26. Touch START. *(Oven cooks: HI, 3 minutes.)*

At Pause, add potatoes and onion. Cover. Touch START. *(Oven cooks: 90, 10 minutes.)*

At Pause, add flour mixture; blend well. Stir in clam-water mixture, clams, milk, salt, and pepper. Cover. Touch START. *(Oven cooks: HI, 1 minute.)*

At Pause, stir. Cover. Touch START. *(Oven cooks: HI, 5 minutes.)*

4 to 6 servings

Recipe No. 27

Minestrone Soup

Preset Cooking Time: 1 hour 3 minutes

- 1 pound beef for stew, trimmed and cut into ½-inch cubes
- 5 cups hot water
- 1 medium onion, chopped
- ½ teaspoon basil
- ¼ teaspoon pepper
- 1 clove garlic, minced
- ½ cup thinly sliced carrots
- 1 can (16 ounces) whole tomatoes, broken up
- 1½ cups sliced zucchini
- 1 cup shredded cabbage
- 1 can (16 ounces) kidney beans, drained
- ½ cup uncooked vermicelli, broken into 1-inch pieces
- 2 tablespoons chopped parsley
- 1 teaspoon salt
- Grated Parmesan or Romano cheese

Combine beef, hot water, onion, basil, pepper, and garlic in 4-quart microproof casserole. Cover and place in oven. Set recipe number 27. Touch START. *(Oven cooks: HI, 25 minutes.)*

At Pause, add carrots and tomatoes. Cover. Touch START. *(Oven cooks: HI, 8 minutes.)*

At Pause, add zucchini, cabbage, beans, vermicelli, parsley, and salt. Cover. Touch START. *(Oven cooks: 50, 25 minutes; stands: 0, 5 minutes.)*

Sprinkle each serving generously with cheese before serving.

6 to 8 servings

Recipe No. 28

Chicken in the Pot

Preset Cooking Time: 1 hour 15 minutes

- Boiling water
- 1 chicken (4 pounds), cut up, giblets except liver and kidney reserved
- 5 to 6 cups hot water
- 4 large carrots, cut into chunks
- 3 medium stalks celery, cut into chunks, tops reserved
- 1 medium onion, cut into quarters
- 1 small parsnip, peeled and cut into chunks
- 1 tablespoon chicken bouillon granules
- ⅛ teaspoon pepper
- Minced parsley

Pour boiling water over chicken to rinse; drain well. Arrange chicken and giblets in 4-quart microproof casserole. Add remaining ingredients except parsley; add more hot water to cover chicken if necessary. Cover and place in oven. Set recipe number 28. Touch START. *(Oven cooks: HI, 1 hour; stands: 0, 15 minutes.)*

Discard celery tops. Divide parsley among individual soup bowls. Ladle soup over parsley.

4 to 6 servings

The boiling water rinse reduces fat and helps eliminate foam. If desired, soup can be strained after cooking and broth served separately. Arrange chicken and vegetables on serving platter, and sprinkle with parsley.

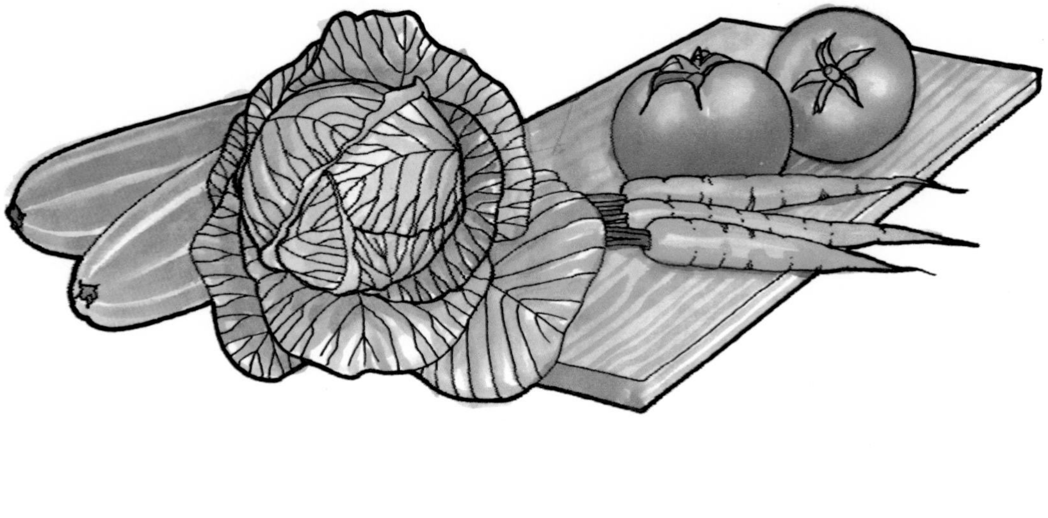

Recipe No. 29

Japanese Cauliflower Soup

Preset Cooking Time: 28 minutes

- 3 tablespoons butter or margarine
- 1/4 cup all-purpose flour
- 1/8 teaspoon ground nutmeg
- 4 cups chicken broth
- 1 head cauliflower (2 1/2 pounds), broken into florets
- 1/4 cup heavy cream or undiluted evaporated milk
- 1 egg yolk
- Minced parsley

Place butter in 2-quart microproof casserole or soup tureen. Place in oven. Set recipe number 29. Touch START. *(Oven cooks: HI, 2 minutes.)*

At Pause, add flour and nutmeg; stir until smooth. Blend in broth. Cover. Touch START. *(Oven cooks: HI, 7 minutes.)*

At Pause, add cauliflower; blend well. Cover. Touch START. *(Oven cooks: HI, 15 minutes.)*

At Pause, remove soup from oven; let stand 10 minutes. Transfer soup in batches to blender or food processor container; cover and purée. Return to casserole. Cover and place in oven. Touch START. *(Oven cooks: HI, 4 minutes.)*

Combine cream and egg yolk; blend well. Add small amount warm soup to egg yolk mixture; blend well; gradually blend into soup. Sprinkle with parsley and serve immediately.

4 servings

You can make a lower-calorie soup by substituting whole or undiluted evaporated skim milk for the heavy cream.

If desired, 4 cups water and 4 teaspoons chicken bouillon granules can be substituted for the chicken broth.

Recipe No. 30

Meatball Soup

Preset Cooking Time: 22 minutes

- 1/2 pound lean ground beef
- 1/4 pound ground pork
- 1/2 cup cornmeal
- 1 large egg
- 1 can (28 ounces) whole tomatoes, broken up
- 1/2 cup water
- 1 small onion, diced
- 1 tablespoon chopped green chilies
- 1 teaspoon chili powder
- 1/2 teaspoon salt
- 1/4 teaspoon marjoram
- 1/4 teaspoon pepper
- 1 clove garlic, minced

Combine beef, pork, cornmeal, and egg; blend well. Shape into 1/2-inch balls; set aside. Combine remaining ingredients in 2-quart microproof casserole or soup tureen. Cover and place in oven. Set recipe number 30. Touch START. *(Oven cooks: HI, 5 minutes.)*

At Pause, drop meatballs into soup. Cover. Touch START. *(Oven cooks: HI, 5 minutes.)*

At Pause, stir. Cover. Touch START. *(Oven cooks: HI, 7 minutes; stands:* 0, 5 *minutes.)*

4 to 6 servings

Recipe No. 31

Hearty Cheese and Frank Soup

Preset Cooking Time: 23 minutes

- 1/2 cup sliced celery
- 1 medium carrot, thinly sliced
- 1/4 cup chopped onion
- 1/4 cup butter or margarine
- 2 tablespoons all-purpose flour
- 2 cans (13 3/4 ounces each) chicken broth
- 1/2 pound frankfurters, sliced
- 2 cups (8 ounces) shredded Cheddar cheese
- 1 1/2 cups milk or half-and-half

Combine celery, carrot, onion, and butter in 3-quart microproof casserole or soup tureen. Cover and place in oven. Set recipe number 31. Touch START. *(Oven cooks: HI, 4 minutes.)*

At Pause, stir. Cover. Touch START. *(Oven cooks: HI, 4 minutes.)*

At Pause, add flour; stir until smooth. Stir in broth and frankfurters. Cover. Touch START. *(Oven cooks: HI, 10 minutes.)*

At Pause, add cheese; stir until melted. Stir in milk. Cover. Touch START. *(Oven cooks: 50, 5 minutes.)*

6 servings

Recipe No. 32

Instant Soups, Soup Mixes

Preset Cooking Time: about 2 minutes

- 1 envelope (1¼ ounces) instant soup mix
- ⅔ cup water

Combine soup mix and water in 8-ounce microproof mug or cup; blend well. Place in oven. Insert temperature probe. Cover with waxed paper. Set recipe number 32. Touch START. *(Oven cooks: HI, about 2 minutes to 150°F; holds warm: 10.)*

Let stand 5 minutes before serving.

1 serving

Recipe No. 33

Cappuccino

Preset Cooking Time: 3½ minutes

- 2 cups milk
- ¼ cup semisweet chocolate pieces
- 2 teaspoons sugar
- 2 teaspoons instant coffee powder
- ½ cup brandy
- Whipped cream

Combine milk, chocolate, sugar, and coffee in 4-cup glass measure. Place in oven. Set recipe number 33. Touch START. *(Oven cooks: HI, 2 minutes.)*

At Pause, stir. Touch START. *(Oven cooks: HI, 1½ minutes.)*

Stir until sugar is dissolved. Divide among 4 mugs. Stir 2 tablespoons brandy into each mug. Top each with dollop of whipped cream before serving. Sprinkle with cinnamon or nutmeg, if desired.

4 servings

Recipe No. 34 ⊞

Hot Buttered Rum

Preset Cooking Time: 1½ minutes

- ¼ cup rum
- 2 teaspoons brown sugar
- 1½ teaspoons unsalted butter
- Dash nutmeg
- 1 stick cinnamon

Combine rum and brown sugar in tall microproof mug or cup. Add water to fill two-thirds full. Place in oven. Set recipe number 34. Touch START. *(Oven cooks: HI, 1½ minutes.)*

Add butter and stir until melted. Sprinkle with nutmeg. Insert cinnamon stick as stirrer.

1 serving

Recipe No. 35 ⊞

Hot Cranberry Punch

Preset Cooking Time: 11 minutes

- 3 cups cranberry juice
- 1 cup apple juice
- ½ cup orange juice
- 3 tablespoons lemon juice
- 3 tablespoons sugar
- Whole cloves
- 1 stick cinnamon
- 1 orange, sliced

Combine juices, sugar, 4 cloves, and cinnamon in 2-quart microproof casserole. Cover and place in oven. Set recipe number 35. Touch START. *(Oven cooks: HI, 11 minutes.)*

Stir until sugar is dissolved. Strain into warmed punch bowl. Stick cloves into orange slices and float slices on punch as garnish.

8 servings

Rinsing the punch bowl with hot water is a good way to warm it before adding punch.

⊞ *Recipe can be increased.* *See "Quantity", page 12.*

Recipe No. 36

Hot Devilish Daiquiri

Preset Cooking Time: 6½ minutes

- ½ cup light rum
- 1½ cups hot water
- 1 can (6 ounces) frozen lemonade concentrate
- 1 can (6 ounces) frozen limeade concentrate
- ¼ cup sugar
- 2 sticks cinnamon
- 8 whole cloves

Pour rum into 1-cup glass measure; set aside. Combine remaining ingredients in 2-quart microproof casserole; blend well. Place in oven. Set recipe number 36. Touch START. *(Oven cooks: HI, 6 minutes.)*

At Pause, remove from oven; set aside. Place rum in oven. Touch START. *(Oven cooks: HI, 30 seconds.)*

Remove rum from oven. Ignite and pour flaming rum over hot juice mixture. Ladle into punch cups, and serve. Garnish with lemon slice and whole clove, if desired.

8 to 10 servings

Recipe No. 37 ⊞

Irish Coffee

Preset Cooking Time: 2 minutes

- 3 tablespoons Irish whiskey
- 1 tablespoon instant coffee powder
- 2 teaspoons sugar
- Whipped cream

Pour whiskey into 8-ounce microproof mug or cup. Add coffee and sugar. Add water to fill three-fourths full; blend well. Place in oven. Set recipe number 37. Touch START. *(Oven cooks: HI, 2 minutes.)*

Stir until sugar is dissolved. Top with dollop of whipped cream. Do not stir. Coffee should be sipped through the layer of cream.

1 serving

Recipe No. 38 ⊞

Russian Tea Mix

Preset Cooking Time: 2 minutes

- 1 jar (9 ounces) powdered orange breakfast drink
- 1 package (3 ounces) lemonade mix
- 1½ cups instant unsweetened tea
- ⅓ cup sugar
- 1 teaspoon cinnamon
- 1 teaspoon ground cloves
- ¾ teaspoon ginger
- ¼ teaspoon nutmeg
- 1 cup water or cider

Combine all ingredients except water. Store in covered jar or container until ready to use. To make 1 serving, place 1 to 2 teaspoons mix in 8-ounce microproof mug or cup. Add water or cider; blend well. Place in oven. Set recipe number 38. Touch START. *(Oven cooks: HI, 2 minutes.)* Stir before serving.

64 servings (about 3 cups mix)

For a lower-calorie drink, omit the sugar. If you'd like to serve your guests the regular drink but fix a low-calorie one for yourself, place 1 cup water, 1½ teaspoons instant unsweetened tea, ½ teaspoon grated orange peel, and 1 whole clove in microproof mug. Cook on HI 1½ minutes. If desired, artificial sweetener equal to 2 teaspoons sugar, or to taste, can be added after mixture is heated. Stir with cinnamon stick.

⊞ *Recipe can be increased. See "Quantity", page 12.*

West Coast Cocoa (page 58), Cappuccino (page 55), Hot Devilish Daiquiri →

Recipe No. 39 ⊞

Spicy Apple Drink

Preset Cooking Time: 10 minutes

- 1 quart apple cider
- 1/4 cup firmly packed brown sugar
- 2 sticks cinnamon
- 8 whole cloves
- 1/2 medium lemon, thinly sliced
- Pinch mace
- Pinch nutmeg
- 1 medium orange, thinly sliced

Combine cider, brown sugar, cinnamon, cloves, lemon, mace, and nutmeg in 2-quart glass measure; stir until brown sugar is dissolved. Place in oven. Set recipe number 39. Touch START. *(Oven cooks: HI, 10 minutes.)*

Strain into 4 mugs. Garnish with orange slices before serving.

4 servings

Recipe No. 41 ⊞

West Coast Cocoa

Preset Cooking Time: 7 minutes

- 1/3 cup unsweetened cocoa powder
- 1/4 cup sugar
- 3 cups milk
- 2 teaspoons grated orange peel
- 1/4 teaspoon almond extract
- 4 sticks cinnamon

Combine cocoa and sugar in 4-cup glass measure. Add 1/2 cup milk; blend to make smooth paste. Stir in remaining 2 1/2 cups milk, orange peel, and almond extract; stir until sugar is dissolved. Place in oven. Set recipe number 41. Touch START. *(Oven cooks: 70, 7 minutes.)*

Pour into 4 mugs. Insert cinnamon sticks as stirrers.

4 servings

Recipe No. 40 ⊞

Tomato Warmer

Preset Cooking Time: 6 minutes

- 2 1/2 cups tomato juice
- 1 can (10 1/2 ounces) beef broth
- 1/4 cup lemon juice
- 1 teaspoon prepared horseradish
- 1 teaspoon parsley flakes
- 1/2 teaspoon celery salt
- 1/4 cup dry sherry (optional)

Combine all ingredients except sherry in 4-cup glass measure. Place in oven. Set recipe number 40. Touch START. *(Oven cooks: HI, 6 minutes.)*

Pour into 6 mugs. Stir 2 teaspoons sherry into each mug before serving.

6 servings

Recipe No. 42

Hot Milk

Preset Cooking Time: about 3 minutes

- 1 cup (8 ounces) milk

Pour milk into microproof mug or cup. Place in oven. Insert temperature probe. Set recipe number 42. Touch START. *(Oven cooks: 70, about 3 minutes to 140°F; holds warm: 10.)*

1 serving

This is an ideal way to heat milk for hot chocolate or any milk-based beverage.

Recipe No. 43

Hot Water

Preset Cooking Time: about 1¾ minutes

1 cup (8 ounces) water

Pour water into microproof mug or cup. Place in oven. Insert temperature probe. Set recipe number 43. Touch START. *(Oven cooks: HI, about 1¾ minutes to 150°F)*

1 serving

⊞ *Recipe can be increased. See "Quantity", page 12.*

Recipe No. 44 ⊞

Hot Water for Instant Beverages

Preset Cooking Time: 1½ minutes

1 cup (8 ounces) water

Pour water into microproof mug or cup. Place in oven. Set recipe number 44. Touch START. *(Oven cooks: HI, 1½ minutes.)*

1 serving

This is an ideal way to heat water for tea, instant coffee, bouillon, etc.

Converting Your Own Sandwich Recipes

The enormous variety of sandwich combinations you can heat in your microwave oven will tickle your imagination, and they are so easy to do. Combine meats and cheeses, eggs, salads, and vegetables; make "Dagwoods" or elegant tea sandwiches; and, of course, you'll want to cook the old standbys, hot dogs and hamburgers. Sandwiches heat in seconds, so be careful not to overcook — the bread can become tough and chewy. Heat breads until warm, not hot, and cheese just until it begins to melt. You can warm meat sandwiches, filled only with several thin slices of meat per sandwich, on HI as follows:

1 sandwich	45 to 50 seconds
2 sandwiches	1 to 1½ minutes
4 sandwiches	2 to 2½ minutes

Follow these tips when adapting or creating your own sandwiches:

- ☐ The best breads to use for warmed sandwiches are day-old, full-bodied breads such as rye and whole wheat, and breads rich in eggs and shortening, like French or Italian and other white breads.
- ☐ Heat sandwiches on paper napkins, paper towels, or paper plates to absorb the steam and prevent sogginess. Cover with a paper towel to prevent splattering. More simply, you can wrap each sandwich in a paper towel. Remove wrapping immediately after warming.
- ☐ Thin slices of meat heat more quickly and taste better than one thick slice. The slower-cooking thick slice often causes bread to overcook before meat is hot.
- ☐ Moist fillings, such as that in a Sloppy Joe or a barbecued beef sandwich, should generally be heated separately from the rolls, to prevent sogginess.
- ☐ The browning dish can be used to enhance your grilled cheese, Reuben, or bacon sandwich. Brown the buttered outer side of bread before inserting filling.

Recipe No. 45

Bacon Cheesewiches

Preset Cooking Time: 3½ minutes

½ cup (2 ounces) grated Cheddar cheese
1 tablespoon mayonnaise
2 teaspoons catsup
1 large egg, hard-cooked and chopped
2 slices bacon
2 hamburger buns, split

Combine cheese, mayonnaise, catsup, and egg; blend well; set aside. Place bacon on paper towel-lined microproof plate. Place in oven. Cover with paper towel. Set recipe number 45. Touch START. *(Oven cooks: HI, 2 minutes.)*

At Pause, remove from oven. Break each slice in half; set aside. Spread half of the cheese mixture on bottom half of each bun. Place on microwave roasting rack. Place in oven. Touch START. *(Oven cooks: 50, 1 minute.)*

At Pause, place 2 halves bacon on each sandwich. Cover with tops of buns. Touch START. *(Oven cooks: 50, 30 seconds.)*

2 sandwiches

Recipe No. 46

Beef Tacos

Preset Cooking Time: 7 minutes

1 pound lean ground beef
1 small onion, chopped
1 envelope (1¼ ounces) taco seasoning mix
10 taco shells
1½ cups (6 ounces) shredded Cheddar cheese, divided
2 cups shredded lettuce
2 medium tomatoes, chopped
1 avocado, peeled and diced
Dairy sour cream (optional)
Hot pepper sauce (optional)

Crumble beef into 2-quart microproof casserole. Add onion. Place in oven. Set recipe number 46. Touch START. *(Oven cooks: HI, 2 minutes.)*

At Pause, stir to break up beef. Touch START. *(Oven cooks: HI, 3 minutes.)*

At Pause, remove from oven. Stir beef; drain. Stir in seasoning mix. Stand taco shells in large, shallow, microproof baking dish. Divide beef mixture among shells. Top each with about 1 tablespoon cheese. Place in oven. Touch START. *(Oven cooks: HI, 2 minutes.)*

Remove tacos from oven. Top each with lettuce, tomatoes, remaining cheese, and avocado. Pass sour cream and hot pepper sauce separately.

10 tacos

Recipe No. 47

Cheeseburgers

Preset Cooking Time: 2½ minutes

1 pound lean ground beef
Salt and pepper, to taste
4 slices process American cheese
4 hamburger buns, split and toasted

Preheat microproof browning dish according to manufacturer's directions. While dish is heating, season beef with salt and pepper. Shape into 4 patties. Place on browning dish in oven. Set recipe number 47. Touch START. *(Oven cooks: HI, 2 minutes.)*

At Pause, turn patties over. Top each with 1 slice cheese. Touch START. *(Oven cooks: HI, 30 seconds.)*

Serve on toasted buns.

4 cheeseburgers

Recipe No. 48 ⊞

Coney Island Hot Dog

Preset Cooking Time: $1\frac{1}{4}$ minutes

1 jumbo hot dog (3 ounces)
1 hot dog bun, split
Prepared mustard
2 tablespoons drained sauerkraut
Pickle relish, chili, grated cheese, chopped onion (optional)

Score opposite sides of hot dog in several places. Place on microproof plate. Place in oven. Set recipe number 48. Touch START. *(Oven cooks: HI,* 1 *minute.)*

At Pause, remove from oven. Place hot dog in bun. Place in oven. Touch START. *(Oven cooks: HI,* 15 *seconds.)*

Top with mustard, sauerkraut, and selected garnish.

1 serving

Because the hot dog is large, it takes longer to cook than it takes for the bun to become hot. The hot dog is cooked first, then added to the bun.

Recipe No. 49 ⊞

Hot Dog

Preset Cooking Time: 50 seconds

1 hot dog (1.6 ounces)
1 hot dog bun, split
Prepared mustard (optional)
Pickle relish (optional)

Score opposite sides of hot dog in several places. Place on microproof plate. Place in oven. Set recipe number 49. Touch START. *(Oven cooks:* 80, 50 *seconds.)*

Place hot dog in bun. Top with mustard and relish.

1 serving

Recipe No. 50 ⊞

Precooked Sausages, Bratwurst, Polish Sausage, Knockwurst

Preset Cooking Time: $1\frac{3}{4}$ minutes

1 sausage (3 ounces)
1 hot dog bun, split

Score opposite sides of sausage in several places. Place on microwave roasting rack. Place in oven. Set recipe number 50. Touch START. *(Oven cooks:* 80, $1\frac{1}{2}$ *minutes.)*

At Pause, remove sausage from rack. Drain rack and wipe clean with paper towel. Place sausage in bun. Place on rack in oven. Touch START. *(Oven cooks: HI,* 15 *seconds.)*

1 serving

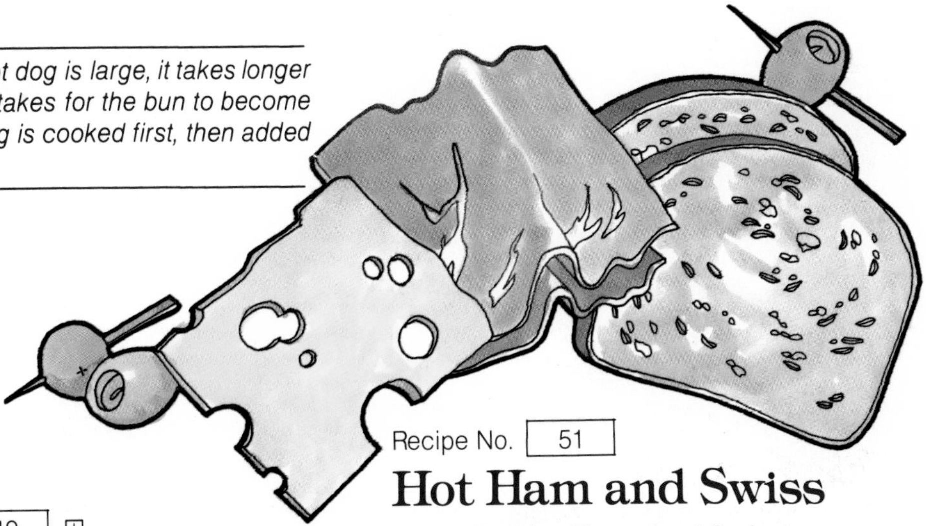

Recipe No. 51

Hot Ham and Swiss

Preset Cooking Time: about 3 minutes

2 slices rye bread
Butter or margarine
Mayonnaise
2 thin slices boiled ham
1 slice Swiss cheese

Spread bread with butter and mayonnaise. Place ham and cheese between bread slices. Place on microwave roasting rack. Place in oven. Insert temperature probe at least 1 inch into center of sandwich. Set recipe number 51. Touch START. *(Oven cooks: HI, about* 1 *minute to* 110°*F; stands:* 0, 2 *minutes.)*

1 sandwich

⊞ *Recipe can be increased. See "Quantity", page 12.*

Recipe No. 52

Hot Tuna Buns

Preset Cooking Time: 2 minutes

- 1 can (6½ to 7 ounces) tuna, drained and flaked
- 1 cup chopped celery
- ¼ cup mayonnaise
- 2 tablespoons catsup
- 1 teaspoon lemon juice
- Salt and pepper, to taste
- 4 hamburger buns, split

Combine tuna, celery, mayonnaise, catsup, and lemon juice. Season with salt and pepper. Spoon mixture onto bottom halves of buns; cover with tops of buns. Place 2 sandwiches on microwave roasting rack. Place in oven. Set recipe number 52. Touch START. *(Oven cooks:* 80, 1 *minute.)*

At Pause, remove sandwiches from oven. Place remaining 2 sandwiches on rack in oven. Touch START. *(Oven cooks:* 80, 1 *minute.)*

4 sandwiches

Recipe No. 53 ⊞

Denver Sandwich

Preset Cooking Time: 2 minutes

- 1 large egg
- 3 tablespoons diced boiled ham
- 1 tablespoon minced onion
- 1 teaspoon minced green pepper
- 1 hamburger bun, split and toasted, or 2 slices bread, toasted

Combine egg, ham, onion, and green pepper in 1-cup glass measure; beat with fork. Pour into small, shallow, microproof bowl. Place in oven. Set recipe number 53. Touch START. *(Oven cooks:* 60, 1 *minute.)*

At Pause, stir carefully. Touch START. *(Oven cooks:* 60, 1 *minute.)*

Serve on toasted bun.

1 sandwich

⊞ *Recipe can be increased. See "Quantity", page 12.*

← *Reuben Sandwich*

Recipe No. 54

Italian Meatball Sandwich

Preset Cooking Time: 9 minutes

- 1 pound lean ground beef
- 1 cup cooked rice
- 1 small onion, finely chopped
- 2 large eggs, lightly beaten
- 1 tablespoon Italian seasoning
- 1 jar (15 ounces) spaghetti sauce
- 1 loaf (1 pound) French or Italian bread, cut in half lengthwise
- Grated Parmesan cheese

Combine beef, rice, onion, eggs, and seasoning; blend well. Shape into 8 balls. Arrange meatballs in circle on microwave roasting rack. Place in oven. Set recipe number 54. Touch START. *(Oven cooks: HI, 3 minutes.)*

At Pause, turn over. Touch START. *(Oven cooks: HI, 2 minutes.)*

At Pause, remove meatballs from oven. Place in microproof casserole. Top with sauce. Cover and place in oven. Touch START. *(Oven cooks: HI, 4 minutes.)*

Spoon meatballs and sauce onto bottom half of loaf. Sprinkle generously with cheese. Cover with top of loaf, slice in half, and serve hot.

4 sandwiches

Recipe No. 55 ⊞

Reuben Sandwich

Preset Cooking Time: 1¾ minutes

- 4 slices rye or pumpernickel bread
- Butter or margarine
- 6 ounces corned beef, thinly sliced
- ½ cup drained sauerkraut
- 2 heaping tablespoons Thousand Island dressing
- 2 slices Swiss cheese

Toast bread; spread lightly with butter. Layer remaining ingredients evenly over 2 slices toast. Place on microwave roasting rack. Place in oven. Set recipe number 55. Touch START. *(Oven cooks:* 80, 1 *minute.)*

At Pause, top with remaining 2 slices toast. Touch START. *(Oven cooks:* 80, 45 *seconds.)*

2 sandwiches

Recipe No. 56 ⊞

Roast Beef 'n Swiss Rolls

Preset Cooking Time: 1½ minutes

- 1½ tablespoons butter or margarine, softened
- ⅓ teaspoon prepared mustard
- ¼ teaspoon poppy seed
- ⅛ teaspoon onion powder
- 2 large hard rolls, split
- 2 thin slices roast beef
- 2 slices Swiss cheese

Combine butter, mustard, poppy seed, and onion powder; blend well. Spread rolls with butter mixture. Place 1 slice each beef and cheese on bottom half of each roll. Place on microwave roasting rack. Place in oven. Set recipe number 56. Touch START. *(Oven cooks:* 50, 1 *minute.)*

At Pause, cover with tops of rolls. Touch START. *(Oven cooks:* 50, 30 *seconds.)*

2 sandwiches

Recipe No. 57

Barbecued Beef-on-a-Bun

Preset Cooking Time: 18¾ minutes

- 1 pound top round steak
- ¼ cup butter or margarine
- 1½ tablespoons cornstarch
- ¼ cup beef broth
- ¼ cup lemon juice
- ½ cup chili sauce
- 1 tablespoon brown sugar
- 1 tablespoon instant minced onion
- 1 tablespoon Worcestershire sauce
- 1 teaspoon prepared horseradish
- ½ teaspoon salt
- ¼ teaspoon paprika
- ¼ teaspoon hot pepper sauce
- 1 small clove garlic, minced
- 6 heated buns

Cut steak across grain into very thin strips; set aside. Place butter in 2½-quart microproof casserole. Place in oven. Set recipe number 57. Touch START. *(Oven cooks: HI,* 45 *seconds.)*

At Pause, add steak; stir to coat. Cover. Touch START. *(Oven cooks:* 50, 5 *minutes.)*

At Pause, stir. Cover. Touch START. *(Oven cooks:* 50, 3 *minutes.)*

At Pause, dissolve cornstarch in broth and lemon juice. Add to steak. Add remaining ingredients except buns; blend well. Cover. Touch START. *(Oven cooks:* 50, 10 *minutes.)*

Let stand 2 minutes before serving on buns.

6 sandwiches

It's hard to imagine a sandwich that is not improved by warming the buns first. Cook 6 buns on 20 for 2 to 3 minutes; 4 buns take 1 *to* 1½ *minutes.*

⊞ *Recipe can be increased. See "Quantity", page 12.*

Sausage and Pepper Heroes (page 66), Hot Dogs (page 61) →

Recipe No. 58

Pizza Burgers

Preset Cooking Time: 6¾ minutes

- ½ pound lean ground beef
- 1 tablespoon finely chopped onion
- ½ cup pizza sauce
- ¼ teaspoon salt
- Dash pepper
- ⅛ teaspoon cinnamon
- ½ cup (2 ounces) shredded mozzarella cheese, divided
- 4 hamburger buns, split

Crumble beef into 1½-quart microproof casserole. Add onion. Place in oven. Set recipe number 58. Touch START. *(Oven cooks: HI, 2 minutes.)*

At Pause, stir to break up beef. Touch START. *(Oven cooks: HI, 1 minute.)*

At Pause, remove from oven; drain. Add pizza sauce, salt, pepper, and cinnamon; blend well. Place in oven. Touch START. *(Oven cooks: HI, 3 minutes.)*

At Pause, remove from oven. Stir in ¼ cup cheese. Arrange bottom halves of buns on microwave roasting rack. Top with beef mixture. Top with remaining cheese. Cover with tops of buns. Place in oven. Touch START. *(Oven cooks: 80, 45 seconds.)*

4 sandwiches

Recipe No. 59

Sausage and Pepper Heroes

Preset Cooking Time: 7 minutes

- 4 Italian sausages
- ½ cup barbecue sauce
- 1 medium green pepper, seeded and cut into strips
- 4 hero rolls

Score sausages on opposite sides in several places. Place on microwave roasting rack. Place in oven. Cover with paper towel. Set recipe number 59. Touch START. *(Oven cooks: HI, 3 minutes.)*

At Pause, remove from oven; set aside. Combine barbecue sauce and green pepper in 2-cup glass measure. Place in oven. Touch START. *(Oven cooks: HI, 2½ minutes.)*

At Pause, remove from oven. Split rolls in half without cutting all the way through. Place 1 sausage in each roll. Top each with sauce. Wipe rack clean with paper towel. Arrange rolls on rack. Place in oven. Touch START. *(Oven cooks: 50, 1½ minutes.)*

4 sandwiches

If you prefer, Spicy Barbecue Sauce (page 178) can be substituted for ready-made sauce.

A Baker's Dozen

Treat your family and friends to the rich aromas of hot-from-the-oven bread, sweet rolls, muffins, and coffee cakes. For a quick and easy surprise breakfast or coffee break, count on the short cooking time of the microwave oven. Bread cooked in the microwave has an excellent texture and flavor, but does not brown or develop crust — there is no hot air to dry the surface as in conventional baking. For best results, if you like the browned look for your bread and muffins, use dark flours, brown sugar, molasses, and spices. Because a crust doesn't form, bread cooked in the microwave oven has the remarkable characteristic of rising higher than in conventional cooking. With tender, loving care you'll soon succeed in making homemade bread, muffins, and sweet rolls a constant addition to your menus. Our Honey Corn Bread Ring (page 68) may be your favorite!

Breads, such as Zucchini-Nut Bread (page 74), and cakes are tested for doneness just as in conventional cooking (above left). Custard cups arranged in a circle may be used to make muffins (above). Raising bread dough is a snap. A cup of water helps provide a moist environment (left).

Converting Your Recipes

When adapting "quick bread" recipes, you will find it necessary to reduce the amount of leavening (baking powder or soda) by about one-quarter the normal amount. A bitter aftertaste is apparent if too much leavening is used in biscuits or muffins. Since foods rise higher in the microwave oven, you will not see a loss in volume from the reduction or soda or baking powder. If a recipe contains buttermilk or sour cream, do not change the amount of soda, since it serves to counteract the sour taste and does not act only as a leavening agent. When using a mix where leavening cannot be reduced, allow the batter or dough to stand about 10 minutes before cooking to reduce some of the gas. Yeast doughs need not be changed but may cook more evenly if cooked in a bundt or ring mold shape rather than the conventional loaf pan. And observe the following tips:

- ☐ To raise yeast dough, place 1 cup water in 2-cup glass measure. Cook on HI 3 minutes, or until boiling. Place dough in oven next to water. Set Cook Control at "1" (lowest possible setting) and timer at 10 minutes. When timer beeps, leave dough in oven another 20 minutes, or until double in bulk.
- ☐ Because breads rise higher than in a conventional oven, use a larger loaf pan.
- ☐ Fill paper-lined muffin cups only half full to allow for muffins rising higher.
- ☐ You can prepare your own "brown 'n serve" rolls. Bake them in the microwave oven. Brown in the conventional oven just before serving.
- ☐ When preparing yeast dough, use a glass measure and the temperature probe set at 120°F to heat liquids.

Recipe No. 60

Caramel Nut Sticky Buns

Preset Cooking Time: 4 minutes

- 1/3 cup firmly packed brown sugar
- 3 tablespoons butter or margarine
- 1 tablespoon water
- 1 teaspoon cinnamon
- 1/3 cup chopped nuts
- 1 package (10 ounces) refrigerator biscuits, separated

Combine brown sugar, butter, water, and cinnamon in 4-cup microproof ring mold. Place in oven. Set recipe number 60. Touch START. *(Oven cooks: HI, 1 minute.)*

At Pause, remove from oven. Stir in nuts. Cut each biscuit into quarters. Place in brown sugar mixture. Stir carefully to coat each piece. Push biscuits toward outside of mold. Place in oven. Touch START. *(Oven cooks: HI, 3 minutes.)*

Let stand 2 minutes. Pull biscuits apart to serve.

6 servings

Recipe No. 61

Honey Corn Bread Ring

Preset Cooking Time: 13 minutes

- 1 cup all-purpose flour
- 1 cup cornmeal
- 3/4 cup milk
- 1/3 cup honey
- 1/4 cup shortening
- 2 large eggs
- 2 teaspoons baking powder

Combine all ingredients; stir just until blended. Pour into lightly greased 8-cup microproof ring mold. Place in oven. Set recipe number 61. Touch START. *(Oven cooks: HI, 8 minutes; stands: 0, 5 minutes.)* If bread is rising unevenly, touch STOP, and rotate mold one-quarter turn. Touch START.

16 servings

Honey Corn Bread Ring, Pineapple Zucchini Bread (page 72) →

Recipe No. 62

Dandy Dumplings

Preset Cooking Time: 19 minutes

- 1 cup all-purpose flour
- 1½ teaspoons baking powder
- ½ teaspoon salt
- 3 tablespoons shortening
- ½ cup milk
- 1 tablespoon minced parsley
- 2½ cups chicken, beef, or vegetable broth

Combine flour, baking powder, and salt. Cut in shortening until mixture is consistency of fine meal. Add milk and parsley; stir just until moistened; set aside. Pour broth into 2-quart microproof casserole. Place in oven. Set recipe number 62. Touch START. *(Oven cooks: HI, 8 minutes.)*

At Pause, immediately drop batter by rounded teaspoonfuls into boiling broth. Touch START. *(Oven cooks: HI, 6 minutes.)*

At Pause, cover. Touch START. *(Oven cooks: HI, 5 minutes.)*

Let stand 2 minutes before transferring dumplings to serving dish with slotted spoon.

16 dumplings

Recipe No. 63

Garlic Parmesan Bread

Preset Cooking Time: 1 minute

- ½ cup butter or margarine, softened
- 2 or 3 cloves garlic, minced
- 1 loaf (1 pound) French, Italian, or sourdough bread
- ½ cup grated Parmesan cheese
- Paprika

Combine butter and garlic; blend well; set aside. Cut loaf into 1-inch thick slices without cutting all the way through. Spread slices with garlic butter. Sprinkle with cheese and paprika. Place loaf on microwave roasting rack. Place in oven. Set recipe number 63. Touch START. *(Oven cooks: 80, 1 minute.)*

12 servings

Recipe No. 64

Oatmeal Muffins

Preset Cooking Time: 7½ minutes

- 3 tablespoons chopped nuts
- 2 tablespoons brown sugar
- Dash nutmeg
- ⅔ cup firmly packed brown sugar
- ½ cup vegetable oil
- ½ cup buttermilk or sour milk
- 2 large eggs, beaten
- 1 cup all-purpose flour
- ⅔ cup rolled oats
- 1 teaspoon baking powder
- ½ teaspoon baking soda
- ½ teaspoon salt

Combine nuts, 2 tablespoons brown sugar, and nutmeg; set aside. Combine ⅔ cup brown sugar, oil, buttermilk, and eggs; blend well. Add remaining ingredients except nut mixture; stir just until moistened. Spoon one third of the batter into 6 paper-lined microproof muffin or custard cups, filling cups half full. Sprinkle with one third of the nut mixture. Place in oven. If using custard cups, arrange in circle. Set recipe number 64. Touch START. *(Oven cooks: HI, 2½ minutes.)*

At Pause, remove from oven. Repeat as above for 6 more muffins. Touch START. *(Oven cooks: HI, 2½ minutes.)*

At Pause, repeat as above for remaining 6 muffins. Touch START. *(Oven cooks: HI, 2½ minutes.)*

Let stand 3 minutes before serving.

18 muffins

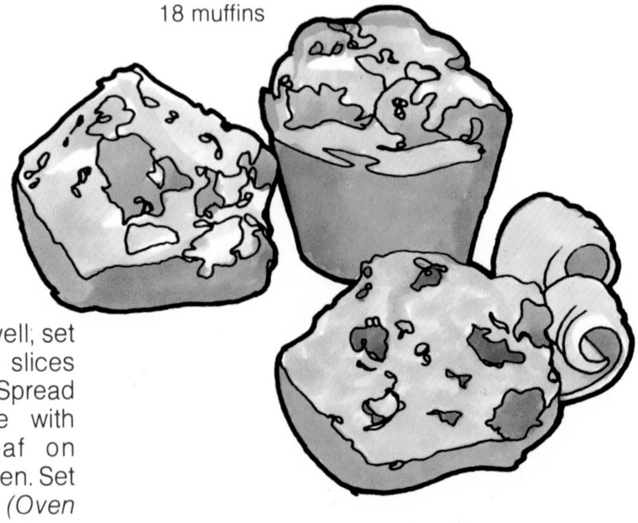

Recipe No. 65

Raisin Bran Muffins

Preset Cooking Time: 6 minutes

- 1 large egg
- 1 cup buttermilk
- 1 1/4 cups all-purpose flour
- 1 cup raisin bran cereal
- 3/4 cup firmly packed brown sugar
- 1/4 cup chopped nuts (optional)
- 1/4 cup vegetable oil
- 1 teaspoon baking soda
- 1/4 teaspoon salt

Combine egg and buttermilk; blend well. Add remaining ingredients; blend well. Spoon batter into 6 paper-lined microproof muffin or custard cups, filling cups two-thirds full. Place in oven. If using custard cups, arrange in circle. Set recipe number 65. Touch START. *(Oven cooks: HI, 3 minutes.)*

At Pause, remove from oven. Repeat as above for remaining 6 muffins. Touch START. *(Oven cooks: HI, 3 minutes.)*

Let stand 3 minutes before serving.

12 muffins

Recipe No. 66

Sour Cream Coffeecake

Preset Cooking Time: 11 minutes

- 1/2 cup chopped nuts
- 1/3 cup firmly packed brown sugar
- 2 tablespoons all-purpose flour
- 2 tablespoons butter or margarine
- 1/4 teaspoon cinnamon
- 1/8 teaspoon salt
- 1/2 cup butter or margarine, softened
- 1/2 cup sugar
- 2 large eggs
- 1/2 teaspoon vanilla
- 1 1/2 cups all-purpose flour
- 1/2 teaspoon baking soda
- 1/2 teaspoon baking powder
- 1/2 cup dairy sour cream

Combine nuts, brown sugar, 2 tablespoons flour, 2 tablespoons butter, cinnamon, and salt; mix until crumbly; set aside. Cream 1/2 cup butter and sugar with electric mixer until light and fluffy. Add eggs and vanilla; blend well. Sift 1 1/2 cups flour, baking soda, and baking powder into separate bowl. Alternately beat flour mixture and sour cream into creamed mixture. Spread half of the batter in 8-inch round microproof baking dish. Sprinkle half of the nut mixture over batter. Carefully spread remaining batter on top. Sprinkle with remaining nut mixture. Place in oven. Set recipe number 66. Touch START. *(Oven cooks: 60, 4 minutes.)*

At Pause, rotate dish one-quarter turn. Touch START. *(Oven cooks: HI, 4 minutes, stands: 0, 3 minutes.)*

Serve warm.

9 servings

Recipe No. 67

Welsh Rabbit on Toast

Preset Cooking Time: 12 minutes

- 4 cups (1 pound) shredded sharp Cheddar cheese
- 4 teaspoons butter or margarine
- 3/4 teaspoon Worcestershire sauce
- 1/2 teaspoon salt
- 1/2 teaspoon paprika
- 1/4 teaspoon dry mustard
- 1/4 teaspoon cayenne
- 2 large eggs, lightly beaten
- 1 cup flat beer or ale, at room temperature
- 4 to 6 slices French bread, toasted

Combine cheese, butter, Worcestershire, salt, paprika, mustard, and cayenne in 2-quart microproof casserole; blend well. Cover and place in oven. Set recipe number 67. Touch START. *(Oven cooks: 50, 3 minutes.)*

At Pause, stir. Cover. Touch START. *(Oven cooks: 50, 3 minutes.)*

At Pause, remove from oven. Stir small amount cheese mixture into eggs; gradually stir into remaining cheese mixture; blend well. Gradually blend in beer. Cover and place in oven. Touch START. *(Oven cooks: 50, 3 minutes.)*

At Pause, stir through several times. Cover. Touch START. *(Oven cooks: 50, 3 minutes.)*

Stir thoroughly and briskly. Arrange toast in individual shallow bowls and ladle cheese mixture over top.

4 to 6 servings

Recipe No. 68

Pineapple Zucchini Bread

Preset Cooking Time: 14½ minutes

- ¾ cup sugar
- ½ cup vegetable oil
- 2 large eggs
- 1 can (8¼ ounces) crushed pineapple
- 1¾ cups all-purpose flour
- 1 cup grated zucchini
- 1 teaspoon cinnamon
- ½ teaspoon baking powder
- ½ teaspoon baking soda
- ½ cup chopped nuts
- ¼ cup graham-cracker crumbs

Grease bottom and sides of 9×5-inch microproof loaf pan; set aside. Combine sugar, oil, and eggs; blend well. Add pineapple, flour, zucchini, cinnamon, baking powder, and baking soda; mix well. Stir in nuts. Pour into prepared pan; spread evenly. Place in oven. Set recipe number 68. Touch START. *(Oven cooks:* 50, 10 *minutes.)*

At Pause, sprinkle the graham-cracker crumbs evenly over top. Touch START. *(Oven cooks: HI, 4½ minutes.)*

Let stand 10 minutes before turning out of pan onto wire rack. Cool completely before slicing.

12 to 18 servings

Recipe No. 69

Blueberry Muffins

Preset Cooking Time: 5 minutes

- 1½ cups all-purpose flour
- ⅓ cup firmly packed brown sugar
- 1 teaspoon cinnamon
- ½ teaspoon baking powder
- ½ teaspoon baking soda
- ½ teaspoon salt
- ¾ cup buttermilk
- ¼ cup vegetable oil
- 1 large egg
- ⅔ cup blueberries

Combine flour, brown sugar, cinnamon, baking powder, baking soda, and salt. Add buttermilk, oil, and egg; stir vigorously just until moistened. Stir in blueberries. Spoon batter into 6 paper-lined microproof custard or muffin cups, filling cups two-thirds full. Place in oven. If using custard cups, arrange in circle. Set recipe number 69. Touch START. *(Oven cooks: HI, 2½ minutes.)*

At Pause, remove from oven. Repeat as above for the remaining 6 muffins. Touch START. *(Oven cooks: HI, 2½ minutes.)*

Let stand 2 minutes before serving.

12 muffins

Recipe No. 70

Molasses Buttermilk Bread

Preset Cooking Time: 9½ minutes

- ½ cup all-purpose flour
- ½ cup whole wheat flour
- ½ cup cornmeal
- 1 teaspoon baking soda
- ½ teaspoon salt
- 1 cup buttermilk
- ⅓ cup molasses
- 2 tablespoons vegetable oil
- 1 large egg, lightly beaten
- ⅓ cup raisins or currants

Lightly grease 6-cup microproof ring mold; set aside. Combine flours, cornmeal, baking soda, and salt; mix lightly. Set aside. Combine buttermilk, molasses, oil, and egg; blend well. Add to flour mixture; blend well. Stir in raisins. Pour batter into prepared mold. Place in oven. Set recipe number 70. Touch START. *(Oven cooks:* 70, 5 *minutes.)*

At Pause, rotate. Touch START. *(Oven cooks:* 70, 4½ *minutes.)*

Let stand 10 minutes before turning out of mold onto wire rack. Cool completely before slicing.

10 to 12 servings

Zucchini-Nut Bread (page 74), →
Raisin Bran Muffins (page 71),
Oatmeal Muffins (page 70)

Recipe No. 71

Zucchini-Nut Bread

Preset Cooking Time: 25 minutes

- 1 cup sugar, divided
- 2 teaspoons cinnamon
- 1 cup grated zucchini
- 2 large eggs
- ½ cup vegetable oil
- ½ cup plain yogurt
- 1 teaspoon vanilla
- 1¾ cups all-purpose flour
- ⅔ cup chopped walnuts
- 1 teaspoon baking soda
- 1 teaspoon salt

Lightly grease 6-cup microproof ring mold. Combine 2 teaspoons sugar and cinnamon; sprinkle over greased surface of mold. Shake to spread evenly; discard excess; set mold aside. Combine remaining sugar, zucchini, eggs, oil, yogurt, and vanilla; blend well. Add remaining ingredients; mix well. Pour into prepared mold. Place in oven. Set recipe number 71. Touch START. *(Oven cooks: 70, 15 minutes; 0, 10 minutes.)* If bread is rising unevenly, touch STOP, and rotate dish one-quarter turn. Touch START.

Turn out of mold onto wire rack. Cool completely before slicing.

12 to 18 servings

Recipe No. 72

Raisin-Nut Ring

Preset Cooking Time: 12 minutes

- 3 tablespoons butter or margarine
- ⅓ cup firmly packed brown sugar
- 2 tablespoons corn syrup
- ½ cup chopped nuts
- ¼ cup raisins
- 1 package (10 ounces) refrigerator buttermilk biscuits, separated

Place butter in 4-cup microproof ring mold. Place in oven. Set recipe number 72. Touch START. *(Oven cooks: HI, 1 minute.)*

At Pause, remove from oven. Stir in brown sugar and corn syrup. Spread evenly over bottom of mold. Sprinkle evenly with nuts and raisins. Place in oven. Touch START. *(Oven cooks: HI, 1 minute.)*

At Pause, arrange biscuits over nuts and raisins. Touch START. *(Oven cooks: 50, 7 minutes; stands: 0, 3 minutes.)* If bread is rising unevenly, touch STOP, and rotate mold one-quarter turn. Touch START.

Invert mold onto serving plate. Allow syrup to drizzle down sides of ring before removing mold.

10 servings

CONVENIENCE BREADS

Food	Amount	Cook Control Setting	Time	Special Notes
Hamburger buns, hot dog rolls, frozen	1 lb.	30 (defrost)	3½-4½ minutes	Use original microproof container, paper plate, or towels. Place on microproof rack, turn over after 2 minutes.
Room temperature:	1	80 (reheat)	5-10 seconds	
	2	80 (reheat)	10-15 seconds	
	4	80 (reheat)	15-20 seconds	
	6	80 (reheat)	20-25 seconds	
Doughnuts, sweet rolls, muffins	1	80 (reheat)	10-15 seconds	Place on paper plate or towel. Add 15 seconds if frozen.
	2	80 (reheat)	20-25 seconds	
	4	80 (reheat)	35-40 seconds	
	6	80 (reheat)	45-50 seconds	
Whole coffee cake, frozen	10-13 oz.	80 (reheat)	1½-2 minutes	Place on paper plate or towel.
Room temperature:	10-13 oz.	80 (reheat)	1-1½ minutes	Place on paper plate or towel.
French bread, frozen	1 lb.	80 (reheat)	1½-2 minutes	Place on paper plate or towel.
Room temperature:	1 lb.	80 (reheat)	20-30 seconds	
English muffins, waffles, frozen	2	HI (max. power)	30-45 seconds	Place on paper towels. Toast in toaster after defrosting, if desired.
Corn bread mix	15 oz.	50 (simmer) HI (max. power)	10 minutes 3-4 minutes	Use 9" round dish, paper-lined custard cups, or microproof muffin tray. Turn dish if rising unevenly. Let stand 5 minutes before serving.

Ring the Dinner Bell for Meat

Cooking meat in the microwave oven offers tremendous advantages over the conventional range. For juiciness and flavor, the microwave method excels. It also stretches your meat dollar by reducing shrinkage. And you can defrost, cook, and reheat in minutes while your kitchen remains cool and comfortable.

If some of your guests or family prefer beef rare and others well done, the microwave oven solves the problem. After the roast is carved, a few seconds in the microwave oven will bring slices of rare roast to medium or well done. In addition, meat for the barbecue is enhanced by precooking in the microwave. You get that wonderful charcoal flavor without the long watchful cooking that often results in burned or blackened meat. Microwave roasting methods are similar to dry roasting in your conventional oven. This means that the better, tender cuts of meat are recommended for best results. Less tender cuts should be marinated or tenderized and cooked at low power settings. As in conventional cooking, they are braised or stewed to achieve tenderness.

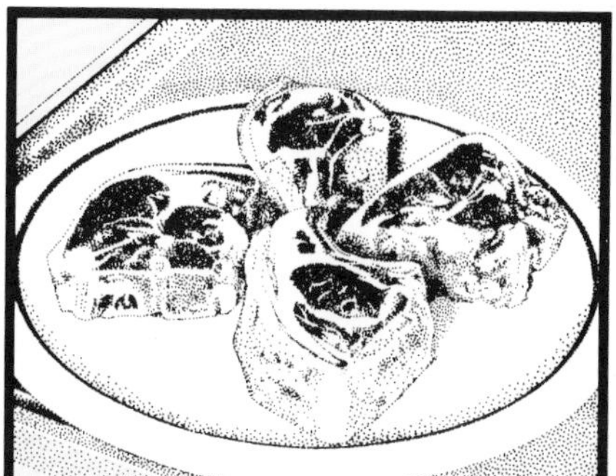

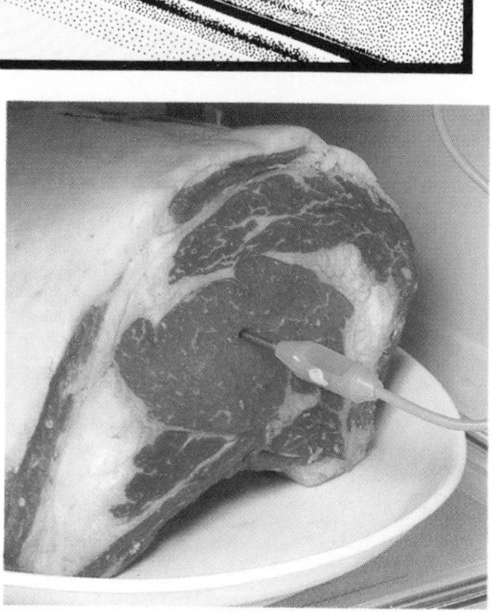

Meatloaf may be cooked in a loaf, but a ring mold is best. You can make your own ring mold by using a small straight-sided glass in baking dish (above). Food arrangement for microwave cooking is illustrated with lamb chops: the narrow bony end is placed toward the center of the dish (above right). Placement of the temperature probe in a rib roast (right).

Some people believe that meat does not brown in microwave ovens. Wrong! Any meat that cooks more than 10 minutes will brown in your microwave oven. True, individual steaks, chops, ground meat patties, chops, and thin cuts of meat that cook quickly will brown best with a microproof browning dish.

Using the browning dish for Cheeseburgers (page 58)→

Converting Your Recipes

Charts on the following pages outline microwave thawing and cooking times for the standard cuts of meat. The temperature probe eliminates any guesswork or troublesome arithmetic. For converting casseroles, meatloaf, meat in sauces, and recipes that call for less tender cuts of meat, you're sure to find a similar recipe here to guide your own creations. Adapt your conventional recipes by matching ingredients and methods as closely as possible. Experiment as much as you like. Here are some helpful hints:

- ☐ For best results, cook evenly shaped, boned, rolled, and tied small roasts.
- ☐ Recipe times here presume meat is at refrigerator temperature. If your meal requires lengthy preparation, during which the meat may reach room temperature, reduce cooking times.
- ☐ Baste, marinate, or season meat just as you would for conventional cooking.
- ☐ You can use a microwave roasting rack to elevate meat from its drippings during cooking.
- ☐ Use a tight cover and a 40 or 50 setting for the less tender cuts of meat such as chuck, bottom round, brisket, and stewing meat cooked in liquid.
- ☐ Check dishes that use relatively long cooking times to be sure liquid has not evaporated. Add liquid as necessary.
- ☐ Enhance the color and flavor of ground beef patties, steaks, meatloaf, and roasts by using one of the following: powdered brown gravy mix; a liquid browning agent; Worcestershire, soy sauce or steak sauce; paprika; cooked bacon; tomato sauce; or dehydrated onion soup mix.
- ☐ Most ground beef recipes call for lean meat. If you are using regular ground beef, drain fat before adding sauce ingredients.
- ☐ Large cuts not usually cooked on the charcoal grill, such as ham, leg of lamb, pork roast, turkey, and whole chicken, may be partially cooked in the microwave oven and finished on the grill for a lovely charcoal flavor and a browned crispness. It's also a great time saver for spareribs.

Using the Defrosting Guide

1. You may defrost meat within its original paper or plastic wrappings. Remove all metal rings, wire twist ties, and all foil wrapping.
2. Defrost in the microwave oven only as long as necessary, since standing time will complete the thawing process. Separate items like chops, bacon, and hot dogs as soon as possible. If pieces are not thawed, distribute evenly in oven and continue defrosting.
3. Slightly increase the time for weights larger than on the chart. Do not double.
4. If you do not plan immediate cooking, follow the guide for only one-half to three-fourths of recommended time. Place meat in refrigerator until needed.
5. Programmed Defrost may be used. See Use & Care Manual for information.

DEFROSTING GUIDE — MEAT

Meat	Amount	Cook Control Setting	Time (in minutes per pound)	Standing Time (in minutes)	Special Notes
Ground beef	1-lb. 2-lbs. 1/4-lb. patty	30 (defrost) 30 (defrost) 30 (defrost)	5-6 8-9 1 per patty	5 5 2	Turn over once. Remove thawed portions with fork. Return remainder. Freeze in doughnut shape. Depress center when freezing. Defrost on plate.
Pot roast, chuck	under 4 lbs. over 4 lbs.	30 (defrost) 70 (roast)	3-5 3-5	10 10	Turn over once. Turn over once.
Rib roast, rolled	3 to 4 lbs. 6 to 8 lbs.	30 (defrost) 70 (roast)	6-8 6-8	30-45 90	Turn over once. Turn over twice.
Rib roast, bone in		70 (roast)	5-6	45-90	Turn over twice.
Rump roast	3 to 4 lbs. 6 to 7 lbs.	30 (defrost) 70 (roast)	3-5 3-5	30 45	Turn over once. Turn over twice.
Round steak		30 (defrost)	4-5	5-10	Turn over once.
Flank steak		30 (defrost)	4-5	5-10	Turn over once.
Sirloin steak	1/2" thick	30 (defrost)	4-5	5-10	Turn over once.
Tenderloin Steaks	 2 or 3 2 to 3 lbs.	30 (defrost) 30 (defrost)	5-6 4-5	10 8-10	Turn over once. Turn over once.
Stew beef	2 lbs.	30 (defrost)	3-5	8-10	Turn over once. Separate.
Lamb					
Cubed for stew		30 (defrost)	7-8	5	Turn over once. Separate.
Ground lamb	under 4 lbs. over 4 lbs.	30 (defrost) 70 (roast)	3-5 3-5	30-45 30-45	Turn over once. Turn over twice.
Chops	1" thick	30 (defrost)	5-8	15	Turn over twice.
Leg	5-8 lbs.	30 (defrost)	4-5	15-20	Turn over twice.
Pork					
Chops	1/2" 1"	30 (defrost) 30 (defrost)	4-6 5-7	5-10 10	Separate chops halfway through defrosting time.
Spareribs, country-style ribs		30 (defrost)	5-7	10	Turn over once.
Roast	under 4 lbs. over 4 lbs.	30 (defrost) 70 (roast)	4-5 4-5	30-45 30-45	Turn over once. Turn over twice.
Bacon	1-lb.	30 (defrost)	2-3	3-5	Defrost until strips separate.
Sausage, bulk	1 lb.	30 (defrost)	2-3	3-5	Turn over once. Remove thawed portions with fork. Return remainder.
Sausage links	1 lb.	30 (defrost)	3-5	4-6	Turn over once. Defrost until pieces can be separated.
Hot dogs		30 (defrost)	5-6	5	

DEFROSTING GUIDE — MEAT

Meat	Amount	Cook Control Setting	Time (in minutes per pound)	Standing Time (in minutes)	Special Notes
Veal					
Roast	3 to 4 lbs. 6 to 7 lbs.	30 (defrost) 70 (roast)	5-7 5-7	30 90	Turn over once. Turn over twice.
Chops	1/2" thick	30 (defrost)	4-6	20	Turn over once. Separate chops and continue defrosting.
Variety Meat					
Liver		30 (defrost)	5-6	10	Turn over once.
Tongue		30 (defrost)	7-8	10	Turn over once.

Using the Cooking Guide

1. Meat should be completely thawed before cooking.
2. Place meat fat side down on microwave roasting rack set in glass baking dish.
3. Meat may be covered lightly with waxed paper to stop splatters.
4. Use the temperature probe for the most accurate cooking of larger cuts. Place probe sensor as horizontally as possible in the densest area, avoiding fat pockets or bone.
5. Unless otherwise noted, times given for steaks and patties will give medium doneness.
6. Ground meat to be used for casseroles should be cooked briefly first; crumble it into a microproof dish and cook covered with a paper towel. Then drain off any fat and add meat to casserole.
7. During standing time, the internal temperature of roasts will rise between 5°F and 15°F. Hence, standing time is considered an essential part of the time required to complete cooking.
8. Cutlets and chops that are breaded are cooked at the same time and cook control setting as shown on chart for unbreaded.

COOKING GUIDE — MEAT

Meat	Amount	First Cook Control Setting And Time	Second Cook Control Setting And Time	or	Temperature Probe And Cook Control Setting	Standing Time (in minutes)	Special Notes
Beef							
Ground beef	Bulk	HI (max. power) 2½ minutes per pound	Stir. HI (max. power) 2½ minutes per pound			5	Crumble in dish, cook covered.
Ground beef patties, 4 oz., 1/2" thick	1	HI (max. power) 1 minute	Turn over. HI (max. power) 1-1½ minutes				Shallow baking dish.
	2	HI (max. power) 1-1½ minutes	Turn over. HI (max. power) 1-1½ minutes				Shallow baking dish.
	4	HI (max. power) 3 minutes	Turn over. HI (max. power) 3-3½ minutes				Shallow baking dish.
Meatloaf	2 lbs.	HI (max. power) 12-14 minutes		or	HI (max. power) 160°	5-10	Glass loaf dish or glass ring mold.

COOKING GUIDE — MEAT

Meat	Amount	First Cook Control Setting And Time	Second Cook Control Setting And Time	or	Temperature Probe And Cook Control Setting	Standing Time (in minutes)	Special Notes
Beef rib roast, boneless		HI (max. power) Rare: 4-5 minutes per pound Medium: 5-6 minutes per pound Well: 6-7 minutes per pound	Turn over. 70 (roast) 3-4 minutes per pound 5-6 minutes per pound 6-7 minutes per pound	or	Turn over once. 70 (roast) 120° 130° 140°	10 10 10	Glass baking dish with microproof roasting rack.
Rib roast, bone in		HI (max. power) Rare: 3-4 minutes per pound Medium: 4-5 minutes per pound Well: 5-6 minutes per pound	Turn over. 70 (roast) 3-4 minutes per pound 3-5 minutes per pound 5-6 minutes per pound	or	Turn over once. 70 (roast) 120° 130° 140°	10	Glass baking dish with microproof roasting rack.
Beef rump, other less tender cuts		HI (max. power) 5 minutes per pound	Turn over. 50 (simmer) 10 minutes per pound			10-15	Casserole with tight cover. Requires liquid.
Beef brisket, boneless, fresh or corned	2½-3½ lbs.	HI (max. power) 5 minutes per pound	Turn over. 50 (simmer) 20 minutes per pound			10-15	4-quart casserole Dutch oven with tight cover. Water to cover.
Top round steak		HI (max. power) 5 minutes per pound	Turn over. 50 (simmer) 5 minutes per pound			10-15	Casserole with tight cover. Requires liquid.
Sirloin steak	3/4 to 1" thick	HI (max. power) 4½ minutes per pound	Drain dish and turn over. HI (max. power) 2 minutes per pound			10-15	Shallow cooking dish or browning dish preheated on HI (max. power) 8 minutes.
Minute steak or cube steak,	4, 6-oz. steaks	HI (max. power) 1-2 minutes	Drain dish and turn over. HI (max. power) 1-2 minutes				Browning dish preheated on HI (max. power) 8 minutes.
Tenderloin	4, 8-oz. steaks	HI (max. power) Rare: 5 minutes Med: 6 minutes Well: 9 minutes	Drain, turn steak. HI (max. power) 1-2 minutes 2-3 minutes 2-3 minutes			10-15	Browning dish preheated on HI (max. power) 8 minutes.
Rib eye or strip steak	1½ to 2 lbs.	HI (max. power) Rare: 4 minutes Med: 5 minutes Well: 7 minutes	Drain, turn steak. HI (max. power) ½-1 minute 1-2 minutes 2-3 minutes			10-15	Browning dish preheated on HI (max. power) 8 minutes.
Lamb Ground lamb patties	1-2 lbs.	HI (max. power) 4 minutes	Turn over. HI (max. power) 4-5 minutes				Browning dish preheated on HI (max. power) 7 minutes.
Lamb chops	1-1½ lbs. 1" thick	HI (max. power) 8 minutes	Turn over. HI (max. power) 7-8 minutes				Browning dish preheated on HI (max. power) 7 minutes.
Lamb leg or shoulder roast, bone in		70 (roast) Medium: 4-5 minutes per pound Well: 5-6 minutes per pound	Cover end of leg bone with foil. Turn over. 70 (roast) Medium: 4-5 minutes per pound Well: 5-6 minutes per pound	or	Turn over once. Cover end of leg bone with foil. 145° 165°	5 10	12×7-inch dish with microproof roasting rack.

COOKING GUIDE — MEAT

Meat	Amount	First Cook Control Setting And Time	Second Cook Control Setting And Time	or	Temperature Probe And Cook Control Setting	Standing Time (in minutes)	Special Notes
Lamb roast, boneless		70 (roast) 5-6 minutes per pound	Turn over. 70 (roast) 5-6 minutes per pound	or	Turn over once. 70 (roast) 150°	10	12 × 7-inch dish with microproof roasting rack.
Veal: Shoulder or rump roast, boneless	2-5 lbs.	70 (roast) 9 minutes per pound	Turn over. 70 (roast) 9-10 minutes per pound	or	Turn over once. 70 (roast) 155°	10	12 × 7-inch dish with microproof roasting rack.
Veal cutlets or loin chops	1/2" thick	HI (max. power) 2 minutes per pound	Turn over. HI (max. power) 2-3½ minutes per pound				Browning dish preheated on HI (max. power) 7-10 minutes.
Pork: Pork chops	1/2" thick	HI (max. power) 6 minutes per pound	Turn over. HI (max. power) 5-6 minutes per pound			5	Browning dish preheated on HI (max. power) 7 minutes
Spareribs		70 (roast) 6-7 minutes per pound	Turn over. 70 (roast) 6-7 minutes per pound			10	12 × 7-inch dish with microproof roasting rack.
Pork loin roast, boneless	3-5 lbs.	HI (max. power) 6 minutes per pound	Turn over. 70 (roast) 5-6 minutes per pound	or	Turn over once. 70 (roast) 165°	10	12 × 7-inch dish with microproof roasting rack.
Pork loin, center cut	4-5 lbs.	HI (max. power) 5-6 minutes per pound	Turn over. 70 (roast) 4-5 minutes per pound	or	Turn over once. 70 (roast) 165°	10	13 × 9-inch dish with microproof roasting rack.
Ham, boneless, precooked		70 (roast) 5-7 minutes per pound	Turn over. 70 (roast) 5-7 minutes per pound	or	Turn over once. 70 (roast) 120°	10	12 × 7-inch dish with microproof roasting rack.
Center cut ham slice	1-1½ lbs.	70 (roast) 5 minutes per pound	Turn over. 70 (roast) 5-6 minutes per pound	or	Turn over once. 70 (roast) 120°	10	12 × 7-inch baking dish.
Smoked ham shank		70 (roast) 4-5 minutes per pound	Turn over. 70 (roast) 4-5 minutes per pound	or	Turn over once. 70 (roast) 120°	10	12 × 7-inch dish with microproof roasting rack.
Canned ham	3 lbs.	70 (roast) 5-6 minutes per pound	70 (roast) 5-6 minutes per pound	or or	70 (roast) 120°	10	12 × 7-inch dish with microproof roasting rack.
	5 lbs.	70 (roast) 4-5 minutes per pound	Turn over. 70 (roast) 4-5 minutes per pound	or	Turn over once. 70 (roast) 120°	10	12 × 7-inch dish with microproof roasting rack.
Sausage patties	12-oz.	HI (max. power) 2 minutes	Turn over. HI (max. power) 1½-2 minutes per pound				Browning dish preheated on HI (max. power) 7 minutes.
Sausage	16 oz.	HI (max. power) 3 minutes	Stir. HI (max. power) 1-2 minutes				Crumble into 1½-quart dish, covered.
Pork sausage links	1/2 lb.	Pierce casing HI (max. power) 1 minute	Turn over. HI (max. power) 1-1½ minutes				Browning dish preheated on HI (max. power) 7 minutes.
	1 lb.	HI (max. power) 2 minutes	HI (max. power) 1½-2 minutes				

COOKING GUIDE — MEAT

Meat	Amount	First Cook Control Setting And Time	Second Cook Control Setting And Time	or	Temperature Probe And Cook Control Setting	Standing Time (in minutes)	Special Notes
Bratwurst, precooked		70 (roast) 5 minutes per pound	Rearrange. 70 (roast) 4-5 minutes per pound				Pierce casing. Casserole.
Polish sausage, knockwurst, ring bologna		80 (reheat) 2-2½ minutes per pound	Rearrange 80 (reheat) 2-2½ minutes per pound				Pierce casing. Casserole.
Hot dogs	1	80 (reheat) 25-30 seconds					Shallow dish.
	2	80 (reheat) 25-40 seconds					Shallow dish.
	4	80 (reheat) 50-55 seconds					Shallow dish.
Bacon 2 slices		HI (max. power) 2-2½ minutes					Dish; slices between paper towels
4 slices		HI (max. power) 4-4½ minutes					Dish; slices between paper towels
6 slices		HI (max. power) 5-6 minutes					Roasting rack, slices covered with paper towels
8 slices		HI (max. power) 6-7 minutes					Roasting rack, slices covered with paper towels

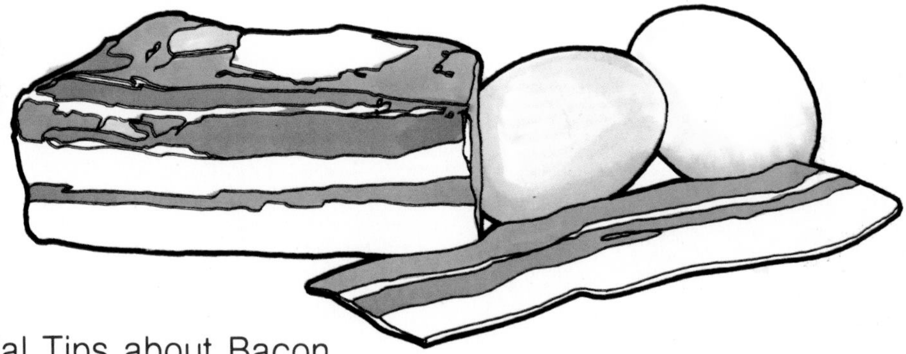

Special Tips about Bacon

- ☐ Cook bacon on a paper-lined plate, and cover with paper towels or waxed paper to prevent splatters and absorb drippings.
- ☐ To reserve drippings, cook bacon on a meat rack in a baking dish or on a microwave bacon rack. Bacon can also be cooked, in slices or cut up, in a casserole and removed, if necessary, with a slotted spoon.
- ☐ For bacon that is soft rather than crisp, cook at the minimum timing.
- ☐ Bacon varies in quality. The thickness and amount of sugar and salt used in curing will affect browning and timing. Cook thicker slices a bit longer than the chart indicates. You will also find that sweeter bacon cooks more quickly.
- ☐ Sugar in bacon causes brown spots to appear on the paper towels. If the bacon tends to stick a bit to the towel, it is due to an extra high amount of sugar.

Recipe No. 73

All-American Meatballs

Preset Cooking Time: 20 minutes

- 1 pound lean ground beef
- 1 medium potato, peeled and coarsely grated
- 2 tablespoons onion soup mix
- 1 tablespoon parsley flakes
- 1 large egg, lightly beaten
- 2 cups beef broth
- 1 tablespoon Worcestershire sauce
- 2 tablespoons cornstarch
- 2 tablespoons water

Combine beef, potato, soup mix, parsley, and egg; blend well. Shape into twelve 1½-inch balls. Combine broth and Worcestershire in 2-quart microproof casserole. Add meatballs. Cover and place in oven. Set recipe number 73. Touch START. *(Oven cooks:* 70, 10 *minutes.)*

At Pause, dissolve cornstarch in water. Stir into casserole. Cover. Touch START. *(Oven cooks:* 70, 3 *minutes.)*

At Pause, stir. Cover. Touch START. *(Oven cooks:* 70, 2 *minutes; stands:* 0, 5 *minutes.)*

4 servings

Recipe No. 74

Barbecued Beef, Chili, Stew, Hash, Meatballs

Preset Cooking Time: 4 minutes

- 1 can (16 ounces) barbecued beef, chili, stew, hash, or meatballs

Pour beef mixture into microproof casserole. Place in oven. Insert temperature probe into beef mixture, and cover. Set recipe number 74. Touch START. *(Oven cooks:* 80, *about* 2 *minutes to* 110°*F.)*

At Pause, stir. Cover. Touch START. *(Oven cooks:* 80, *about* 2 *minutes to* 150°*F; holds warm:* 10.)

1 to 2 servings

Recipe No. 75

Horseradish-Onion Beef Roast

Preset Cooking Time: 21 minutes

- 1 beef round rump roast, boneless (3½ pounds)
- ½ cup prepared horseradish
- 1 tablespoon steak sauce
- 1 clove garlic, minced
- 1 envelope (1½ ounces) onion soup mix, divided
- ¼ cup cold water
- 2 tablespoons all-purpose flour
- Dash pepper

Remove string from roast. Cut roast in half horizontally without cutting all the way through; open gently. Slash inside of roast all over, without cutting all the way through. Combine horseradish, steak sauce, and garlic; spread over cut surfaces of roast. Press cut surfaces together; tie roast securely with string. Place in shallow 2½- to 3-quart microproof baking dish. Sprinkle with half of the soup mix. Place in oven. Cover with waxed paper. Set recipe number 75. Touch START. *(Oven cooks:* 70, 10 *minutes.)*

At Pause, turn over. Cover. Touch START. *(Oven cooks:* 70, 7 *minutes.)*

At Pause, remove from oven. Transfer roast to warmed serving platter, and cover with aluminum foil to keep warm while preparing gravy. (Internal temperature of roast will rise to 140°F, medium rare.)

Pour drippings into 4-cup glass measure; skim fat. Add water to equal 1 cup liquid. Combine remaining soup mix, ¼ cup cold water, and flour; blend well. Stir into drippings. Place in oven. Touch START. *(Oven cooks: HI,* 2 *minutes.)*

At Pause, stir vigorously and thoroughly with wire whisk. Touch START. *(Oven cooks: HI,* 2 *minutes.)*

Add pepper; stir vigorously. Pass gravy with sliced roast.

6 to 8 servings

COOKING/DEFROSTING GUIDE — CONVENIENCE BEEF

Food	Amount	Cook Control Setting	Time (in minutes)	or	Temperature Probe Setting	Special Notes
Barbecued beef, chili, stew, hash, meatballs, etc.	16 oz. or less (cans)	80 (reheat)	3-5	or	150°	Remove from cans to microproof plate or casserole, cover. Stir halfway through cooking time.
Stuffed peppers, cabbage rolls, chow mein, etc.	16-32 oz. (cans)	80 (reheat)	5-9	or	150°	
Barbecued beef, chili, stew, corned beef hash, meatballs, patties in sauce, gravy	8-16 oz. package (frozen)	HI (max. power)	5-11	or	150°	Remove from foil container to microproof casserole, cover. Slit plastic pouches
Dry casserole mixes, cooked hamburger added	6½-8 oz. package	HI (max. power)	18-22	or	150°	Remove mix from package to 3-quart microproof casserole. Cover. Stir once.

Recipe No. 76

Beef Stew

Preset Cooking Time: 1 hour 40 minutes

- 2 pounds beef for stew, trimmed and cut into 1½-inch cubes
- ½ teaspoon salt
- 1 envelope (1½ ounces) brown gravy mix with mushrooms
- 1½ cups water
- 3 medium stalks celery, cut into 1-inch chunks
- 4 medium carrots, cut into chunks
- 4 medium potatoes, peeled and cut in half
- 1 large onion, sliced

Arrange beef in 3-quart microproof casserole. Sprinkle with salt. Blend gravy mix with water; pour over beef. Place in oven. Set recipe number 76. Touch START. *(Oven cooks:* 50, 10 *minutes.)*

At Pause, add vegetables; stir to coat evenly with sauce. Cover. Touch START. *(Oven cooks:* 30, 30 *minutes.)*

At Pause, stir. Cover. Touch START. *(Oven cooks:* 30, 30 *minutes.)*

At Pause, stir. Cover. Touch START. *(Oven cooks:* 30, 30 *minutes.)*

4 to 6 servings

Recipe No. 77

Beef Shanghai

Preset Cooking Time: 9 minutes

- 2 tablespoons vegetable oil
- 1 top round or sirloin steak, boneless (1 pound), cut into thin strips
- 1 can (16 ounces) whole tomatoes, broken up
- 1 medium onion, finely chopped
- 1 clove garlic, minced
- 1 teaspoon salt
- ⅛ teaspoon pepper
- 2 large green peppers, seeded and cut into thin strips
- 2 teaspoons cornstarch
- 2 tablespoons soy sauce

Pour oil into 3-quart microproof casserole. Add beef; stir to coat. Add tomatoes, onion, garlic, salt, and pepper. Cover and place in oven. Set recipe number 77. Touch START. *(Oven cooks: HI, 2 minutes.)*

At Pause, stir. Cover. Touch START. *(Oven cooks: HI, 2 minutes.)*

At Pause, add green peppers. Dissolve cornstarch in soy sauce; stir into beef mixture. Cover. Touch START. *(Oven cooks: HI, 5 minutes.)*

Serve over hot rice, and sprinkle with chow mein noodles.

4 servings

Recipe No. 78

Boiled Beef Carbonnade

Preset Cooking Time: 1 hour 30 minutes

1 lean beef heel of round roast (3 pounds)
1 small onion, sliced
1 medium carrot, sliced
5 peppercorns
1/8 teaspoon white pepper
1 bay leaf
1 can (12 ounces) beer
Salt, to taste

Place roast, onion, carrot, peppercorns, pepper, and bay leaf in 4-quart microproof casserole. Pour in beer. Add water to cover roast. Cover and place in oven. Set recipe number 78. Touch START. *(Oven cooks: HI, 30 minutes.)*

At Pause, turn roast over. Add water to cover roast if necessary. Cover. Touch START. *(Oven cooks:* 50, 1 *hour.)*

Let stand 10 minutes. Strain broth; skim fat. Slice roast thinly, and season with salt. Serve with broth.

6 servings

Recipe No. 79

Chili con Carne

Preset Cooking Time: 20 minutes

1 pound lean ground beef
1/2 cup minced onion
1/2 cup chopped green pepper
1 clove garlic, minced
1 can (16 ounces) whole tomatoes, broken up
1 can (16 ounces) kidney beans
1 to 2 tablespoons chili powder, to taste
1 teaspoon salt

Crumble beef into 2-quart microproof casserole. Add onion, green pepper, and garlic. Place in oven. Set recipe number 79. Touch START. *(Oven cooks: HI, 2 minutes.)*

At Pause, stir. Touch START. *(Oven cooks: HI, 2 minutes.)*

At Pause, remove from oven; drain. Add remaining ingredients; blend well. Cover and place in oven. Touch START. *(Oven cooks:* 70, 9 *minutes.)*

At Pause, stir. Cover. Touch START. *(Oven cooks: 70, 7 minutes.)*

Let stand 5 minutes before serving.

4 servings

Recipe No. 80

Eggplant Parthenon

Preset Cooking Time: 23 minutes

2 eggplants (1 pound each)
1 pound ground lamb
2 medium onions, chopped
2 cloves garlic, minced
1 beef bouillon cube
1/2 cup hot water
1 can (8 ounces) tomato sauce, divided
2 tablespoons chopped parsley
1 teaspoon oregano
1/2 teaspoon salt
1/4 teaspoon pepper
1/4 teaspoon cinnamon
1/2 cup dry bread crumbs

Wash eggplants; cut in half lengthwise. Pierce skin in several places. Place, cut-sides down, on microwave roasting rack. Place in oven. Set recipe number 80. Touch START. *(Oven cooks: HI,* 5 *minutes.)*

At Pause, remove from oven. Scoop out pulp, leaving 1-inch thick shells. Chop pulp; set aside shells and pulp. Crumble lamb into 2-quart glass measure. Add onions and garlic. Place in oven. Touch START. *(Oven cooks: HI,* 5 *minutes.)*

At Pause, remove from oven. Stir; drain. Dissolve bouillon in hot water; stir into lamb mixture. Stir in 1/2 cup tomato sauce and eggplant pulp. Cover and place in oven. Touch START. *(Oven cooks:* 80, 8 *minutes.)*

At Pause, remove from oven. Stir in parsley, oregano, salt, pepper, and cinnamon. Place eggplant shells in shallow, oval, microproof baking dish. Fill shells with lamb mixture. Sprinkle with bread crumbs. Drizzle remaining tomato sauce over the crumbs. Place in oven. Touch START. *(Oven cooks:* 80, 5 *minutes.)*

4 servings

← *Eggplant Parthenon, Stuffed Green Peppers (page 93), Eggs in Nests (page 135)*

Recipe No. 81

Favorite Meatloaf

Preset Cooking Time: about 17 minutes

- 1 can (8 ounces) tomato sauce
- 1/4 cup firmly packed brown sugar
- 1 teaspoon prepared mustard
- 2 pounds lean ground beef
- 1/4 cup cracker crumbs
- 2 large eggs, lightly beaten
- 1 medium onion, minced
- 1 1/4 teaspoons salt
- 1/4 teaspoon pepper

Combine tomato sauce, brown sugar, and mustard; set aside. Combine remaining ingredients. Add 1/2 cup tomato sauce mixture; blend well. Fill 8-cup microproof ring mold. Pour remaining tomato sauce mixture evenly over top. Place in oven. Insert temperature probe into center of meatloaf. Set recipe number 81. Touch START. *(Oven cooks: HI, about* 12 *minutes to* 160°*F; stands:* 0, 5 *minutes.)*

6 servings

Recipe No. 82

Oriental Beef

Preset Cooking Time: 11 minutes

- 1/2 cup soy sauce
- 1/2 cup dry sherry
- 1/2 cup water
- 1 tablespoon sugar
- 1 clove garlic, minced
- 2 thin slices fresh ginger, minced
- 1 sirloin steak, boneless (1 1/2 to 2 pounds), cut into thin strips
- 1/2 medium bunch broccoli
- 1/2 pound bean sprouts
- 6 green onions, cut into 2-inch pieces
- 1 can (5 ounces) sliced water chestnuts, drained

Combine soy sauce, sherry, water, sugar, garlic, and ginger in 2-quart microproof casserole. Add steak; stir to coat. Cover and let stand at room temperature 2 hours, stirring occasionally. Cut broccoli stems diagonally into thin slices; break florets into individual pieces. Rinse bean sprouts in cold water; drain. Combine broccoli, bean sprouts, green onions, and water chestnuts. Push marinated steak to center of casserole. Arrange vegetables around steak. Cover and place in oven. Touch START. *(Oven cooks: HI,* 11 *minutes.)*

Let stand 2 minutes before serving with hot rice.

4 to 6 servings

You can substitute 1 *package (*10 *ounces) frozen broccoli spears, thawed, for fresh broccoli. If fresh bean sprouts are unavailable, substitute 2 cups drained canned bean sprouts.*

Recipe No. 83

One-Step Lasagna

Preset Cooking Time: 37 minutes

- 1 pound lean ground beef
- 1 jar (15 ounces) spaghetti sauce
- 1/2 cup water
- 1 teaspoon salt
- 1 package (8 ounces) lasagna noodles
- 2 cups ricotta cheese, drained
- 3 cups (12 ounces) shredded mozzarella cheese, divided
- 1/2 cup grated Parmesan cheese
- Chopped parsley

Crumble beef into 2-quart microproof casserole. Place in oven. Set recipe number 83. Touch START. *(Oven cooks: HI,* 3 *minutes.)*

At Pause, stir to break up beef. Touch START. *(Oven cooks: HI, 2 minutes.)*

At Pause, remove from oven. Stir; drain. Stir in spaghetti sauce, water, and salt. Spread one third of the beef mixture in 11 × 7-inch microproof baking dish. Arrange half of the noodles over sauce. Spread with 1 cup ricotta cheese. Sprinkle with 1 cup mozzarella cheese. Repeat layers once. Top with remaining beef mixture. Sprinkle with Parmesan cheese. Double wrap with plastic wrap, and place in oven. Touch START. *(Oven cooks:* 50, 30 *minutes.)*

At Pause, sprinkle with remaining 1 cup mozzarella cheese. Do not cover. Touch START. *(Oven cooks:* 50, 2 *minutes.)*

Sprinkle with parsley, and serve with additional Parmesan cheese, if desired.

6 servings

Garlic Parmesan Bread (page 70), Green Beans Italiano (page 159), One-Step Lasagna →

Recipe No. 84

Rib Roast, bone in (rare)

Preset Cooking Time: 25 to 35 minutes

1 envelope (1½ ounces) onion soup mix
1 rib roast, bone in (5 pounds)
1 pound mushrooms, sliced

Rub soup mix all over roast. Place roast, fat-side down, in shallow microproof baking dish. Sprinkle mushrooms over top and sides of roast. Place in oven. Insert temperature probe horizontally into densest part of roast without touching fat or bone. Set recipe number 84. Touch START. *(Oven cooks: HI, 10 to 15 minutes to 90°F.)*

At Pause, turn roast on its side. Spoon juices and mushrooms over top. Touch START. *(Oven cooks:* 70, 15 to 20 *minutes to* 120°*F; holds warm:* 10.)

Spoon juices and mushrooms over roast. Cover with aluminum foil and let stand 10 minutes before serving. (Internal temperature of roast will rise to 135°F.)

6 to 8 servings

Recipe No. 85

Rib Roast, bone in (medium)

Preset Cooking Time: 25 to 40 minutes

1 envelope (1½ ounces) onion soup mix
1 rib roast, bone in (5 pounds)
1 pound mushrooms, sliced

Rub soup mix all over roast. Place roast, fat-side down, in shallow microproof baking dish. Sprinkle mushrooms over top and sides of roast. Place in oven. Insert temperature probe horizontally into densest part of roast without touching fat or bone. Set recipe number 85. Touch START. *(Oven cooks: HI,* 10 *to* 15 *minutes to* 90°*F.)*

At Pause, turn roast on its side. Spoon juices and mushrooms over top. Touch START. *(Oven cooks:* 70, 15 *to* 25 *minutes to* 130°*F; holds warm:* 10.)

Spoon juices and mushrooms over roast. Cover with aluminum foil and let stand 10 minutes before serving. (Internal temperature of roast will rise to 145°F.)

6 to 8 servings

Rare Rib Roast goes great with a green salad →

Recipe No. 86

Stuffed Cabbage

Preset Cooking Time: 36 minutes

- 1 head (about 1 1/2 pounds) cabbage, cored, blemished leaves discarded
- 1/4 cup water
- 1 pound lean ground beef
- 1/2 pound ground pork
- 3/4 cup cooked rice
- 1 large egg, lightly beaten
- 1 tablespoon chopped parsley
- 1 clove garlic, minced
- 1 teaspoon salt
- 1/2 teaspoon thyme
- 1/4 teaspoon pepper
- 1/4 cup butter or margarine
- 2 cans (8 ounces each) tomato sauce

Place cabbage and water in 3-quart microproof casserole. Cover and place in oven. Set recipe number 86. Touch START. *(Oven cooks: HI, 6 minutes.)*

At Pause, remove from oven; drain. Let stand to cool slightly. Separate 6 to 8 large outside leaves, discarding tough centers; set aside. Combine beef, pork, rice, egg, parsley, garlic, salt, thyme, and pepper; blend well. Divide mixture evenly among large outside cabbage leaves, wrapping leaves tightly around mixture. Line bottom of 13×9-inch microproof baking dish with some of the remaining cabbage leaves. Top with stuffed cabbage rolls. Cover with remaining leaves. Dot with butter. Cover with tomato sauce. Cover with plastic wrap and place in oven. Touch START. *(Oven cooks:* 80, 15 *minutes.)*

At Pause, baste with pan juices. Touch START. *(Oven cooks:* 80, 10 *minutes;* 10, 5 *minutes.)*

Discard top leaves before serving.

4 servings

Recipe No. 87

Short Ribs of Beef

Preset Cooking Time: 1 hour 10 minutes

- 2 pounds meaty beef chuck short ribs
- 1 medium onion, sliced
- 4 medium potatoes, peeled and cut in half
- 4 medium carrots, cut into 1-inch chunks
- 1 clove garlic, minced
- 1/2 teaspoon salt
- 1/2 cup dry red wine
- 1 tablespoon microwave browning sauce

Arrange ribs, bone-side up, in 3-quart microproof casserole. Arrange onion over ribs. Arrange potatoes and carrots around ribs. Sprinkle with garlic and salt. Combine wine and browning sauce; pour over ribs and vegetables. Cover and place in oven. Set recipe number 87. Touch START. *(Oven cooks:* 30, 1 *hour;* 20, 10 *minutes.)*

4 servings

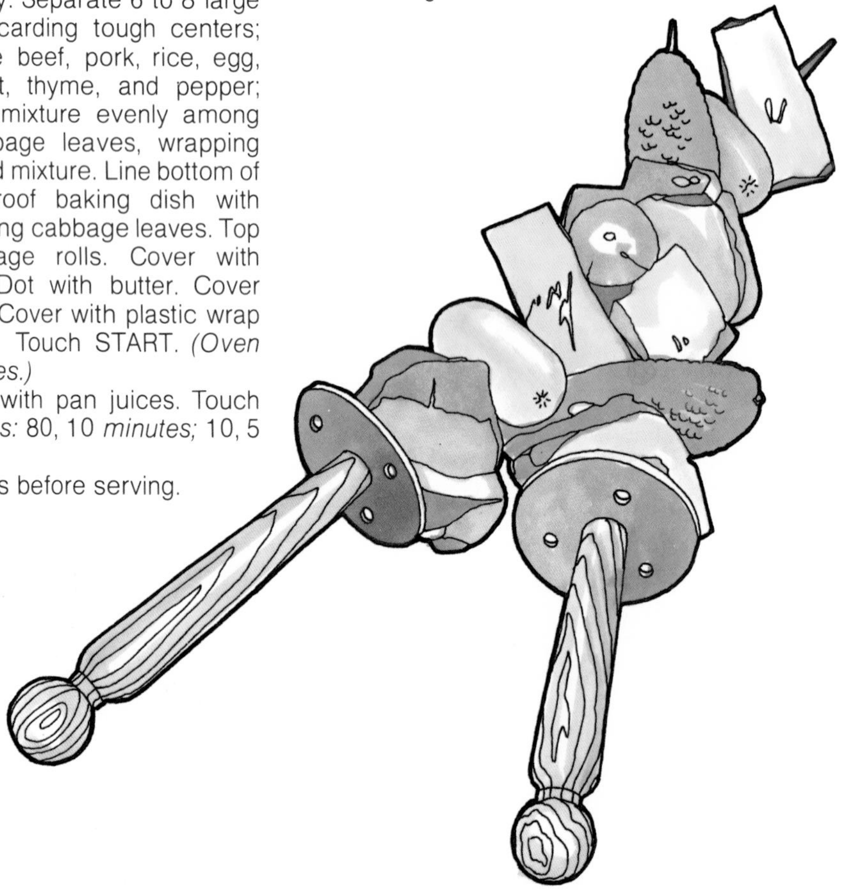

Recipe No. 88

Shish Kabobs

Preset Cooking Time: 6 minutes

- ½ cup wine vinegar
- ½ cup vegetable oil
- ½ cup water
- ¼ cup soy sauce
- 1 teaspoon onion salt
- 1 teaspoon oregano
- 1 clove garlic, cut in half
- 1 sirloin steak or lamb shoulder roast, boneless (2 pounds), cut into 1-inch cubes
- ½ pound small mushrooms
- 12 very firm cherry tomatoes
- 1 green pepper, seeded and cut into 1-inch squares

Combine vinegar, oil, water, soy sauce, onion salt, oregano, and garlic. Add meat. Refrigerate 5 to 6 hours, stirring occasionally. Thread meat cubes and vegetables alternately on 6 long wooden skewers. Arrange on microwave roasting rack, or microproof plate or pie plate, spoke fashion. Brush with marinade. Place in oven. Set recipe number 88. Touch START. *(Oven cooks: HI, 6 minutes.)* Brush with marinade before serving.

6 servings

Recipe No. 89

Corned Beef Hash, Country Style

Preset Cooking Time: 6 minutes

- 1 can (15 ounces) corned beef hash
- 2 English muffins, split and toasted
- 4 teaspoons Dijon mustard
- ½ cup (2 ounces) shredded Cheddar cheese
- 1 tablespoon minced parsley

Preheat microproof browning dish according to manufacturer's directions. Remove hash from can by opening both ends and sliding knife around hash. Slice into 4 patties. Arrange patties in circle on browning dish in oven. Set recipe number 89. Touch START. *(Oven cooks: HI, 2 minutes.)*

At Pause, turn patties over. Touch START. *(Oven cooks: HI, 2 minutes.)*

At Pause, slide 1 half muffin under each patty. Spread mustard on patties, and sprinkle with cheese. Touch START. *(Oven cooks: HI, 2 minutes.)*

Sprinkle with parsley; serve immediately.

4 servings

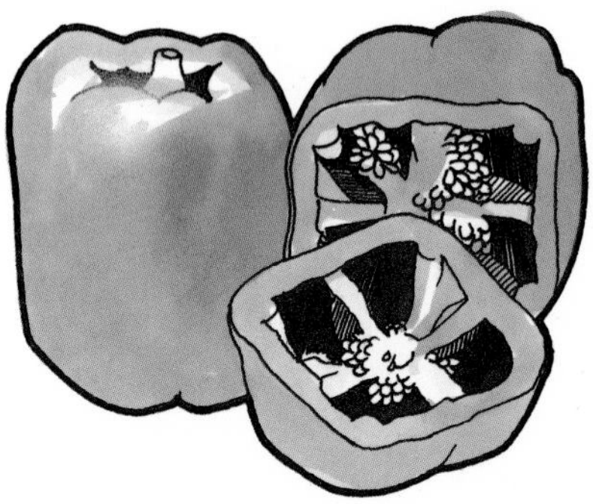

Recipe No. 90 ⊞

Tomato Swiss Steak

Preset Cooking Time: 1 hour 3 minutes

- ¼ cup all-purpose flour
- 1 teaspoon salt
- ¼ teaspoon pepper
- 1 round or flank steak (1 pound), ½ inch thick
- 1 large onion, sliced
- ½ green pepper, seeded and cut into strips
- 1 can (6 ounces) tomato paste
- 1 cup beef broth, or 1 cup water plus 1 beef bouillon cube

Combine flour, salt, and pepper. Place steak on cutting board; pound half of the flour mixture into both sides of steak with meat mallet. Cut steak in half; place in 8-inch round or oval microproof baking dish. Sprinkle with remaining flour mixture. Spread onion, green pepper, and tomato paste over steak. Add broth to cover. Double wrap with plastic wrap. Place in oven. Set recipe number 90. Touch START. *(Oven cooks: HI, 3 minutes; 30, 1 hour.)*

2 servings

Recipe No. 91

Veal Shoulder or Rump Roast, boneless

Preset Cooking Time: 36 minutes to 1 hour 35 minutes

1 veal shoulder or rump roast, boneless (2 to 5 pounds)

Place roast, fat-side down, on microwave roasting rack in 12 × 7-inch microproof baking dish. Place in oven. Insert temperature probe horizontally into densest part of roast without touching fat. Cover lightly with waxed paper. Set recipe number 91. Touch START. *(Oven cooks:* 70, 18 *to* 45 *minutes to* 90°*F.)*

At Pause, turn over. Cover. Touch START. *(Oven cooks:* 70, 18 *to* 50 *minutes to* 155°*F; holds warm:* 10.)

(Internal temperature of roast will rise to 170°F.)

4 to 8 servings

Recipe No. 92

Veal Cordon Bleu

Preset Cooking Time: 4½ minutes

2 veal cutlets (¼ pound each), ½ inch thick
1 slice Swiss cheese, cut in half
2 thin slices boiled ham
1½ tablespoons all-purpose flour
1 large egg
1 tablespoon water
¼ cup dry bread crumbs
1½ tablespoons butter or margarine
1 tablespoon chopped parsley
2 tablespoons dry vermouth

Cut veal cutlets in half. Place each piece between 2 sheets of waxed paper. Pound with smooth-surfaced meat mallet until veal is ⅛ inch thick; set aside. Fold each piece cheese in half. Place 1 piece cheese on each slice ham. Roll ham around cheese 3 times, being certain that finished roll is smaller than pieces of veal. Place 1 ham roll on 1 slice veal. Top with another slice veal. Press edges of veal together to seal. Repeat with remaining ham roll and veal. Place flour on sheet of waxed paper. Beat egg and water lightly. Place bread crumbs on separate sheet of waxed paper. Dip veal "sandwiches" in flour, then in egg mixture. Coat well with bread crumbs; set aside. Place butter and parsley in 8-inch round microproof baking dish. Place in oven. Set recipe number 92. Touch START. *(Oven cooks: HI, 30 seconds.)*

At Pause, add veal "sandwiches." Touch START. *(Oven cooks: HI, 2 minutes.)*

At Pause, turn over. Touch START. *(Oven cooks: HI, 2 minutes.)*

Transfer veal to serving platter. Add vermouth to butter in baking dish; blend well. Pour over veal before serving.

2 servings

Recipe No. 93

Beef Roulade

Preset Cooking Time: 54 minutes

1 top round steak (2 pounds), ½ inch thick
½ cup chopped celery with leaves
¼ cup chopped onion
2 tablespoons butter or margarine
1 cup soft bread crumbs
¼ teaspoon rosemary
¼ teaspoon thyme
¼ teaspoon pepper
1 can (10¾ ounces) cream of mushroom soup, undiluted

Pound steak with meat mallet. Cut into six 3-inch strips; set aside. Combine celery, onion, and butter in 4-cup glass measure. Place in oven. Set recipe number 93. Touch START. *(Oven cooks: HI, 4 minutes.)*

At Pause, remove from oven. Blend in bread crumbs, rosemary, thyme, and pepper. Spread over steak strips. Roll strips around stuffing; fasten with wooden toothpicks. Arrange in 2-quart microproof baking dish. Spoon soup over rolls. Place in oven. Touch START. *(Oven cooks:* 50, 20 *minutes.)*

At Pause, turn over. Spoon soup over rolls. Touch START. *(Oven cooks:* 50, 25 *minutes; stands:* 0, 5 *minutes.)*

6 servings

Recipe No. 94

Tenderloin of Beef Supreme

Preset Cooking Time: 20 minutes

- 1 beef loin tenderloin roast (2 pounds)
- 3 tablespoons onion soup mix
- ½ pound fresh mushrooms, sliced

Place roast in shallow microproof baking dish. Pat soup mix all over roast. Arrange mushrooms on top. Place in oven. Cover with waxed paper. Set recipe number 94. Touch START. *(Oven cooks: HI, about* 5 *minutes to* 90°*F.)*

At Pause, turn over. Spoon juices and mushrooms over roast. Cover. Touch START. *(Oven cooks:* 70, *about* 10 *minutes, to* 120°*F;* 10, 5 *minutes.)*

4 servings

Recipe No. 95

Pot Roast in Sherry

Preset Cooking Time: 1 hour 10 minutes

- 1 envelope (1½ ounces) onion soup mix
- 1 lean beef chuck roast (3 pounds), trimmed
- ½ cup dry sherry
- ½ cup beef broth

Cut a 1-inch strip from open end of cooking bag. Pat soup mix all over roast. Place in cooking bag in shallow microproof baking dish. Pour sherry and broth over roast. Tie bag loosely with removed strip. Place in oven. Set recipe number 95. Touch START. *(Oven cooks:* 70, 10 *minutes;* 50, 45 *minutes.)*

At Pause, turn over. Squeeze sides of bag to baste roast. Touch START. *(Oven cooks:* 30, 10 *minutes; stands:* 0, 5 *minutes.)* Use drippings to make Easy Gravy (page 173), if desired.

6 to 8 servings

Recipe No. 96

Stuffed Green Peppers

Preset Cooking Time: 16 minutes

- 4 large green peppers
- ¼ cup water
- 1 pound lean ground beef
- 1 small onion, finely chopped
- 1 large egg
- 1 cup catsup, separated
- 1½ cups cooked rice
- 3 tablespoons minced parsley
- 1 clove garlic, minced
- ½ teaspoon salt
- ¼ teaspoon pepper

Remove tops from peppers; discard seeds and membranes. Rinse in cold water. Place upside down on paper towels to drain. Combine beef and onion in 2-quart microproof bowl. Place in oven. Set recipe number 96. Touch START. *(Oven cooks: HI,* 3 *minutes.)*

At Pause, stir to break up beef; drain. Touch START. *(Oven cooks: HI, 2 minutes.)*

At Pause, remove from oven. Stir in remaining ingredients, except 4 tablespoons catsup. Fill peppers with beef mixture, mounding on top. Arrange upright in circle in round or oval microproof baking dish just large enough to accommodate peppers. Top with remaining 4 tablespoons catsup. Cover lightly with waxed paper. Touch START. *(Oven cooks:* 60, 5 *minutes.)*

At Pause, rotate dish. Touch START. *(Oven cooks:* 60, 6 *minutes.)*

Let stand, covered, 5 minutes before serving.

4 servings

Recipe No. 97

Pepper Steak

Preset Cooking Time: 16¾ minutes

- 1 top round steak (1½ pounds), ½ inch thick
- 1 tablespoon vegetable oil
- 1 clove garlic, minced
- 2 teaspoons cornstarch
- 2 tablespoons soy sauce
- 2 green peppers, cut into 1-inch cubes (2 cups)
- 1 cup thinly sliced onions
- 2 large stalks celery, sliced
- ½ cup water
- 1 jar (2 ounces) chopped pimiento, drained
- 1 teaspoon instant beef bouillon granules
- 1 teaspoon salt
- ¼ teaspoon pepper

Cut steak into ¼-inch wide strips; set aside. Pour oil into 2-quart microproof casserole. Place in oven. Set recipe number 97. Touch START. *(Oven cooks: HI, 45 seconds.)*

At Pause, add steak and garlic; stir to coat. Touch START. *(Oven cooks: 50, 7 minutes.)*

At Pause, cover. Touch START. *(Oven cooks: 50, 3 minutes.)*

At Pause, dissolve cornstarch in soy sauce. Stir into steak mixture. Blend in remaining ingredients. Cover. Touch START. *(Oven cooks: HI, 6 minutes.)*

Let stand 5 minutes before serving.

4 servings

Recipe No. 98

Zucchini Lasagna

Preset Cooking Time: 31 minutes

- 6 cups sliced zucchini
- ¼ cup water
- 1 pound lean ground beef
- 2 cans (8 ounces each) tomato sauce
- ¼ pound mushrooms, chopped
- 1 small onion, minced
- 1 clove garlic, minced
- 1 teaspoon basil
- ½ teaspoon oregano
- ½ teaspoon thyme
- ½ teaspoon salt
- ¼ teaspoon pepper
- ¼ cup dry bread crumbs
- 12 ounces low-fat cottage cheese, drained
- 1 cup (4 ounces) shredded mozzarella cheese
- ⅓ cup grated Parmesan cheese

Place zucchini and water in 1½-quart microproof casserole. Cover and place in oven. Set recipe number 98. Touch START. *(Oven cooks: HI, 7 minutes.)*

At Pause, remove from oven. Drain; set aside. Crumble beef into 2-quart glass measure. Place in oven. Touch START. *(Oven cooks: HI, 4 minutes.)*

At Pause, remove from oven. Stir to break up beef; drain. Stir in tomato sauce, mushrooms, onion, garlic, and seasonings. Place in oven. Touch START. *(Oven cooks: HI, 8 minutes.)*

At Pause, remove from oven. Layer one-third of the zucchini in 11 × 7-inch microproof baking dish. Sprinkle with 1 tablespoon bread crumbs. Top with one-third of the beef mixture and half of the cottage cheese and mozzarella cheese. Repeat layers once. Top with remaining zucchini, beef mixture, and bread crumbs. Sprinkle with Parmesan cheese. Place in oven. Cover with waxed paper. Touch START. *(Oven cooks: HI, 12 minutes.)*

Let stand, covered, 5 minutes before serving.

8 to 10 servings

← *Veal Parmigiana (page 96)*

Recipe No. 99

Veal Parmigiana

Preset Cooking Time: 9 minutes

- 4 veal cutlets (1/4 pound each)
- 1 medium egg
- 1/4 teaspoon salt
- 1/3 cup grated Parmesan cheese
- 3 tablespoons cracker crumbs
- 2 tablespoons vegetable oil
- 1/4 cup dry vermouth
- 1 medium onion, minced
- 1 cup (4 ounces) shredded mozzarella cheese
- 1 can (6 ounces) tomato paste
- 1/8 teaspoon pepper
- 1/8 teaspoon oregano

Place each veal cutlet between 2 sheets of waxed paper. Pound with smooth-surfaced meat mallet until veal is 1/4 inch thick; set aside. Beat egg and salt in shallow dish. Combine Parmesan cheese and cracker crumbs on sheet of waxed paper. Dip veal in egg mixture, then in crumb mixture; set aside. Preheat microwave browning dish according to manufacturer's directions. Pour oil into browning dish. Place cutlets on browning dish in oven. Cover loosely with waxed paper. Set recipe number 99. Touch START. *(Oven cooks: HI, 1 1/2 minutes.)*

At Pause, turn over. Cover. Touch START. *(Oven cooks: HI, 1 1/2 minutes.)*

At Pause, pour vermouth over veal. Sprinkle with onion. Top with mozzarella cheese and tomato paste. Sprinkle with pepper and oregano. Cover. Touch START. *(Oven cooks: 60, 6 minutes.)*

4 servings

Recipe No. 100

Hungarian Goulash

Preset Cooking Time: 1 hour 25 minutes

- 2 pounds beef for stew, cut into 1-inch cubes
- 4 large tomatoes, peeled and cut into chunks
- 1 medium onion, coarsely chopped
- 1 1/2 tablespoons paprika
- 1 teaspoon salt
- 1/2 teaspoon pepper
- 1 container (8 ounces) dairy sour cream

Combine beef, tomatoes, onion, paprika, salt, and pepper in 3-quart microproof casserole. Place in oven. Set recipe number 100. Touch START. *(Oven cooks: 50, 25 minutes.)*

At Pause, stir. Touch START. *(Oven cooks: 50, 30 minutes.*

At Pause, stir. Touch START. *(Oven cooks: 50, 25 minutes; 20, 5 minutes.)*

Blend in sour cream. Serve over hot noodles.

4 to 6 servings

Recipe No. 101

Enchilada Casserole

Preset Cooking Time: 15 minutes

- 1 3/4 pounds lean ground beef
- 1 cup chopped onion
- 2 cloves garlic, minced
- 1 can (16 ounces) tomato purée
- 1 envelope (1 5/8 ounces) taco seasoning mix
- 6 corn tortillas
- 3 cups (12 ounces) shredded Cheddar cheese, divided

Crumble beef into 2-quart glass measure. Add onion and garlic; mix lightly. Place in oven. Set recipe number 101. Touch START. *(Oven cooks: HI, 3 minutes.)*

At Pause, stir through several times. Touch START. *(Oven cooks: HI, 2 minutes.)*

At Pause, stir in purée and seasoning mix. Touch START. *(Oven cooks: HI, 3 minutes.)*

At Pause, remove from oven. Layer tortillas, beef mixture, and 2 1/2 cups cheese in 2-quart round microproof casserole. Cover and place in oven. Touch START. *(Oven cooks: HI, 7 minutes.)*

Sprinkle with remaining 1/2 cup cheese. Cut into wedges to serve.

4 to 6 servings

Recipe No. 102

Lamb Leg or Shoulder Roast, bone in (medium)

Preset Cooking Time: 32 minutes to 1 hour 20 minutes

1 lamb leg or shoulder roast, bone in (4 to 8 pounds)

Place lamb, fat-side down, on microwave roasting rack in 12×7-inch microproof baking dish. Place in oven. Insert temperature probe horizontally into densest part of lamb without touching fat or bone. Cover lightly with waxed paper. Set recipe number 102. Touch START. *(Oven cooks:* 70, 16 *to* 40 *minutes to* 90°*F.)*

At Pause, turn over. Cover end of leg bone with aluminum foil. Cover lamb with waxed paper. Touch START. *(Oven cooks:* 70, 16 *to* 40 *minutes to* 145°*F; holds warm:* 10.*)*

8 to 12 servings

Recipe No. 103

Lamb Leg or Shoulder Roast, bone in (well done)

Preset Cooking Time: 40 minutes to 1 hour 36 minutes

1 lamb leg or shoulder roast, bone in (4 to 8 pounds)

Place lamb, fat-side down, on microwave roasting rack in 12×7-inch microproof baking dish. Place in oven. Insert temperature probe horizontally into densest part of lamb without touching fat or bone. Cover with waxed paper. Set recipe number 103. Touch START. *(Oven cooks:* 70, 20 *to* 48 *minutes to* 90°*F.)*

At Pause, turn over. Cover end of leg bone with aluminum foil. Cover lamb with waxed paper. Touch START. *(Oven cooks:* 70, 20 *to* 48 *minutes to* 165°*F; holds warm:* 10.*)*

8 to 12 servings

Recipe No. 104

Zesty Lamb Chops

Preset Cooking Time: 20 minutes

½ cup catsup
2 tablespoons Worcestershire sauce
1 tablespoon prepared mustard
4 shoulder lamb chops (1¾ pounds)
½ cup coarsely chopped onion
1 clove garlic, minced

Combine catsup, Worcestershire, and mustard; set aside. Arrange lamb in single layer in microproof baking dish. Sprinkle with onion and garlic. Place in oven. Cover with waxed paper. Set recipe number 104. Touch START. *(Oven cooks: HI,* 5 *minutes.)*

At Pause, spread catsup mixture over lamb. Cover. Touch START. *(Oven cooks:* 60, 15 *minutes.)*

4 servings

Recipe No. 105

Lamb Ragout

Preset Cooking Time: 56 minutes

1 pound lamb for stew, cut into 1-inch cubes
1 envelope (⅝ ounce) brown gravy mix
3 medium carrots, cut into chunks
2 medium stalks celery, cut into chunks
2 medium potatoes, peeled and cut into cubes
1 cup water
¼ cup dry red wine
2 tablespoons all-purpose flour
1 teaspoon salt
½ teaspoon Worcestershire sauce
⅛ teaspoon pepper
1 clove garlic, minced

Combine lamb and gravy mix in 3-quart microproof casserole. Place in oven. Set recipe number 105. Touch START. *(Oven cooks:* 50, 5 *minutes.)*

At Pause, stir. Touch START. *(Oven cooks:* 50, 5 *minutes.)*

At Pause, add remaining ingredients; blend well. Cover. Touch START. *(Oven cooks:* 50, 23 *minutes.)*

At Pause, stir. Cover. Touch START. *(Oven cooks:* 50, 23 *minutes.)*

Let stand 3 to 4 minutes before serving.

4 servings

Recipe No. 106

Herbed Leg of Lamb (medium)

Preset Cooking Time: 50 minutes

- 2 cloves garlic, divided
- 1 butterflied boneless lamb leg roast (4 pounds)
- 1½ tablespoons soy sauce
- 1 tablespoon dry mustard
- 1 teaspoon salt
- 1 teaspoon lemon juice
- ½ teaspoon thyme
- ¼ teaspoon rosemary
- ⅛ teaspoon pepper

Cut 1 clove garlic in half; rub all over lamb. Cut both cloves into slivers. Slit outside of lamb at intervals; insert garlic slivers into slits. Combine remaining ingredients; blend well. Spread all over lamb. Place on microwave roasting rack in shallow microproof baking dish. Place in oven. Cover lightly with waxed paper. Set recipe number 106. Touch START. *(Oven cooks: 70, 20 minutes.)*

At Pause, turn over. Cover. Touch START. *(Oven cooks: 70, 20 minutes; 10, 10 minutes.)*

6 to 8 servings

Recipe No. 107

Herbed Leg of Lamb (well done)

Preset Cooking Time: 1 hour

Follow directions for preparing lamb in recipe number 106 (above). Place lamb on microwave roasting rack in shallow microproof baking dish. Place in oven. Cover lightly with waxed paper. Set recipe number 107. Touch START. *(Oven cooks: 70, 25 minutes.)*

At Pause, turn over. Cover. Touch START. *(Oven cooks: 70, 25 minutes; 10, 10 minutes.)*

6 to 8 servings

Recipe No. 108 ⊞

Bacon

Preset Cooking Time: 4½ minutes

- 4 slices bacon

Place bacon on paper towel on microproof plate. Place in oven. Cover with paper towel. Set recipe number 108. Touch START. *(Oven cooks: HI, 4½ minutes.)*

1 serving

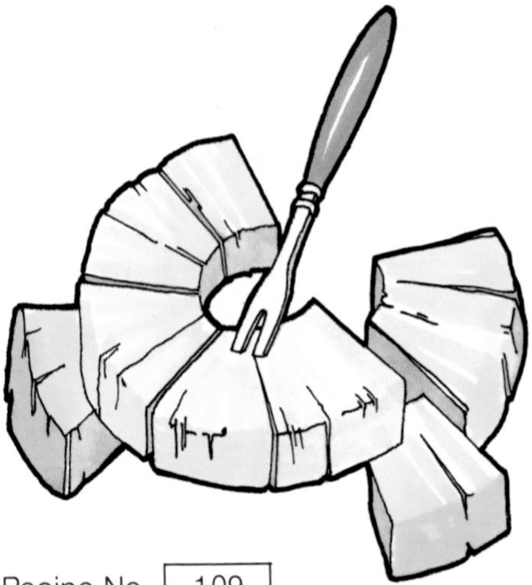

Recipe No. 109

Baked Ham with Pineapple

Preset Cooking Time: 27 minutes

- 1 precooked ham (3 pounds)
- ¼ cup firmly packed brown sugar
- 1 can (4 ounces) pineapple slices, drained, 2 teaspoons juice reserved
- Whole cloves

Place ham, fat-side down, in shallow microproof baking dish. Place in oven. Set recipe number 109. Touch START. *(Oven cooks: 70, 20 minutes.)*

At Pause, remove from oven. Turn ham over. Combine brown sugar and reserved juice; blend to make paste. Spread over top of ham. Arrange pineapple slices on top, attaching with toothpicks if necessary. Stud ham with cloves. Place in oven. Touch START. *(Oven cooks: 70, 7 minutes.)*

Cover with aluminum foil, and let stand 10 minutes before slicing.

8 to 10 servings

Recipe No. 110

Barbecued Spareribs

Preset Cooking Time: 40 minutes

- 2½ pounds pork spareribs, cut into individual ribs
- 1 can (8 ounces) tomato sauce
- 2 tablespoons onion flakes
- 1 tablespoon brown sugar
- 1 tablespoon lemon juice
- 1 teaspoon Worcestershire sauce
- 1 teaspoon prepared mustard
- ½ teaspoon salt
- ¼ teaspoon pepper
- ¼ teaspoon hot pepper sauce

Cut a 1-inch strip from open end of cooking bag. Arrange ribs in bag in large microproof baking dish; tie bag with removed strip. Place in oven. Set recipe number 110. Touch START. *(Oven cooks:* 50, 15 *minutes.)*

At Pause, remove from oven. Open bag; turn ribs over; drain. Combine remaining ingredients; blend well. Pour over ribs in bag. Close bag. Place in oven. Touch START. *(Oven cooks:* 50, 15 *minutes; stands:* 0, 10 *minutes.)*

4 servings

Recipe No. 111

Country Style Ribs

Preset Cooking Time: 1 hour 5 minutes

- 3 pounds meaty country style pork ribs
- ½ cup barbecue sauce
- 3 tablespoons olive oil
- 1 tablespoon wine vinegar
- 1 tablespoon chopped onion
- 1 teaspoon chopped parsley
- ½ teaspoon salt
- ⅛ teaspoon pepper
- 1 clove garlic, minced

Cut a 1-inch strip from open end of cooking bag. Arrange ribs in bag in large microproof baking dish; tie bag with removed strip. Place in oven. Set recipe number 111. Touch START. *(Oven cooks:* 50, 35 *minutes.)*

At Pause, remove from oven. Open bag; turn ribs over; drain. Combine remaining ingredients; blend well. Pour over ribs in bag. Close bag. Place in oven. Touch START. *(Oven cooks:* 50, 25 *minutes;* 20, 5 *minutes.)*

14 to 6 servings

You can substitute ½ cup Spicy Barbecue Sauce (page 178) for ready-made sauce, if desired.

Recipe No. 112

Center Cut Ham Slice

Preset Cooking Time: about 15 minutes

- 1 center cut ham slice (1 pound)

Place ham in 12×7-inch microproof baking dish. Place in oven. Insert temperature probe horizontally into center of ham without touching fat or bone. Set recipe number 112. Touch START. *(Oven cooks:* 70, *about* 5 *minutes to* 90°*F.)*

At Pause, turn over. Touch START. *(Oven cooks:* 70, *about* 5 *minutes to* 120°*F; stands:* 0; 5 *minutes.)*

2 servings

Recipe No. 113

Precooked Ham

Preset Cooking Time: 35 minutes to 1 hour 15 minutes

- 1 precooked ham (3 to 5 pounds)

Place ham on microwave roasting rack in 12×7-inch microproof baking dish. Place in oven. Insert temperature probe horizontally into center of ham. Cover lightly with waxed paper. Set recipe number 113. Touch START. *(Oven cooks:* 70, 15 *to* 35 *minutes to* 90°*F.)*

At Pause, turn over. Cover. Touch START. *(Oven cooks:* 70, 15 *to* 35 *minutes to* 120°*F; stands:* 0; 5 *minutes.)*

6 to 10 servings

Recipe No. 114

Orange Ginger Pork Chops

Preset Cooking Time: 17 minutes

- 6 lean pork loin chops (1½ pounds), trimmed
- ¼ cup orange juice
- 2 teaspoons ginger
- ½ teaspoon salt
- ½ teaspoon garlic powder
- 6 strips orange peel
- ½ cup dairy sour cream

Place pork chops in rectangular microproof baking dish. Pour juice over chops. Place in oven. Cover with waxed paper. Set recipe number 114. Touch START. *(Oven cooks:* 70, 6 *minutes.)*

At Pause, turn over. Cover. Touch START. *(Oven cooks:* 70, 6 *minutes.)*

At Pause, sprinkle with ginger, salt, and garlic powder. Place 1 strip orange peel on each chop. Cover. Touch START. *(Oven cooks: HI,* 5 *minutes.)*

Discard orange peel. Top each chop with dollop of sour cream. Let stand, covered, 5 minutes before serving.

6 servings

Recipe No. 115

Pork Loin Roast, boneless

Preset Cooking Time: 33 to 36 minutes (about 12 minutes per pound)

- 1 pork loin roast, boneless (3 pounds)

Place roast, fat-side down, on microwave roasting rack in 12×7-inch microproof baking dish. Place in oven. Insert temperature probe horizontally into densest part of roast without touching fat. Cover lightly with waxed paper. Set recipe number 115. Touch START. *(Oven cooks:* 50, *about* 18 *minutes to* 120°F.*)*

At Pause, turn over. Cover. Touch START. *(Oven cooks:* 50, 15 *to* 18 *minutes to* 160°F; *10, 10 minutes.)*

6 servings

← *Honey-Glazed Pork Roast*

Recipe No. 116

Honey-Glazed Pork Roast

Preset Cooking Time: 52 minutes

- ¼ cup honey
- 2 tablespoons orange juice
- 1 teaspoon cornstarch
- ¾ teaspoon cinnamon
- 1 pork loin roast, boneless (3 pounds)

Combine honey, juice, cornstarch, and cinnamon in 2-cup glass measure. Stir until cornstarch is dissolved. Place in oven. Set recipe number 116. Touch START. *(Oven cooks: HI,* 1 *minute.)*

At Pause, remove from oven; set aside. Place roast, fat-side down, in microwave roasting rack in shallow microproof baking dish. Cover with plastic wrap and place in oven. Touch START. *(Oven cooks:* 50, 25 *minutes.)*

At Pause, turn over. Cover. Touch START. *(Oven cooks:* 50, 25 *minutes.)*

At Pause, brush on half of the honey glaze. Do not cover. Touch START. *(Oven cooks: HI,* 1 *minute.)*

Brush on remaining glaze. Let stand 10 minutes before serving.

6 to 8 servings

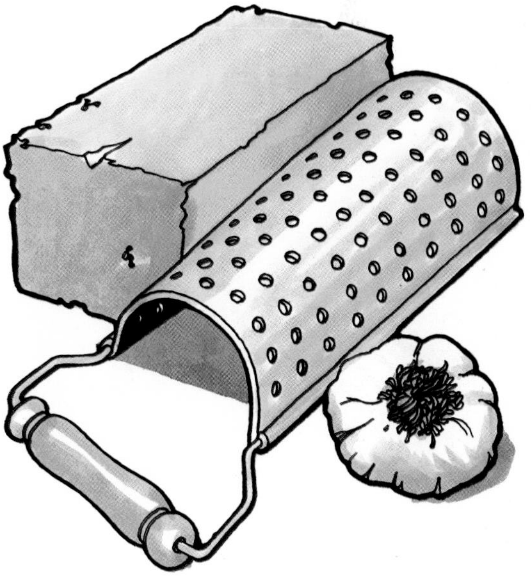

Recipe No. 117 ⊞

Sausage

Preset Cooking Time: 5 minutes

1 package (1 pound) bulk pork sausage

Crumble sausage into 1½-quart microproof casserole. Cover and place in oven. Set recipe number 117. Touch START. *(Oven cooks: HI, 3 minutes.)*

At Pause, stir to break up sausage. Cover. Touch START. *(Oven cooks: HI, 2 minutes.)*

Drain before serving.

2 servings

Recipe No. 118

Stuffed Pork Chops

Preset Cooking Time: 25¾ minutes

- 2 tablespoons butter or margarine
- 1 cup coarse dry bread crumbs
- ½ cup chopped apple
- 2 tablespoons chopped raisins
- 2 tablespoons sugar
- 2 tablespoons minced onion
- ½ teaspoon salt
- ¼ teaspoon pepper
- Pinch sage
- 2 tablespoons hot water
- 8 thin pork loin chops (1 pound), trimmed
- ½ envelope (⅜ ounce) brown gravy mix

Place butter in 1-quart microproof bowl. Place in oven. Set recipe number 118. Touch START. *(Oven cooks: HI, 45 seconds.)*

At Pause, remove from oven. Add bread crumbs, apple, raisins, sugar, onion, salt, pepper, and sage; stir lightly. Add hot water; stir just until moistened. Place 4 chops in 8-inch microproof baking dish. Divide stuffing evenly over chops. Cover with remaining 4 chops; press together lightly. Sprinkle with gravy mix. Place in oven. Cover with waxed paper. Touch START. *(Oven cooks: 50, 20 minutes.)*

At Pause, baste with pan juices. Cover. Touch START. *(Oven cooks: 20, 5 minutes.)*

4 servings

Recipe No. 119

Sweet and Sour Pork

Preset Cooking Time: 29 minutes

- 4 medium carrots, thinly sliced
- ¼ cup vegetable oil
- 2 pounds lean boneless pork, cut into ¾-inch cubes
- 2 medium green peppers, seeded and sliced
- 1 medium onion, sliced
- ¼ cup cornstarch
- 1 can (16 ounces) pineapple chunks, drained, ½ cup juice reserved
- ½ cup firmly packed brown sugar
- ½ cup soy sauce
- ¼ cup wine vinegar
- 1 tablespoon Worcestershire sauce
- ½ teaspoon pepper
- ¼ teaspoon hot pepper sauce

Place carrots and oil in 3-quart microproof casserole; stir to coat. Cover and place in oven. Set recipe number 119. Touch START. *(Oven cooks: HI, 4 minutes.)*

At Pause, add pork, green peppers, and onion; mix lightly. Cover. Touch START. *(Oven cooks: HI, 5 minutes.)*

At Pause, dissolve cornstarch in reserved pineapple juice. Stir in remaining ingredients except pineapple. Add to pork mixture; blend well. Stir in pineapple. Cover. Touch START. *(Oven cooks: 50, 10 minutes.)*

At Pause, stir. Cover. Touch START. *(Oven cooks: 50, 10 minutes.)*

Serve over hot rice, and sprinkle with chow mein noodles.

8 servings

⊞ *Recipe can be increased. See "Quantity", page 12.*

All Seasons Rice (page 143), Sweet and Sour Pork →

Recipe No. 120

Smoked Ham Shank

Preset Cooking Time: 16 to 20 minutes

1 smoked ham shank (2 pounds)

Place ham, fat-side down, on microwave roasting rack in 12×7-inch microproof baking dish. Place in oven. Insert temperature probe horizontally into densest part of ham without touching fat or bone. Cover lightly with waxed paper. Set recipe number 120. Touch START. *(Oven cooks:* 70, 8 *to* 10 *minutes to* 90°F.)

At Pause, turn over. Cover. Touch START. *(Oven cooks:* 70, 8 *to* 10 *minutes to* 120°*F; holds warm:* 10.)

4 servings

Recipe No. 121

Liver Venetian Style

Preset Cooking Time: 18 minutes

4 slices bacon
2 medium onions, thinly sliced
1 pound sliced calves livers
Salt and pepper, to taste

Place bacon in microproof casserole. Cover and place in oven. Set recipe number 121. Touch START. *(Oven cooks: HI,* 4 *minutes.)*

At Pause, remove from oven. Transfer bacon to paper towels to drain, reserving drippings in casserole. Add onions to drippings; stir to coat. Cover and place in oven. Touch START. *(Oven cooks: HI,* 5 *minutes.)*

At Pause, push onions to side of casserole. Add liver; turn to coat both sides. Cover. Touch START. *(Oven cooks:* 50, 5 *minutes.)*

At Pause, turn over. Cover. Touch START. *(Oven cooks:* 50, 4 *minutes.)*

Season liver with salt and pepper, and serve topped with onions and crumbled bacon.

4 servings

Prime Time Poultry

Chicken, turkey, duck, and Cornish hen are especially juicy, tender, and flavorful when cooked in a microwave oven. Because they require less attention than other meats, they are great favorites for microwave cooks on those days when too many things seem to be happening at once. Poultry turns out golden brown but not crisp. If you have crisp-skin lovers at your table, you can satisfy them by crisping the skin in a conventional oven at 450°F, after the microwave cooking. You can also avoid the frustrations of long barbecue cooking by partially cooking poultry in the microwave oven, then finishing it off on the charcoal grill. Try the tasty recipes suggested here and then adapt your own. You'll even want to experiment with new recipes when you discover how much easier it is to cook poultry in your microwave oven than in the conventional oven.

A browning sauce may be brushed on poultry before cooking if you prefer a more-browned appearance than the microwave normally provides (above left). The best arrangement for chicken parts (above). Turning Microwave Fried Chicken (page 114) in a browning dish (left).

Converting Your Recipes

Conventional one-dish poultry recipes that call for cut-up pieces are easy to adapt for the microwave. The temperature probe can help achieve accurate doneness in whole-chicken recipes as well as in casseroles. Refer to the comparative chicken recipes on page 34 to guide you in converting your favorite dishes. Here are some good tips to follow:

- ☐ To obtain uniform doneness and flavor, cook poultry weighing no more than 14 pounds in the microwave oven. Poultry over 14 pounds should be cooked conventionally.
- ☐ Butter- or oil-injected turkeys often have uneven concentrations of fat and thus cook unevenly. For best results, use uninjected turkeys.
- ☐ Conventional pop-up indicators for doneness do not work correctly in the microwave.
- ☐ The temperature probe may be used in cooking whole poultry. Insert the probe in the fleshy part of the inside thigh muscle without touching the bone.
- ☐ Poultry pieces prepared in a cream sauce should be cooked on 70 to prevent the cream from separating or curdling.
- ☐ Chicken coated with a crumb mixture cooks to crispness more easily if left uncovered.
- ☐ Less tender game birds should be cooked on 70 on a microwave roasting rack. Pour off fat as necessary. For best results, marinate game birds before cooking.
- ☐ Standing time is essential to complete cooking. Allow up to 15 minutes standing time for whole poultry depending upon size. The internal temperature will rise approximately 15°F during 15 minutes standing time. Chicken pieces and casseroles need only 5 minutes standing time.

Using the Defrosting Guide

1. Poultry can be defrosted within the original paper or plastic wrapping. Remove all metal rings, wire twist ties, and any aluminum foil. Since it is difficult to remove metal clamps from legs of frozen turkey, they need not be removed until after defrosting. The metal must be at least 1 inch from oven walls.
2. Defrost only as long as necessary. Poultry should be cool in the center when removed from the oven.
3. To speed defrosting during standing time, poultry may be placed in a cold-water bath.
4. Separate cut-up chicken pieces as soon as partially thawed.
5. Wing and leg tips and area near breast bone may begin cooking before center is thoroughly defrosted. As soon as these areas appear thawed, cover them with small strips of aluminum foil; this foil should be at least 1 inch from oven walls.
6. Programmed Defrost offers another thawing method. See Use & Care Manual for instructions.

DEFROSTING GUIDE — POULTRY

Food	Amount	Minutes (per pound)	Cook Control Setting	Standing Time (in minutes)	Special Notes
Capon	6-8 lbs.	2	70 (roast)	60	Turn over once. Immerse in cold water for standing time.
Chicken, cut up	2-3 lbs.	5-6	30 (defrost)	10-15	Turn every 5 minutes. Separate pieces when partially thawed.
Chicken, whole	2-3 lbs.	6-8	30 (defrost)	25-30	Turn over once. Immerse in cold water for standing time.
Cornish hens	1, 1-1½ lbs. 2, 1-1½ lbs. ea.	6-8 8-10	30 (defrost) 30 (defrost)	20 20	Turn over once.
Duckling	4-5 lbs.	4	70 (roast)	30-40	Turn over once. Immerse in cold water for standing time.
Turkey	Under 8 lbs. Over 8 lbs.	3-5 3-5	30 (defrost) 70 (roast)	60 60	Turn over once. Immerse in cold water for standing time.
Turkey breast	Under 4 lbs. Over 4 lbs.	3-5 1 2	30 (defrost) 70 (roast) 50 (simmer)	20 20	Turn over once. Start at 70 (roast), turn over, continue on 50 (simmer).
Turkey drumsticks	1-1½ lbs.	5-6	30 (defrost)	15-20	Turn every 5 minutes. Separate pieces when partially thawed.
Turkey roast, boneless	2-4 lbs.	3-4	30 (defrost)	10	Remove from foil pan. Cover with waxed paper.

Using the Cooking Guide

1. Defrost frozen poultry completely before cooking.
2. Remove the giblets, rinse poultry in cool water, and pat dry.
3. Brush poultry with browning sauce before cooking, if desired.
4. When cooking whole birds, place on a microproof roasting rack in a glass baking dish large enough to catch drippings.
5. Turn over, as directed in Guide, halfway through cooking time.
6. Cook whole poultry covered loosely with a waxed paper tent to prevent splattering. Toward end of cooking time, small pieces of aluminum foil may be used for shielding to cover legs, wing tips, or breast bone area to prevent overcooking. Foil should be at least 1 inch from oven walls.
7. Cover poultry pieces with either glass lid or plastic wrap during cooking and standing time.
8. Use temperature probe inserted in thickest part of thigh, set at 180°F for whole poultry, and at 170°F for parts, including turkey breasts.
9. Standing time completes the cooking of poultry. Cooked whole birds may be covered with aluminum foil during standing time.

COOKING GUIDE — POULTRY

Food	First Cook Control Setting and Time (in minutes)	Second Cook Control Setting and Time (in minutes)	or	Temperature Probe Setting	Standing Time (in minutes)	Special Notes
Chicken, whole, 2-3 pounds	HI (max. power) 3-4 per pound	Turn over. HI (max. power) 4 per pound	or	Turn over. 180°	5 (covered with foil)	Shallow baking dish, roasting rack, breast up.
3-5 pounds	HI (max. power) 4 per pound	Turn over. HI (max. power) 4-5 per pound	or	Turn over. 180°	5	12×7-inch baking dish, roasting rack, breast up.
Chicken, cut up 2½-3½ pounds	HI (max. power) 10	Turn over. HI (max. power) 8-12	or	Turn over. 170°	5	12×7-inch baking dish. Cover.
Chicken, quartered	HI (max. power) 3-4 per pound	Turn over. HI (max. power) 3-4 per pound	or	Turn over. 170°	5	Shallow baking dish, skin side down.
Cornish hens 1-1½ pounds	HI (max. power) 4 per pound	Turn over. HI (max. power) 3 per pound	or	Turn over. 180°	5	Shallow baking dish, breast down. Cover.
Duckling 4-5 pounds	70 (roast) 4 per pound	Turn over. Drain excess fat. 70 (roast) 4 per pound	or	Turn over. 170°	8-10	Shallow baking dish, roasting rack. Cover.
Turkey, whole, 8-14 pounds	HI (max. power) 5 per pound	Turn over. 70 (roast) 4 per pound	or	Turn over. 70 (roast) 180°	10-15 (covered with foil)	Shallow baking dish, 13×9-inch, roasting rack, breast up.
Turkey breast, 3-4 pounds	HI (max. power) 7 per pound	Turn over. 70 (roast) 5 per pound	or	Turn over. 70 (roast) 170°		Shallow baking dish, roasting rack.
Turkey roast, boneless 2-4 pounds	70 (roast) 10 per pound	Turn over. 70 (roast) 9 per pound	or	Turn over. 70 (roast) 170°	10-15	Loaf pan. Cover with plastic wrap.
Turkey parts, 2-3 pounds	70 (roast) 7-8 per pound	Turn over. 70 (roast) 7-8 per pound			5	Shallow baking dish with roasting rack.

Recipe No. 122

Chicken Liver Chow Mein

Preset Cooking Time: 19 minutes

- ½ pound chicken livers, rinsed and drained
- ½ cup sliced celery
- ¼ cup chopped onion
- 3 tablespoons butter or margarine, divided
- 1 envelope (1¾ ounces) mushroom gravy mix
- 1 can (16 ounces) Chinese vegetables
- 1 can (8 ounces) sliced water chestnuts, drained
- 1 tablespoon soy sauce

Cut liver into bite-size pieces; discard membranes; set aside. Combine celery, onion, and 1 tablespoon butter in 3-quart microproof casserole. Cover and place in oven. Set recipe number 122. Touch START. *(Oven cooks: HI, 4 minutes.)*

At pause, stir in gravy mix. Add Chinese vegetables, water chestnuts, and soy sauce; stir until gravy mix is dissolved. Cover. Touch START. *(Oven cooks: HI, 7 minutes.)*

At Pause, remove from oven; set aside. Place liver and remaining 2 tablespoons butter in 4-cup glass measure. Place in oven. Cover with waxed paper. Touch START. *(Oven cooks: 50, 6 minutes.)*

At Pause, remove from oven; drain. Carefully stir liver into vegetable mixture. Cover and place in oven. Touch START. *(Oven cooks: HI, 2 minutes.)*

Let stand, covered, 5 minutes. Serve over hot rice, and sprinkle with chow mein noodles.

4 to 6 servings

Recipe No. 123

Barbecued Chicken

Preset Cooking Time: 25 minutes

- 1 broiler-fryer chicken (2½ pounds), quartered
- ½ cup barbecue sauce
- 1 tablespoon parsley flakes
- 1 tablespoon onion flakes

Arrange chicken in round or oval microproof baking dish, skin-side down, with thickest parts toward outside of dish. Combine remaining ingredients; brush half of the sauce mixture over chicken. Place in oven. Cover with waxed paper. Set recipe number 123. Touch START. *(Oven cooks: HI,* 10 *minutes.)*

At Pause, turn over; brush with remaining sauce. Cover. Touch START. *(Oven cooks: HI,* 10 *minutes;* 20, 5 *minutes.)*

4 servings

Recipe No. 124

Breast of Turkey Jardiniere

Preset Cooking Time: 54 minutes

- 2 medium carrots, cut into 2-inch strips
- 2 medium stalks celery, cut into 2-inch strips
- 1 medium potato, peeled and cut into 2-inch strips
- 1 small onion, cut into 2-inch strips
- 2 tablespoons minced parsley
- 3 tablespoons butter or margarine
- Salt and pepper, to taste
- ½ turkey breast (3 pounds), skinned and boned, if desired
- 2 tablespoons vegetable oil
- ¾ teaspoon paprika

Arrange carrots, celery, potato, onion, and parsley in center of oval microproof baking dish. Dot with butter. Season with salt and pepper. Cover with plastic wrap and place in oven. Set recipe number 124. Touch START. *(Oven cooks: HI,* 7 *minutes.)*

At Pause, stir. Place turkey over vegetables. Combine oil and paprika; brush over turkey. Cover with waxed paper. Touch START. *(Oven cooks: HI,* 7 *minutes;* 70, 30 *minutes.)*

At Pause, rotate. Touch START. *(Oven cooks:* 20, 10 *minutes.)*

4 servings

Recipe No. 125

Chicken Milano

Preset Cooking Time: 16 minutes

- 4 tablespoons olive oil
- 1 teaspoon salt
- ½ teaspoon pepper
- ¼ teaspoon oregano
- ¼ teaspoon basil
- 4 chicken thighs (¼ pound each)
- 1 cup dry bread crumbs
- ½ teaspoon paprika
- 2 medium potatoes, peeled and cut into quarters

Combine oil, salt, pepper, oregano, and basil. Place chicken in mixture and roll to coat all sides. Cover and refrigerate 2 hours. Combine bread crumbs and paprika. Remove 1 piece chicken from marinade; drain. Roll in crumb mixture to coat. Repeat with remaining chicken. Set aside remaining marinade and crumb mixture. Arrange chicken in 9-inch round microproof baking dish, skin-side down, with thickest parts toward outside of dish. Cut ends from potatoes to make quarters even; wipe dry. Roll potatoes in remaining marinade to coat, adding more oil to marinade if necessary. Arrange potatoes around chicken. Place in oven. Cover with waxed paper. Set recipe number 125. Touch START. *(Oven cooks: HI,* 6 *minutes.)*

At Pause, turn chicken and potatoes over. Sprinkle with remaining crumb mixture. Cover. Touch START. *(Oven cooks: HI,* 5 *minutes; stands:* 0, 5 *minutes.)*

2 servings

Recipe No. 126

Chicken Marengo

Preset Cooking Time: 35 minutes

- 1 broiler-fryer chicken (3½ pounds), cut up
- ¼ cup vegetable oil
- 2 cups soft bread crumbs
- 1 package (3 ounces) spaghetti sauce mix
- 2 cups sliced mushrooms
- 1 can (16 ounces) whole tomatoes, broken up
- 1 cup dry white wine

Rinse chicken and pat dry with paper towels. Brush with oil. Combine bread crumbs and sauce mix in plastic bag. Shake chicken, 1 piece at a time, in bag to coat well. Arrange chicken in 3-quart round or oval microproof casserole with thickest parts toward outside of casserole. Place in oven. Set recipe number 126. Touch START. *(Oven cooks: HI, 15 minutes.)*

At Pause, add remaining ingredients. Cover. Touch START. *(Oven cooks: HI, 15 minutes; 30, 5 minutes.)*

4 to 6 servings

Recipe No. 127

Chicken Sukiyaki

Preset Cooking Time: 12 minutes

- ½ cup soy sauce
- ½ cup chicken broth
- ¼ cup dry sherry
- 2 tablespoons sugar
- 2 chicken breasts (½ pound each), skinned, boned, and cut into ½-inch slices
- 1 pound spinach, stems removed
- ½ pound bean sprouts
- ¼ pound pea pods
- ½ cup sliced celery
- 1 medium onion, thinly sliced
- 1 medium bunch green onions, cut into 3-inch strips
- 6 small mushrooms, sliced

Combine soy sauce, broth, sherry, and sugar in 2-cup glass measure; stir until sugar is dissolved. Place in oven. Set recipe number 127. Touch START. *(Oven cooks: HI, 2 minutes.)*

At Pause, remove from oven. Combine remaining ingredients in 3-quart microproof casserole; toss lightly. Pour sauce mixture over chicken mixture. Cover and place in oven. Touch START. *(Oven cooks: HI, 3 minutes.)*

At Pause, stir. Cover. Touch START. *(Oven cooks: HI, 2 minutes.)*

At Pause, stir. Cover. Touch START. *(Oven cooks: HI, 5 minutes.)*

Pass additional soy sauce at table.

4 servings

Recipe No. 128

Chicken Parts

Preset Cooking Time: 7 minutes

- 1 pound chicken parts
- Melted butter
- Seasonings

Arrange chicken in 8-inch round microproof baking dish, skin-side up, with thickest parts toward outside of dish. Brush with butter. Sprinkle with seasonings as desired. Place in oven. Cover with waxed paper. Set recipe number 128. Touch START. *(Oven cooks: HI, 7 minutes.)*

Let stand, covered, 5 minutes before serving.

2 servings

Recipe No. 129

Chicken and Vegetables

Preset Cooking Time: 25 minutes

- 2 medium carrots
- 2 medium stalks celery
- 2 small parsnips, peeled
- 2 small potatoes, peeled
- 1 medium onion
- 2 tablespoons butter or margarine
- 2 tablespoons minced parsley
- ½ teaspoon salt
- ⅛ teaspoon paprika
- Dash pepper
- 2 whole chicken breasts (1 pound each), split, skinned, and boned

Cut all vegetables into 1½ × ¼-inch strips (about 4 cups total). Place in shallow round or oval microproof baking dish. Dot with butter. Season with parsley, salt, paprika, and pepper. Cover with plastic wrap and place in oven. Set recipe number 129. Touch START. *(Oven cooks: HI, 5 minutes.)*

At Pause, stir. Cover. Touch START. *(Oven cooks: HI, 5 minutes.)*

At Pause, arrange chicken over vegetables around outside of dish. Sprinkle with paprika. Cover with plastic wrap. Touch START. *(Oven cooks: HI, 10 minutes; stands: 0, 5 minutes.)*

Spoon vegetables over chicken, and sprinkle with additional parsley before serving.

4 servings

Recipe No. 130

Chicken, Whole

Preset Cooking Time: 26 minutes

- 1 broiler-fryer chicken (3 pounds), giblets removed
- Microwave browning sauce

Rinse chicken in cool water and pat dry. Place chicken, breast-side up, on microwave roasting rack in 12×7-inch microproof baking dish. Brush with browning sauce. Place in oven. Cover with waxed-paper tent. Set recipe number 130. Touch START. *(Oven cooks: HI, 9 minutes.)*

At Pause, turn over. Brush with pan juices. Cover. Touch START. *(Oven cooks: HI, 12 minutes; 30, 5 minutes.)*

4 servings

Recipe No. 131

Chicken, Cut Up

Preset Cooking Time: 27 minutes

- 1 broiler-fryer chicken (3½ pounds), cut up
- Microwave browning sauce

Rinse chicken in cool water and pat dry. Arrange chicken in shallow round or oval microproof baking dish, skin-side down, with thickest parts toward outside of dish and breast in center. Brush chicken with browning sauce. Place in oven. Cover lightly with waxed paper. Set recipe number 131. Touch START. *(Oven cooks: HI, 10 minutes.)*

At Pause, turn over. Brush with pan juices. Touch START. *(Oven cooks: HI, 12 minutes; 20, 5 minutes.)*

4 servings

If desired, you can substitute seasoned sauce or paprika for browning sauce.

Recipe No. 132

Chicken Veronique

Preset Cooking Time: 10 minutes

- 3 cups cooked rice
- 2 cups coarsely cut up cooked chicken
- 1 cup halved seedless green or white grapes
- ½ cup diced celery
- ¾ cup milk
- ¼ cup white wine
- 2 tablespoons butter or margarine
- 2 tablespoons all-purpose flour
- ½ teaspoon chervil
- ½ teaspoon parsley flakes
- ¼ teaspoon tarragon
- Dash white pepper

Combine rice, chicken, grapes, and celery in 1½-quart microproof casserole; mix lightly; set aside. Pour milk and wine into 2-cup glass measure. Place in oven. Set recipe number 132. Touch START. *(Oven cooks: HI, 2 minutes.)*

At Pause, remove from oven; set aside. Place butter in 2-cup glass measure. Place in oven. Touch START. *(Oven cooks: HI, 1 minute.)*

At Pause, stir flour into butter. Touch START. *(Oven cooks: HI, 1 minute.)*

At Pause, remove from oven. Briskly stir milk mixture into flour mixture with wire whisk; stir until smooth. Stir in seasonings. Pour over chicken mixture. Cover and place in oven. Touch START. *(Oven cooks: HI, 6 minutes.)*

Let stand 2 minutes before serving.

4 to 6 servings

Recipe No. 133

Duckling

Preset Cooking Time: 45 minutes

- 1 duckling (4 pounds), giblets removed
- Salt and pepper, to taste

Rinse duckling in cool water and pat dry. Pierce skin all over to allow fat to drain. Place duckling, breast-side up, on microwave roasting rack in 12×7-inch microproof baking dish. Place in oven. Sprinkle with salt and pepper. Cover with waxed-paper tent. Set recipe number 133. Touch START. *(Oven cooks:* 70, 20 *minutes.)*

At Pause, turn over; drain, reserving drippings for Orange Sauce, if desired. Brush with pan juices. Cover. Touch START. *(Oven cooks:* 70, 20 *minutes;* 30, 5 *minutes.)*

Serve with Orange Sauce (page 176).

2 servings

If you like crisp skin, preheat conventional oven to 400°F. Place duckling in conventional oven until skin is brown and crisp.

Recipe No. 134

Easy Baked Chicken

Preset Cooking Time: 30 minutes

- 1 broiler-fryer chicken (3½ pounds), giblets removed
- Salt and pepper
- 2 medium stalks celery, cut into 1-inch chunks
- 1 small onion, cut into quarters
- 2 tablespoons butter or margarine, softened
- ⅛ teaspoon thyme

Rinse chicken in cool water and pat dry. Sprinkle cavity with salt and pepper. Place celery and onion inside cavity. Tie legs together with string; tie wings to body. Place chicken, breast-side up, on microwave roasting rack in 12×7-inch microproof baking dish. Spread with butter; sprinkle with thyme. Place in oven. Set recipe number 134. Touch START. *(Oven cooks: HI,* 10 *minutes.)*

At Pause, turn over. Baste with pan juices. Touch START. *(Oven cooks: HI,* 15 *minutes;* 30, 5 *minutes.)*

4 servings

Recipe No. 135

Garlic Chicken Italiano

Preset Cooking Time: 21 minutes

- ⅓ cup olive oil
- 24 large cloves garlic
- 1 medium stalk celery, thinly sliced
- 2 tablespoons chopped parsley
- 1 teaspoon salt
- ½ teaspoon pepper
- ½ teaspoon oregano
- Pinch nutmeg
- 4 chicken legs (¼ pound each)
- 4 chicken thighs (¼ pound each)

Combine oil, garlic, celery, parsley, salt, pepper, oregano, and nutmeg in shallow microproof baking dish. Add chicken pieces; turn to coat all sides with marinade. Cover and refrigerate at least 3 hours, turning several times during marinating. Cover and place in oven. Set recipe number 135. Touch START. *(Oven cooks: HI,* 8 *minutes.)*

At Pause, turn over. Baste with pan juices. Cover. Touch START. *(Oven cooks: HI,* 8 *minutes;* 10, 5 *minutes.)*

4 servings

Recipe No. 136

Heavenly Cornish Hens

Preset Cooking Time: 27 minutes

- 2 Cornish hens (1½ pounds each)
- 2 tablespoons sherry or water
- 1 envelope (2⅜ ounces) seasoned coating mix for chicken

Split hens lengthwise. Remove backbones. Rinse hens in cool water and pat dry. Brush all over with sherry. Cover with coating mix. Arrange in round or oval microproof baking dish, breast-side down, with thickest parts toward outside of dish. Place in oven. Cover with waxed paper. Set recipe number 136. Touch START. *(Oven cooks: HI,* 10 *minutes.)*

At Pause, turn over. Cover. Touch START. *(Oven cooks: HI,* 12 *minutes;* 10, 5 *minutes.)*

4 servings

Heavenly Cornish Hens →

Recipe No. 137

Microwave Fried Chicken

Preset Cooking Time: 9 minutes

- ½ cup all-purpose flour
- ½ teaspoon salt
- ¼ teaspoon pepper
- ⅛ teaspoon dry mustard
- 1 broiler-fryer chicken (2½ pounds), cut up, backbone and wing tips removed
- 2 tablespoons lemon juice
- 2 tablespoons vegetable oil
- 2 tablespoons butter
- Paprika

Combine flour, salt, pepper, and mustard in paper bag; shake well. Brush chicken with lemon juice. Shake chicken, a few pieces at a time, in seasoned flour. Shake off excess flour. Preheat large microwave browning dish according to manufacturer's directions. Add oil and butter to dish. Arrange chicken on browning dish in oven, skin-side down, without crowding. Cover lightly with waxed paper. Set recipe number 137. Touch START. *(Oven cooks: HI, 4 minutes.)*

At Pause, turn over. Sprinkle with paprika. Cover. Touch START. *(Oven cooks: HI, 5 minutes.)*

4 servings

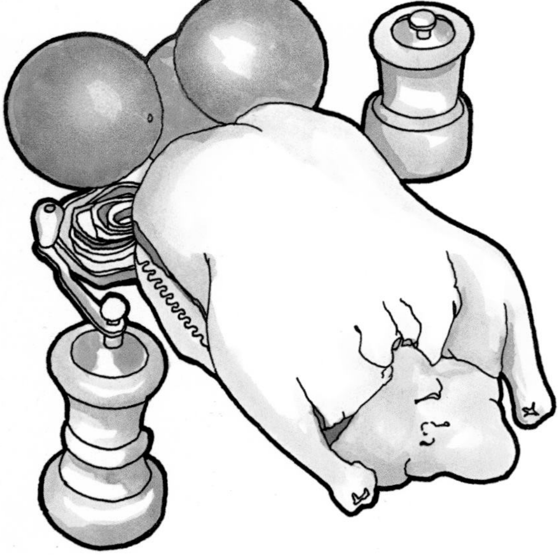

Recipe No. 138

Roast Orange Duckling

Preset Cooking Time: 56 minutes

- 1 duckling (4 pounds), giblets removed
- 1 orange, peeled and cut into chunks
- 1 medium onion, cut into quarters
- ½ cup orange marmalade

Rinse duckling in cool water and pat dry. Place orange and onion pieces in body cavity. Secure neck skin with wooden toothpicks or skewers. Tie legs together with string; tie wings to body. Pierce skin all over to allow fat to drain. Place duckling, breast-side up, on microwave roasting rack in 12×7-inch microproof baking dish; set aside. Place marmalade in 1-cup glass measure. Place in oven. Set recipe number 138. Touch START. *(Oven cooks: HI, 1 minute.)*

At Pause, remove from oven. Spread half of the marmalade over duckling. Place duckling in oven. Touch START. *(Oven cooks:* 70, 25 *minutes.)*

At Pause, turn over. Brush with remaining marmalade. Cover with waxed paper. Touch START. *(Oven cooks:* 70, 25 *minutes;* 30, 5 *minutes.)*

2 servings

If you like crispy skin, place cooked duckling in conventional oven preheated to 350°F; bake 10 minutes until desired crispness is reached.

Microwave Fried Chicken →

Recipe No. 139

Soy Sherry Chicken

Preset Cooking Time: 34 to 40 minutes

- 1 broiler-fryer chicken (3 pounds), giblets removed
- 1/4 cup soy sauce
- 1/4 cup dry sherry
- 1 small onion, sliced
- 3 slices fresh ginger (1/8 inch thick)

Cut off a 1-inch strip from open end of cooking bag. Rinse chicken in cool water and pat dry. Brush generously with soy sauce. Place chicken, breast-side up, in cooking bag in microproof baking dish. Add sherry, any remaining soy sauce, onion, and ginger. Place in oven. Insert temperature probe into thigh. Tie bag loosely with removed strip. Set recipe number 139. Touch START. *(Oven cooks: 80, 24 to 30 minutes to 180°F; 10, 10 minutes.)*

Turn bag over to baste chicken with juices before removing from bag. Discard ginger. Serve with cooking juices and onion.

4 servings

Recipe No. 140

Swiss Coated Chicken

Preset Cooking Time: 5 1/2 minutes

- 1 whole chicken breast (1 pound), split, skinned, and boned
- 1 teaspoon cornstarch
- 1/4 teaspoon paprika
- 1/4 teaspoon white pepper
- 1/3 cup light cream
- 2 tablespoons apple juice
- 1/2 cup (2 ounces) shredded Swiss cheese
- 1 tablespoon chopped parsley

Place chicken in shallow microproof baking dish; set aside. Combine cornstarch, paprika, and pepper. Add cream and apple juice; stir until cornstarch is dissolved. Pour over chicken. Cover and place in oven. Set recipe number 140. Touch START. *(Oven cooks: HI, 1 minute.)*

At Pause, turn chicken over. Stir sauce and baste chicken. Cover. Touch START. *(Oven cooks: HI, 3 minutes.)*

At Pause, stir sauce and baste chicken. Sprinkle with cheese. Do not cover. Touch START. *(Oven cooks: HI, 1 1/2 minutes.)*

Sprinkle with parsley before serving.

2 servings

Recipe No. 141

Tarragon Grilled Chicken

Preset Cooking Time: 27 minutes

- 1/4 cup olive oil
- 1/4 cup dry sherry or chicken broth
- 1 tablespoon onion flakes
- 1 clove garlic, minced
- 1 teaspoon salt
- 1/2 teaspoon tarragon
- 1/8 teaspoon white pepper
- 1 broiler-fryer chicken (3 pounds), quartered

Combine all ingredients except chicken. Arrange chicken in shallow oval microproof baking dish, skin-side down, with thickest parts toward outside of dish. Brush with half of the oil mixture. Place in oven. Cover with waxed paper. Set recipe number 141. Touch START. *(Oven cooks: HI, 10 minutes.)*

At Pause, turn over. Brush generously with remaining oil mixture. Cover. Touch START. *(Oven cooks: HI, 12 minutes; 10, 5 minutes.)*

4 servings

This chicken dish is delicious when finished on a charcoal grill. Prepare chicken as directed above. Cook in microwave oven on HI 8 minutes on one side, and 7 to 9 minutes on the other, or until nearly done. Reserve pan juices. Barbecue about 4 inches above hot coals 10 to 12 minutes, or until golden brown. Turn occasionally and brush with reserved juices.

Recipe No. 142

Turkey with Nut Stuffing

Preset Cooking Time: 1 hour 55 minutes

- 1 turkey (12 pounds), neck and giblets removed
- 1 cup chicken broth
- ½ cup butter or margarine
- 2 medium stalks celery, thinly sliced
- 1 large onion, chopped
- 10 cups day-old bread crumbs or ½-inch cubes
- 1 cup coarsely chopped walnuts or pecans
- ¼ cup chopped parsley
- 1 teaspoon poultry seasoning
- ½ teaspoon salt
- 1 tablespoon bottled brown sauce

Rinse turkey in cool water and pat dry; set aside. Place broth and butter in 3-quart microproof casserole. Add celery and onion. Cover and place in oven. Set recipe number 142. Touch START. *(Oven cooks: HI, 5 minutes.)*

At Pause, remove from oven. Add bread crumbs, nuts, parsley, poultry seasoning, and salt; stir lightly. Stuff neck opening with part of stuffing. Secure neck skin with strong wooden toothpicks or skewers. Stuff cavity with remaining stuffing. Tie legs together with strong string; tie wings to body. Place turkey, breast-side up, on microwave roasting rack in large microproof baking dish. Place in oven. Touch START. *(Oven cooks: HI, 20 minutes.)*

At Pause, turn over; drain. Cover with waxed-paper tent. Touch START. *(Oven cooks: 70, 40 minutes.)*

At Pause, baste with brown sauce and pan juices. Rotate pan one-quarter turn. Cover. Touch START. *(Oven cooks: 70, 50 minutes.)*

Remove from oven. Cover with aluminum foil, and let stand 10 minutes before carving.

6 to 8 servings

If you like extra-crisp skin, place turkey in conventional oven preheated to 450°F. Bake 10 to 15 minutes until desired crispness is reached.

Recipe No. 143

Chicken Supreme

Preset Cooking Time: 55 minutes

- 5 slices bacon
- 1 can (10¾ ounces) cream of onion soup, undiluted
- ½ cup dry red wine or dry sherry
- ½ cup chopped onion
- 1 clove garlic, minced
- 1 tablespoon minced parsley
- 1½ teaspoons chicken bouillon granules
- ½ teaspoon salt
- ¼ teaspoon pepper
- ¼ teaspoon thyme
- 6 small potatoes, peeled and cut in half
- 2 medium carrots, thinly sliced
- 1 broiler-fryer chicken (2½ pounds), cut up
- ½ pound mushrooms, sliced

Arrange bacon on paper towel on microproof plate. Place in oven. Cover with paper towel. Set recipe number 143. Touch START. *(Oven cooks: HI, 5 minutes.)*

At Pause, remove from oven; crumble bacon and set aside. Combine soup, wine, onion, garlic, parsley, bouillon, and seasonings; set aside. Place potatoes and carrots in 3-quart microproof casserole. Arrange chicken on top, skin-side down, with thickest parts toward outside of casserole. Pour soup mixture over top. Cover and place in oven. Touch START. *(Oven cooks: HI, 30 minutes.)*

At Pause, rearrange chicken, bringing bottom pieces to top, skin-side up. Sprinkle with bacon and mushrooms. Cover. Touch START. *(Oven cooks: 70, 15 minutes; 10, 5 minutes.)*

4 to 6 servings

Recipe No. 144

Chicken Cacciatore

Preset Cooking Time: 45 minutes

- 1 medium onion, chopped
- 1 medium green pepper, seeded and thinly sliced
- 1 tablespoon butter or margarine
- 1 can (28 ounces) whole tomatoes, broken up
- 1/4 cup all-purpose flour
- 1/2 cup dry red wine or water
- 1 tablespoon parsley flakes
- 1 teaspoon salt
- 1 teaspoon paprika
- 1/2 teaspoon oregano
- 1/4 teaspoon pepper
- 1/4 teaspoon basil
- 1 bay leaf
- 1 clove garlic, minced
- 1 broiler-fryer chicken (3 pounds), cut up

Combine onion, green pepper, and butter in 3-quart microproof casserole. Cover and place in oven. Set recipe number 144. Touch START. *(Oven cooks: HI, 5 minutes.)*

At Pause, add tomatoes and flour; stir until smooth. Stir in the remaining ingredients except chicken. Cover. Touch START. *(Oven cooks: HI, 5 minutes.)*

At Pause, add chicken, placing thickest parts toward outside of casserole and breast in center. Spoon sauce over chicken. Cover. Touch START. *(Oven cooks: HI, 25 minutes; 30, 10 minutes.)*

Discard bay leaf. Serve with hot spaghetti or rice.

4 to 6 servings

← *Chicken Cacciatore*

Catch of the Day

Poaching and steaming have always been the most classic methods of cooking fish. Now, discover the newest "classic" — fish and shellfish microwave-style! So moist, tender, and delicious that you'll never want to cook seafood any other way. And all this with no elaborate procedures: No need to tie the fish in cheesecloth or use a special fish poacher. Shellfish steam to a succulent tenderness with very little water. If you think your microwave oven cooks chicken and meat fast, you'll be amazed at its speed with fish! For best results, fish should be prepared at the last minute. Even standing time is short. So, when planning a fish dinner, have everything ready. *Then* start to cook.

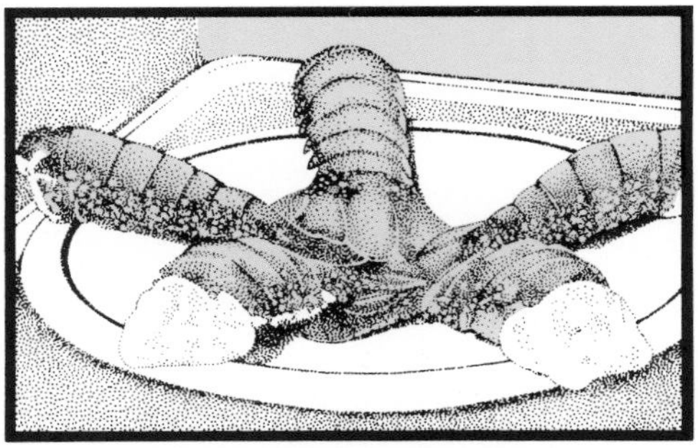

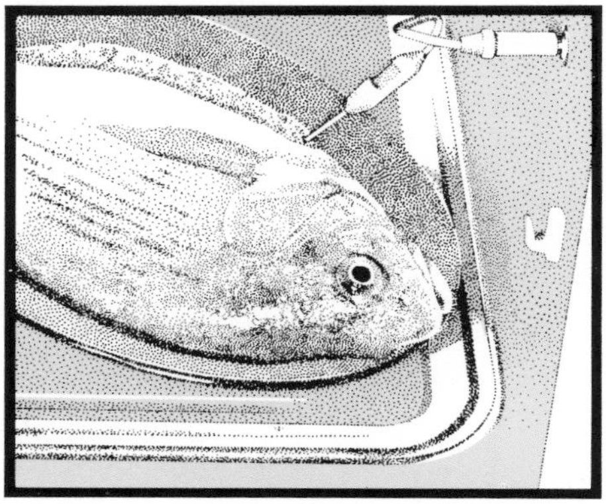

Poached Salmon (page 126) is best prepared in an oval baking dish (top left). Oysters, lobster, and other shellfish should be arranged in a circle with the thichest parts toward the outside of the dish (top right and above left). Stuffed Bass (page 131) with temperature probe inserted (above right).

← *Broccoli (page 151), Salmon Ring (page 129), and Parsley New Potatoes (page 162)*

Converting Your Recipes

If your family likes seafood only when it is fried crackly-crisp, surprise them with a new taste delight when you try traditional fish recipes cooked in the microwave oven. They'll swear fish has been pampered and poached by the most famous French chef. Use the cooking charts and the preset recipes as guides for adapting your own dishes. If you don't find a recipe that matches or comes close to the conventional recipe you want to adapt, follow this general rule of thumb: Begin cooking at 70 or at HI for one-fifth of the time the conventional recipe recommends. Observe, and if it appears to be done earlier, touch "stop" and check. If the dish is not done, continue cooking 30 seconds at a time. As in conventional cooking, the secret to seafood is to watch it carefully, since fish can overcook in seconds. It's best to remove it when barely done and allow standing time to finish the cooking. If you read these simple tips, you'll have excellent results:

- ☐ Most recipes that specify a particular variety of fish will work when any white fish is substituted. When a recipe calls for fresh or thawed frozen fish fillets, use sole, flounder, bluefish, cod, scrod, or any similar fish.
- ☐ Cook fish covered unless it is coated with crumbs, which seal in the juices.
- ☐ When cooking whole fish, the dish should be rotated one-quarter turn twice during the cooking process to help provide even cooking. The odd shape of the fish requires this procedure.
- ☐ Fish is done when the flesh becomes opaque and barely flakes with a fork.
- ☐ Shellfish is done when flesh is opaque and just firm.
- ☐ Shellfish come in their own cooking containers which respond well to microwaves. Clam and mussel shells open before your eyes. Shrimp, crab, and lobster shells turn pink.
- ☐ All seafood recipes freeze well except where otherwise noted.
- ☐ You can use the browning dish for fillets or fish patties. Preheat, add butter or oil and brown on one side for best results.
- ☐ To remove seafood odors from the oven, combine 1 cup water with lemon juice and a few cloves in a small bowl. Cook on HI 3 to 5 minutes.

Using the Defrosting Guide

1. Frozen fish may be thawed in its original wrapper. First discard any aluminum foil, metal rings, or wire twist ties.
2. Remove wrapping when the fish begins to thaw.
3. One pound of fish takes 4 to 6 minutes to nearly thaw on 30.
4. To prevent the outer edges from drying out or beginning to cook, it is best to remove fish from oven before it has completely thawed.
5. Finish defrosting under cold running water, separating fillets.
6. Programmed Defrost may be used. See Use & Care Manual for instructions.

DEFROSTING GUIDE — SEAFOOD

Food	Amount	Cook Control Setting	Time (in minutes)	Standing Time (in minutes)	Special Notes
Fish Fillets	1 lb. 2 lbs.	30 (defrost) 30 (defrost)	4-6 5-7	5 5	Defrost in package on dish. Carefully separate fillets under cold water. Turn once.
Fish steaks	1 lb.	30 (defrost)	4-6	5	Defrost in package on dish. Carefully separate steaks under cold running water.
Whole fish	8-10 oz. 1½-2 lbs.	30 (defrost) 30 (defrost)	4-6 5-7	5 5	Shallow dish; shape of fish determines size. Should be icy when removed. Finish at room temperature. Cover head with aluminum foil. Turn once.
Lobster tails	8 oz. package	30 (defrost)	5-7	5	Remove from package to baking dish.
Crab legs	8-10 oz.	30 (defrost)	5-7	5	Glass baking dish. Break apart and turn once.
Crabmeat	6 oz.	30 (defrost)	4-5	5	Defrost in package on dish. Break apart. Turn once.
Shrimp	1 lb.	30 (defrost)	3-4	5	Remove from package to dish. Spread loosely in baking dish and rearrange during thawing as necessary.
Scallops	1 lb.	30 (defrost)	8-10	5	Defrost in package if in block; spread out on baking dish if in pieces. Turn over and rearrange during thawing as necessary.
Oysters	12 oz.	30 (defrost)	3-4	5	Remove from package to dish. Turn over and rearrange during thawing as necessary.

Using the Cooking Guide

1. Defrost seafood fully; then cook.
2. Remove original wrapping. Rinse under cold running water.
3. Place seafood in microproof baking dish with thick edges of fillets and steaks and thick ends of shellfish toward the outer edge of the dish.
4. Cover dish with plastic wrap or waxed paper.
5. Test often during the cooking period to avoid overcooking.
6. Method and time are the same for seafood in the shell or without the shell.

COOKING/DEFROSTING GUIDE — CONVENIENCE SEAFOOD

Food	Amount	Cook Control Setting	Time (in minutes)	Special Notes
Shrimp croquettes	12 oz. package	80 (reheat)	6-8	Pierce sauce pouch, place on serving plate with croquettes. Cover, turn halfway through cooking time.
Fish sticks, frozen	4 oz. 8 oz.	80 (reheat) 80 (reheat)	2-3 3½-4½	Will not crisp. Cook on serving plate.
Tuna casserole, frozen	11 oz. package	HI (max. power)	4-6	Remove from package to 1-quart casserole. Stir once during cooking and before serving.
Shrimp or crab newburg, frozen pouch	6½ oz.	HI (max. power)	4-6	Place pouch on plate. Pierce pouch. Flex pouch to mix halfway through cooking time. Stir before serving.

COOKING GUIDE — SEAFOOD AND FISH

Food	Cook Control Setting	Time (in Minutes)	or	Temperature Probe Setting	Standing Time (in minutes)	Special Notes
Fish fillets, 1 lb. ½ inch thick,	HI (max. power)	4-5	or	140°	4-5	12 × 7-inch dish, covered.
2 lbs.	HI (max. power)	7-8	or	140°	4-5	
Fish steaks, 1 inch thick, 1 lb.	HI (max. power)	5-6	or	140°	5-6	12 × 7-inch dish, covered.
Whole fish						
8-10 oz.	HI (max. power)	3½-4	or	170°	3-4	Appropriate shallow dish.
1½-2 lbs.	HI (max. power)	5-7	or	170°	5	
Crab legs						
8-10 oz.	HI (max. power)	3-4			5	Appropriate shallow dish, covered. Turn once.
16-20 oz.	HI (max. power)	5-6			5	
Shrimp, scallops						Appropriate shallow dish, covered. Rearrange halfway.
8 oz.	70 (roast)	3-4				
1 lb.	70 (roast)	5-7				
Snails, clams, oysters, 12 oz.	70 (roast)	3-4				Shallow dish, covered. Rearrange halfway.
Lobster tails						
1: 8 oz.	HI (max. power)	3-4			5	Shallow dish. Split shell to reduce curling.
2: 8 oz. each	HI (max. power)	5-6			5	
4: 8 oz. each	HI (max. power)	9-11			5	

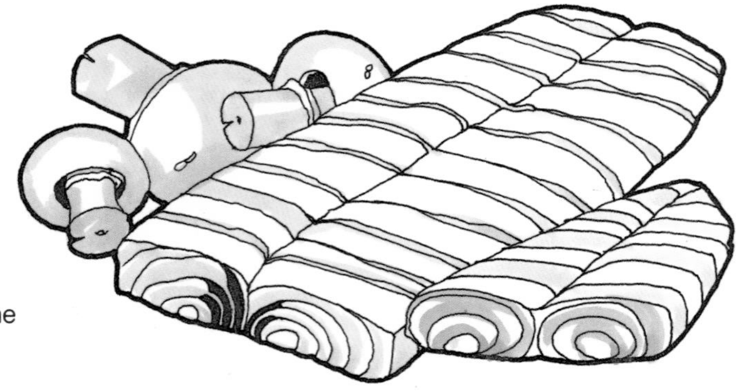

Recipe No. 145 ⊞

Fish Fillets with Mushrooms

Preset Cooking Time: 8 minutes

1 pound fish fillets
2 tablespoons butter or margarine
2 tablespoons dry white wine
½ teaspoon lemon juice
1 medium tomato, peeled and cut into cubes
2 green onions, thinly sliced
½ cup sliced mushrooms
½ teaspoon salt

Arrange fillets in 8-inch round or oval microproof baking dish with thickest parts toward outside of dish. Dot with butter. Combine wine and lemon juice; pour over fillets. Sprinkle with remaining ingredients. Place in oven. Cover with waxed paper. Set recipe number 145. Touch START. *(Oven cooks: HI,* 5 *minutes; stands:* 0, 3 *minutes.)*

2 servings

Recipe No. 146

Fish Fillets

Preset Cooking Time: 8 minutes

1 pound fish fillets, ½ inch thick

Arrange fillets in round or oval microproof baking dish with thickest parts toward outside of dish. Place in oven. Cover with waxed paper. Set recipe number 146. Touch START. *(Oven cooks: HI,* 5 *minutes; stands:* 0, 3 *minutes.)*

2 servings

Recipe No. 147 ⊞

Fish Steaks

Preset Cooking Time: 9 minutes

2 halibut steaks (1/2 pound each), 1 inch thick
2 tablespoons butter, melted
2 teaspoons lemon juice
1/2 teaspoon dillweed (optional)

Arrange fish in round or oval microproof baking dish with thickest parts toward outside of dish. Combine butter and lemon juice; brush over salmon. Sprinkle with dillweed. Place in oven. Cover with waxed paper. Set recipe number 147. Touch START. *(Oven cooks: HI, 6 minutes; stands: 0, 3 minutes.)*

2 servings

Recipe No. 148 ⊞

Grilled Swordfish Steaks

Preset Cooking Time: 5 minutes

2 swordfish or salmon steaks (1/2 pound each)
1 tablespoon vegetable oil
Lemon pepper
Paprika

Brush fish on 1 side with oil. Sprinkle with lemon pepper and paprika; set aside. Preheat 9-inch microwave browning dish according to manufacturer's directions. Arrange fish on preheated dish, seasoned-side down, with thickest parts toward outside of dish. Place in oven. Cover loosely with waxed paper. Set recipe number 148. Touch START. *(Oven cooks: HI, 2 minutes.)*

At Pause, turn over. Cover. Touch START. *(Oven cooks: HI, 1 minute; stands: 0, 2 minutes.)*

2 servings

Recipe No. 149

Tuna-Mushroom Patties

Preset Cooking Time: 9 1/2 minutes

2 tablespoons milk
1 can (10 3/4 ounces) cream of celery soup, undiluted, divided
2 cans (6 1/2 ounces each) tuna, drained
1/2 cup dry bread crumbs
1/2 cup chopped mushrooms
1 large egg, beaten
2 tablespoons instant minced onion
1/4 teaspoon white pepper
2 tablespoons minced parsley

Combine milk and half of the soup in 2-cup glass measure; blend well; set aside. Combine remaining soup, tuna, bread crumbs, mushrooms, egg, onion, and pepper. Shape into 6 patties, using about 1/2 cup mixture for each. Place in shallow microproof baking dish. Place in oven. Cover with waxed paper. Set recipe number 149. Touch START. *(Oven cooks: HI, 8 minutes.)*

At Pause, remove from oven. Place milk mixture in oven. Touch START. *(Oven cooks: HI, 1 1/2 minutes.)*

Stir and pour over tuna patties. Sprinkle with parsley before serving.

6 servings

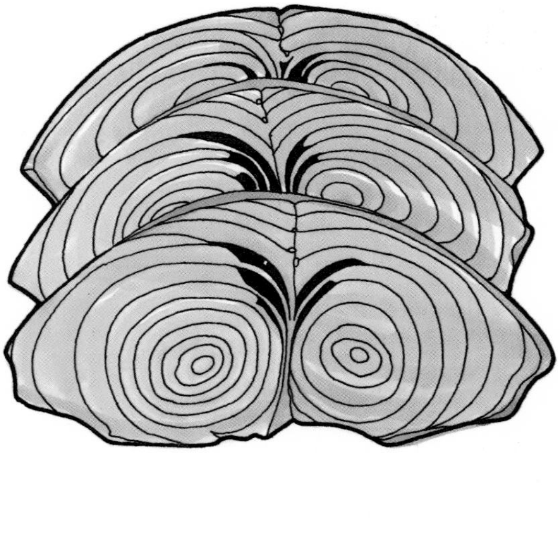

⊞ *Recipe can be increased. See "Quantity", page 12.*

Recipe No. 150

Poached Salmon

Preset Cooking Time: 12 minutes

- 2 cups water
- 1 medium stalk celery, cut into chunks
- ½ medium lemon, sliced
- ½ medium onion, sliced
- 3 tablespoons vinegar
- 2 tablespoons lemon juice
- 1½ teaspoons salt
- 6 whole cloves
- 1 bay leaf
- 4 salmon, swordfish, halibut, or other fish steaks (6 to 8 ounces each)
- Parsley sprigs

Combine all ingredients except fish and parsley in 2-quart microproof casserole. Cover and place in oven. Set recipe number 150. Touch START. *(Oven cooks: HI, 7 minutes.)*

At Pause, add fish; spoon liquid over top. Cover. Touch START. *(Oven cooks: HI, 5 minutes.)*

Carefully turn fish over. Let stand, covered, 5 minutes. Transfer to serving platter. Garnish with parsley. Serve hot or chilled.

4 servings

Recipe No. 151

Scallops Vermouth

Preset Cooking Time: 10 minutes

- ¼ cup butter or margarine
- 1 tablespoon minced onion
- 2 tablespoons all-purpose flour
- 1 pound bay scallops
- ½ cup sliced mushrooms
- ¼ cup dry vermouth
- 2 teaspoons lemon juice
- ½ teaspoon salt
- ⅛ teaspoon pepper
- 1 bay leaf
- ½ cup light cream
- 1 egg yolk
- ½ teaspoon hot pepper sauce (optional)
- 1 tablespoon chopped parsley

Combine butter and onion in 2-quart microproof casserole. Place in oven. Set recipe number 151. Touch START. *(Oven cooks: HI, 2 minutes.)*

At Pause, add flour; blend well. Add scallops, mushrooms, vermouth, lemon juice, salt, pepper, and bay leaf; stir carefully. Cover. Touch START. *(Oven cooks:* 80, 4 *minutes.)*

At Pause, discard bay leaf. Combine cream and egg yolk; blend well. Stir small amount hot liquid into cream mixture; gradually stir mixture into casserole. Add hot pepper sauce; blend well. Cover. Touch START. *(Oven cooks:* 60, 3 *minutes.)*

At Pause, stir. Cover. Touch START. *(Oven cooks:* 60, 1 *minute.)*

Sprinkle with parsley before serving.

4 servings

Recipe No. 152 ⊞

Scampi

Preset Cooking Time: 4 minutes

- 3 tablespoons vegetable oil
- 2 large cloves garlic, minced
- 3 tablespoons minced parsley
- 2 tablespoons dry white wine
- ⅛ teaspoon paprika
- ¾ pound large shrimp, shelled, deveined, and butterflied, tails intact
- Juice of ½ medium lemon
- Salt and pepper, to taste
- Chopped parsley

Combine oil and garlic in oval microproof baking dish just large enough to hold all ingredients. Place in oven. Set recipe number 152. Touch START. *(Oven cooks: HI, 1 minute.)*

At Pause, add parsley, wine, and paprika. Touch START. *(Oven cooks: HI, 1 minute.)*

At Pause, add shrimp, lemon juice, salt, and pepper; stir to coat well. Arrange shrimp with tails toward center of dish. Cover with waxed paper. Touch START. *(Oven cooks: HI, 1 minute.)*

At Pause, stir. Cover. Touch START. *(Oven cooks: HI, 1 minute.)*

Garnish with parsley, and serve immediately.

2 servings

⊞ *Recipe can be increased. See "Quantity", page 12.*

Fillet of Fish Amandine (page 132) →

Recipe No. 153

Shrimp Chow Mein

Preset Cooking Time: 21 minutes

- 1 medium onion, chopped
- 1 cup sliced celery
- 1 green pepper, seeded and cut into thin strips
- 2 tablespoons butter or margarine
- 1 pound fresh bean sprouts, or 1 can (16 ounces) bean sprouts, drained
- 1 can (8 ounces) sliced water chestnuts, drained
- 8 to 10 ounces cooked deveined shelled shrimp
- ½ cup sliced mushrooms
- 2 tablespoons chopped pimiento
- 3 tablespoons cornstarch
- 3 tablespoons soy sauce
- 1 cup water
- 2 teaspoons chicken bouillon granules

Combine onion, celery, green pepper, and butter in 2-quart microproof casserole. Cover and place in oven. Set recipe number 153. Touch START. *(Oven cooks: HI, 10 minutes.)*

At Pause, remove from oven. Add bean sprouts, water chestnuts, shrimp, mushrooms, and pimiento; set aside. Dissolve cornstarch in soy sauce in 4-cup glass measure. Add water and bouillon; blend well. Place soy sauce mixture in oven. Touch START. *(Oven cooks: HI, 3 minutes.)*

At Pause, stir. Touch START. *(Oven cooks: HI, 3 minutes.)*

At Pause, remove from oven. Stir sauce into shrimp mixture. Cover and place in oven. Touch START. *(Oven cooks: HI, 5 minutes.)*

Stir through before serving over hot rice, topped with chow mein noodles.

5 to 6 servings

Recipe No. 154

Shrimp Veracruz

Preset Cooking Time: 12 minutes

- 1 large onion, cut into chunks
- 1 large green pepper, seeded and cut into chunks
- 2 cloves garlic, crushed
- 2 tablespoons vegetable oil
- 1 can (8 ounces) tomato sauce
- ¼ cup dry white wine
- ½ teaspoon oregano
- ½ teaspoon salt
- ¼ teaspoon cumin
- Dash hot pepper sauce
- 1 pound jumbo shrimp, shelled and deveined
- 2 tablespoons chopped parsley

Combine onion, green pepper, garlic, and oil in shallow oval microproof baking dish. Place in oven. Set recipe number 154. Touch START. *(Oven cooks: HI, 3 minutes.)*

At Pause, stir through several times. Add tomato sauce, wine, oregano, salt, cumin, and hot pepper sauce. Touch START. *(Oven cooks: HI, 5 minutes.)*

At Pause, add shrimp. Spoon sauce over shrimp. Touch START. *(Oven cooks: HI, 2 minutes.)*

At Pause, stir. Cover. Touch START. *(Oven cooks: HI, 2 minutes.)*

Garnish with parsley, and serve over hot rice or noodles.

4 servings

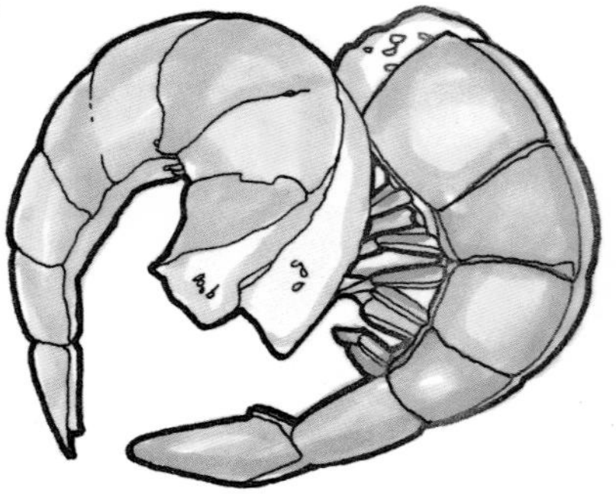

Recipe No. 155

Salmon Ring

Preset Cooking Time: 12 minutes

Paprika
1 can (16 ounces) red salmon, skin and bones discarded
1 cup soft bread crumbs
¾ cup finely chopped celery
2 large eggs, lightly beaten
3 tablespoons minced green onion
2 tablespoons mayonnaise
Pinch dillweed
Minced parsley

Butter 6-cup microproof ring mold; sprinkle with paprika; set aside. Combine all ingredients except parsley; blend well. Turn into prepared mold, spreading evenly. Place in oven. Set recipe number 155. Touch START. *(Oven cooks: HI, 7 minutes;* 20, 5 *minutes.)* Unmold onto serving platter, and garnish with parsley.

4 to 6 servings

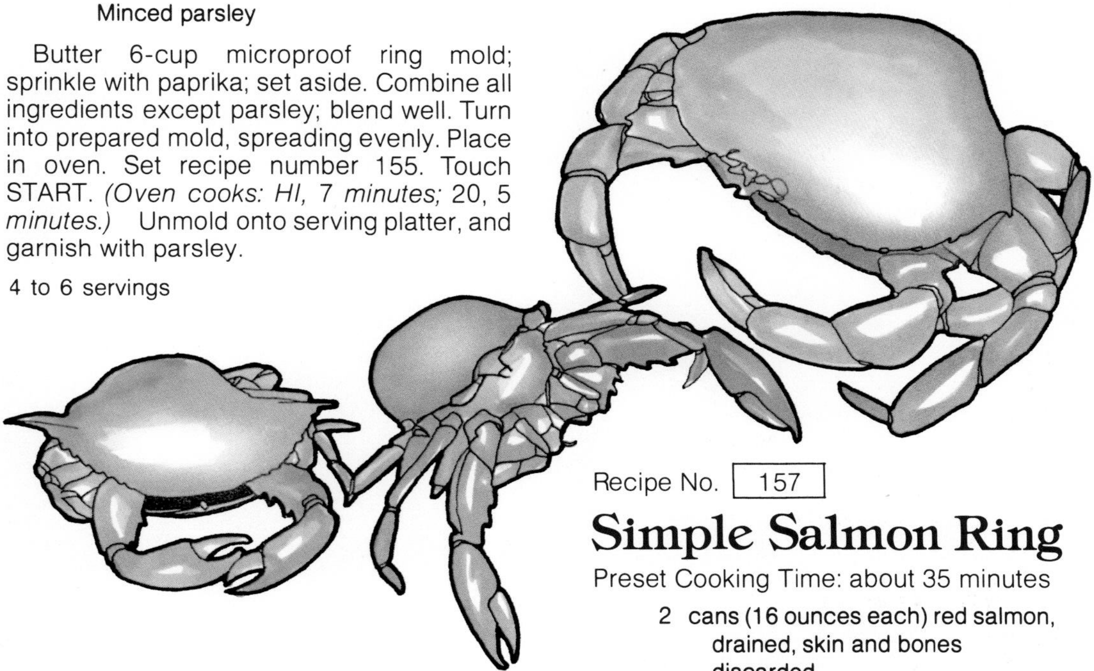

Recipe No. 156

Crab Imperial

Preset Cooking Time: 12 minutes

½ cup chopped onion
2 tablespoons butter or margarine
1½ cups light cream
1 cup sliced mushrooms
3 tablespoons all-purpose flour
3 tablespoons dry white wine
¼ teaspoon salt
⅛ teaspoon pepper
2 egg yolks, lightly beaten
1½ cups crab-meat chunks

Place onion and butter in 2-quart glass measure. Place in oven. Set recipe number 156. Touch START. *(Oven cooks: HI,* 3 *minutes.)*

At Pause, add cream, mushrooms, flour, wine, salt, and pepper; blend well. Touch START. *(Oven cooks: HI,* 5 *minutes.)*

At Pause, blend in egg yolks. Touch START. *(Oven cooks: HI,* 2 *minutes.)*

At Pause, add crab meat; blend well. Touch START. *(Oven cooks:* 70, 2 *minutes.)*

Serve in au gratin dishes, individual custard cups, ramekins, or shells.

4 to 6 servings

Recipe No. 157

Simple Salmon Ring

Preset Cooking Time: about 35 minutes

2 cans (16 ounces each) red salmon, drained, skin and bones discarded
3 slices soft bread, cut into cubes
½ cup milk
¼ cup butter, melted
1 large egg, lightly beaten
½ teaspoon salt

Grease 10-cup microproof ring mold; set aside. Combine all ingredients; blend well. Pack firmly into prepared mold. Place in oven. Insert temperature probe into center of salmon mixture. Cover with waxed paper. Set recipe number 157. Touch START. *(Oven cooks:* 70, *about* 30 *minutes to* 140°*F;* 10, 5 *minutes.)*

Unmold onto serving platter. Serve with Lemon Butter Sauce (page 176) or Hot Lemony Dill Sauce (page 175) in center of ring, if desired.

6 to 8 servings

Recipe No. 158

Stuffed Bass

Preset Cooking Time: about 19½ minutes

- 1 bass (2 pounds), cleaned
- ¼ cup chopped onion
- 2 tablespoons butter or margarine
- ¾ cup dry bread crumbs
- ½ cup chopped mushrooms
- 2 tablespoons minced parsley
- 1 large egg, beaten
- 1 tablespoon lemon juice
- 1 teaspoon salt
- ⅛ teaspoon pepper
- 1 tablespoon bottled brown sauce
- 1 tablespoon water

Rinse bass well in cold water and pat dry; set aside. Place onion and butter in 1½-quart microproof bowl. Place in oven. Set recipe number 158. Touch START. *(Oven cooks: HI, 2 minutes.)*

At Pause, remove from oven. Add remaining ingredients except brown sauce and water; blend well. Spoon stuffing into cavity of bass. Place on oval microproof platter or in 12 × 7-inch microproof baking dish. Combine brown sauce and water; brush over bass.

Place in oven. Insert temperature probe into meatiest part of fish, parallel to spine and close to probe receptacle. Cover dish tightly with plastic wrap, but wrap loosely around probe to vent. Touch START. *(Oven cooks: HI, about 12½ minutes to 170°F; stands: 0, 5 minutes.)*

4 servings

Other whole fish of the same size can be substituted for bass, such as red snapper, lake trout, salmon, or whitefish. Whole stuffed fish can be cooked without the temperature probe; cook on HI, allowing 5 to 7 minutes per pound.

Recipe No. 159 ⊞

Stuffed Mountain Trout

Preset Cooking Time: 5½ minutes

- 2 trout (½ pound each), or one 1-pound trout
- ¼ cup butter or margarine, melted
- ¼ cup instant minced onion
- 4 teaspoons slivered almonds
- 4 teaspoons minced parsley
- 4 to 5 medium mushrooms, sliced (optional)

Rinse trout in cool water and pat dry. Place in shallow microproof baking dish. Brush cavities with some of the butter. Stuff with some of the onion, almonds, parsley, and mushrooms. Pour remaining butter over trout. Sprinkle with remaining onion, almonds, and parsley; arrange remaining mushrooms around trout. Place in oven. Cover with paper towel or waxed paper. Set recipe number 159. Touch START. *(Oven cooks: HI, 5½ minutes.)*

2 servings

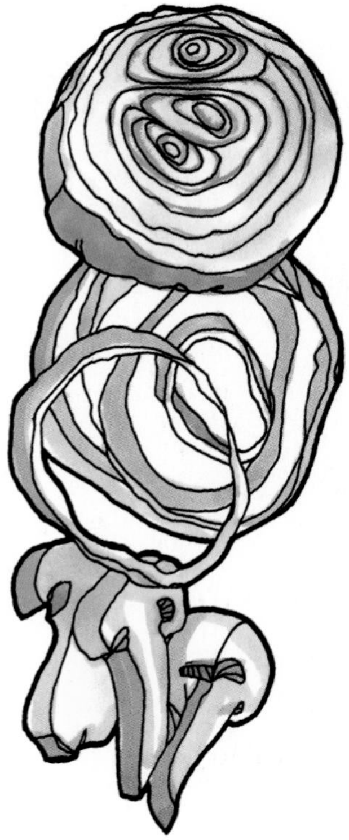

← *Stuffed Mountain Trout*

⊞ *Recipe can be increased. See "Quantity", page 12.*

Recipe No. 160 ⊞

Fillet of Fish Amandine

Preset Cooking Time: 11 minutes

- ½ cup slivered almonds
- ½ cup butter or margarine
- 1 pound fish fillets
- 1 tablespoon lemon juice
- 1 teaspoon chopped parsley
- ½ teaspoon salt
- ¼ teaspoon dillweed
- ⅛ teaspoon pepper

Place almonds and butter in 8-inch microproof baking dish. Place in oven. Set recipe number 160. Touch START. *(Oven cooks: HI, 3 minutes.)*

At Pause, stir. Touch START. *(Oven cooks: HI, 3 minutes.)*

At Pause, remove from oven. Remove almonds from dish with slotted spoon; set aside. Add fillets; turn to coat both sides with butter. Sprinkle with lemon juice, parsley, salt, dillweed, and pepper. Roll up fillets in dish. Place in oven. Cover with waxed paper. Touch START. *(Oven cooks: HI, 4 minutes.)*

At Pause, sprinkle with almonds. Cover. Touch START. *(Oven cooks: HI, 1 minute.)*

Let stand 4 minutes. Serve garnished with lemon wedges, parsley sprigs, or paprika.

2 to 3 servings

⊞ *Recipe can be increased. See "Quantity", page 12.*

Recipe No. 161

Shrimp Creole

Preset Cooking Time: 15 minutes

- 4 green onions, thinly sliced
- ½ cup chopped green pepper
- ¼ cup chopped celery
- 1 clove garlic, minced
- 2 tablespoons butter or margarine
- 1 can (16 ounces) whole tomatoes, drained and chopped
- 1 can (6 ounces) tomato paste
- 2 teaspoons parsley flakes
- 1 teaspoon salt
- ¼ teaspoon cayenne
- 1 package (10 ounces) frozen cooked shrimp, thawed

Combine green onions, green pepper, celery, garlic, and butter in 2-quart microproof casserole. Cover and place in oven. Set recipe number 161. Touch START. *(Oven cooks: HI, 3 minutes.)*

At Pause, add remaining ingredients except shrimp; blend well. Cover. Touch START. *(Oven cooks:* 80, 5 *minutes.)*

At Pause, add shrimp; blend well. Cover. Touch START. *(Oven cooks:* 80, 3 *minutes.)*

At Pause, stir. Cover. Touch START. *(Oven cooks:* 80, 4 *minutes.)*

Stir before serving over hot rice.

4 to 6 servings

A Visit to the Dairy Case

Eggs and cheese are great microwave partners; but they can stand by themselves, too. There's nothing quite like plain scrambled eggs or cheese fondue made in the microwave oven. From the simplest omelets to fancy quiches, the microwave oven can enliven an ordinary breakfast, Sunday brunch, or any meal. The recipes in this chapter are perfect for unexpected guests any time of day. Just remember to have on hand a carton of fresh eggs and some Cheddar or Swiss cheeses that keep well. Then, a little onion and seasonings are all you need to make a quick, easy, and delicious meal. As a special treat, we have included in this chapter a special recipe for Quiche Lorraine (page 138). One reminder: Do not hardboil eggs in the microwave oven. Pressure builds up inside the shell, which causes the egg to burst. Egg yolks should always be carefully pierced before cooking to prevent them from popping. Keep in mind that eggs and cheese are delicate ingredients; handle them with care and you will have delectable results.

Omelet Classique (page 140) is cooked and served in the same dish (above left). Just a flip makes your Sunny-Side-Up Eggs (page 138) become "Over Easy" if that's your preference (above). Refrigerated cheese can be quickly brought to room temperature at 60 for 1 minute (left).

Converting Your Recipes

The best advice for adapting recipes that use eggs and cheese as primary ingredients is "better to undercook than overcook." Cheese and eggs cook so quickly that a few seconds can make the difference between airy excellence and a rubbery disaster. You will be able to make countless variations on the recipes here, substituting vegetables and cooked meat, and adding your own spices and sauces. Conventional soufflé recipes do not adapt to microwave cooking. Microwave soufflé recipes require a special form of stabilization because they cook so quickly; therefore, evaporated milk is used for the cream sauce base. The tips below will guide you to microwave success with all your egg and cheese recipes:

- ☐ Undercook eggs slightly and allow standing time to complete cooking. Eggs become tough when overcooked. Always check doneness to avoid overcooking.
- ☐ Cover poaching or baking eggs to trap steam and ensure even cooking.
- ☐ Eggs are usually cooked at 60 or 70.
- ☐ If you want a soft yolk, remove the egg from oven before whites are completely cooked. A brief standing time allows whites to set without overcooking yolks.
- ☐ Add 1/8 to 1/4 teaspoon vinegar to the water when poaching eggs to help the white coagulate.
- ☐ Cook bacon and egg combinations on HI, since most of the microwaves are attracted to the bacon because of its high fat content.
- ☐ Omelets and scrambled eggs should be stirred at least once during cooking. Fondues and sauces profit from occasional stirring during the cooking time.
- ☐ Cheese melts quickly and makes an attractive topping for casseroles and sandwiches.
- ☐ Cook cheese on 70 or a lower setting for short periods of time to avoid separation and toughening.

COOKING GUIDE — CONVENIENCE EGGS AND CHEESE

Food	Amount	Cook Control Setting	Time (in minutes)	Special Notes
Omelet, frozen	10 oz.	80 (reheat)	4 - 5	Use microproof plate.
Egg substitute	8 oz.	50 (simmer)	4 - 4½	Turn carton over after 1 minute. Open carton after 1½ minutes. Stir every 30 seconds until smooth.
Soufflés: Corn, frozen	12 oz.	HI (max. power)	10 - 12	Use 1½-quart casserole, covered. Rotate casserole twice.
Cheese, frozen	12 oz.	HI (max. power)	11 - 13	Use 1½-quart casserole, covered. Rotate casserole twice.
Spinach, frozen	12 oz.	HI (max. power)	12 - 15	Use 1½-quart casserole, covered. Rotate casserole twice.
Welsh rabbit, frozen	10 oz.	70 (roast)	6 - 7	Use 1½-quart casserole, covered. Stir during cooking time.

Recipe No. 162 ⊞

Cheddar and Onion Egg

Preset Cooking Time: 3 minutes

- 1 teaspoon butter or margarine
- 1 green onion, thinly sliced
- 1 large egg
- 1 heaping tablespoon shredded Cheddar cheese

Combine butter and green onion in microproof custard cup. Place in oven. Set recipe number 162. Touch START. *(Oven cooks: HI, 1 minute.)*

At Pause, carefully break egg into custard cup. Carefully pierce yolk in several places with toothpick. Sprinkle with cheese. Cover with waxed paper. Touch START. *(Oven cooks:* 60, 1 *minute: stands:* 0, 1 *minute.)*

1 serving

Recipe No. 163

Festival Eggs

Preset Cooking Time: 5 minutes

- 6 large eggs
- ½ cup dairy sour cream
- ¼ cup grated Parmesan cheese
- 2 tablespoons chopped green pepper
- 2 tablespoons chopped pimiento
- ½ teaspoon salt
- ¼ teaspoon thyme
- ¼ teaspoon dry mustard
- 2 tablespoons butter or margarine

Beat eggs until frothy in 2-quart microproof casserole. Carefully stir in remaining ingredients. Place in oven. Cover with waxed paper. Set recipe number 163. Touch START. *(Oven cooks: HI, 2 minutes.)*

At Pause, stir. Cover. Touch START. *(Oven cooks: HI, 2 minutes.)*

At Pause, stir. Touch START. *(Oven cooks:* 60, 1 *minute.)*

4 servings

⊞ *Recipe can be increased. See "Quantity", page 12.*

Recipe No. 164

Eggs in Nests

Preset Cooking Time: 7 minutes

- 2 very firm tomatoes (8 ounces each)
- 1 tablespoon parsley flakes
- 1 tablespoon onion flakes
- ⅛ teaspoon salt
- Dash pepper
- 2 large eggs

Slice tops off tomatoes; carefully remove center pulp and seeds leaving a thick shell; discard seeds. Place shells, upside down, on paper towels to drain. Chop pulp. Combine pulp, parsley, onion flakes, salt, and pepper. Fill shells half full with tomato mixture. Place in shallow microproof dish. Break 1 egg into each shell; carefully pierce yolks with toothpick. Place in oven. Cover with waxed paper. Set recipe number 164. Touch START. *(Oven cooks: HI, 2 minutes.)*

At Pause, rotate dish one half turn. Touch START. *(Oven cooks:* 60, 3 *minutes; stands:* 0, 2 *minutes.)*

Serve immediately.

2 servings

An easy way to remove pulp and seeds from tomatoes is to squeeze gently while holding tomato upside down.

Recipe No. 165

Poached Egg

Preset Cooking Time: 3½ minutes

¼ cup water
¼ teaspoon vinegar
Pinch salt
1 large egg

Place water, vinegar, and salt in 6-ounce microproof custard cup. Place in oven. Set recipe number 165. Touch START. *(Oven cooks: HI, 1½ minutes.)*

At Pause, carefully break egg into hot liquid. Carefully pierce yolk in several places with toothpick. Cover with waxed paper. Touch START. *(Oven cooks:* 50, 1 *minute; stands:* 0, 1 *minute.)*

1 serving

Recipe No. 166

Puffy Cheddar Omelet

Preset Cooking Time: 7¾ minutes

4 large eggs, separated
⅓ cup mayonnaise
2 tablespoons water
1 tablespoon butter or margarine
½ cup (2 ounces) grated Cheddar cheese
1 tablespoon minced parsley

Beat egg whites with electric mixer until soft peaks form. Beat yolks, mayonnaise, and water; gently fold whites into yolk mixture; set aside. Place butter in 9-inch microproof pie plate. Place in oven. Set recipe number 166. Touch START. *(Oven cooks: HI, 45 seconds.)*

At Pause, tilt plate to coat evenly with butter. Pour in egg mixture. Touch START. *(Oven cooks:* 60, 6 *minutes.)* If eggs are rising unevenly, touch STOP, and rotate dish one-quarter turn. Touch START.

At Pause, sprinkle with cheese. Touch START. *(Oven cooks:* 60, 1 *minute.)*

Fold omelet in half and then cut in half. Slide onto serving plates. Sprinkle with parsley before serving.

2 servings

Recipe No. 167 ⊞

Scrambled Egg

Preset Cooking Time: 2 minutes

1 large egg
2 tablespoons low-fat milk
6 tablespoons (1½ ounces) shredded Monterey Jack or Cheddar cheese
Salt and pepper, to taste

Break egg into small microproof bowl. Add milk; mix well with fork. Add cheese, salt, and pepper; blend well. Place in oven. Cover with waxed paper. Set recipe number 167. Touch START. *(Oven cooks:* 60, 1 *minute.)*

At Pause, stir. Cover. Touch START. *(Oven cooks:* 60, 1 *minute.)*

Stir before serving.

1 serving

Recipe No. 168 ⊞

Shirred Eggs

Preset Cooking Time: 3½ minutes

1 teaspoon butter or margarine
2 large eggs
1 tablespoon light cream
Salt and pepper, to taste

Place butter in microproof ramekin or small bowl. Place in oven. Set recipe number 168. Touch START. *(Oven cooks:* 70, 30 *seconds.)*

At Pause, carefully break eggs into ramekin. Carefully pierce yolks in several places with toothpicks. Add cream. Cover tightly with plastic wrap. Touch START. *(Oven cooks:* 60, 2 *minutes; stands:* 0, 1 *minute.)*

Season with salt and pepper before serving.

1 serving

⊞ *Recipe can be increased. See "Quantity", page 12.*

Caramel Nut Sticky Buns (page 68), Shirred Eggs, Bacon (Guide, page 81) →

Recipe No. 169

Sunny-Side-Up Eggs

Preset Cooking Time: 1 minute 40 seconds

- 1 tablespoon butter or margarine
- 2 large eggs
- Salt and pepper, to taste

Preheat microwave browning dish according to manufacturer's directions. Place butter in browning dish; let stand until melted. Tilt dish carefully to coat evenly with butter. Carefully break eggs into dish. Carefully pierce yolks in several places with toothpick. Season with salt and pepper. Cover and place in oven. Set recipe number 169. Touch START. *(Oven cooks: HI, 40 seconds; stands:* 0, 1 *minute.)*

1 to 2 servings

Recipe No. 170

Quiche Lorraine

Preset Cooking Time: 28½ minutes

- 6 slices bacon
- 3 green onions, thinly sliced
- 2 cups (8 ounces) shredded Swiss cheese
- 1 baked 9-inch Homemade Pie Shell (page 192)
- 1 can (13 ounces) evaporated milk, undiluted
- 4 large eggs, beaten
- 1 teaspoon prepared mustard
- ¼ teaspoon salt
- ¼ teaspoon nutmeg
- Dash cayenne

Arrange bacon on paper towel-lined microproof plate. Place in oven. Cover with paper towel. Set recipe number 170. Touch START. *(Oven cooks: HI, 7 minutes.)*

At Pause, remove from oven; crumble bacon. Reserve 1 tablespoon each bacon and green onion for topping. Sprinkle remaining bacon, green onions, and cheese in pie shell; set aside. Pour milk into 2-cup glass measure. Place in oven. Touch START. *(Oven cooks: HI, 2½ minutes.)*

At Pause, remove from oven. Combine eggs, mustard, salt, nutmeg, and cayenne. Gradually stir milk into egg mixture. Pour carefully into pie shell. Sprinkle with reserved bacon and green onion. Place in oven. Touch START. *(Oven cooks:* 70, 14 *minutes;* 10, 5 *minutes.)*

6 servings

If you are in a hurry and use a ready-made pie shell, be sure to place it in a microproof pie plate before filling.

Quiche Lorraine →

Recipe No. 171

Fiesta Scramble

Preset Cooking Time: 11 minutes

- 6 large eggs
- 6 tablespoons milk
- 1/8 teaspoon garlic powder
- 1/4 teaspoon salt
- Dash pepper
- 2 tablespoons butter or margarine, cut up
- 2 small tomatoes, peeled and chopped
- 1 can (4 ounces) diced green chilies, drained
- 1 tablespoon minced chives
- 1 cup (4 ounces) grated sharp Cheddar cheese
- 2 tablespoons minced parsley

Beat eggs, milk, garlic powder, salt, and pepper; set aside. Arrange butter, tomatoes, chilies, and chives evenly over bottom of 10-inch microproof pie plate. Place in oven. Set recipe number 171. Touch START. *(Oven cooks: HI, 3 minutes.)*

At Pause, stir. Add egg mixture to tomato mixture. Touch START. *(Oven cooks:* 70, 3 *minutes.)*

At Pause, stir outside of egg mixture toward center. Touch START. *(Oven cooks:* 70, 4 *minutes.)*

At Pause, stir outside of egg mixture toward center. Sprinkle with cheese. Touch START. *(Oven cooks: HI,* 1 *minute.)*

Sprinkle with parsley before serving.

4 servings

Recipe No. 172 ⊞

Omelet Classique

Preset Cooking Time: 8 minutes

- 1 tablespoon butter or margarine
- 4 large eggs
- 4 tablespoons water
- 1/2 teaspoon salt
- 1/8 teaspoon pepper

Place butter in 9-inch microproof pie plate. Place in oven. Set recipe number 172. Touch START. *(Oven cooks: HI,* 30 *seconds.)*

At Pause, combine remaining ingredients; beat with fork. Pour over butter in pie plate. Cover with waxed paper. Touch START. *(Oven cooks:* 60, 3½ *minutes.)*

At Pause, stir lightly. Cover. Touch START. *(Oven cooks:* 60, 2 *minutes; stands:* 0, 2 *minutes.)*

Fold omelet in half and then cut in half. Slide onto serving plates.

2 servings

Before folding omelet, you can top with crumbled cooked bacon, grated Cheddar cheese, chopped cooked ham, or chopped tomato, if desired.

⊞ *Recipe can be increased. See "Quantity", page 12.*

The Grain Belt

The microwave oven provides no significant saving of time when cooking pasta and rice. It takes just as long to rehydrate these products in the microwave oven as it does conventionally. But the convenience of being able to cook and serve in the same dish, and to eliminate scorching and food stuck to pans makes it well worthwhile. Once the pasta is prepared and added to the rest of the ingredients according to the recipe, the casserole cooks in speedy microwave time. Another great advantage the microwave oven offers is that you can reheat pasta, rice, and cereal without adding water or having to stir. No worry about soggy noodles or starchy rice. And they taste as good reheated as when they were freshly cooked!

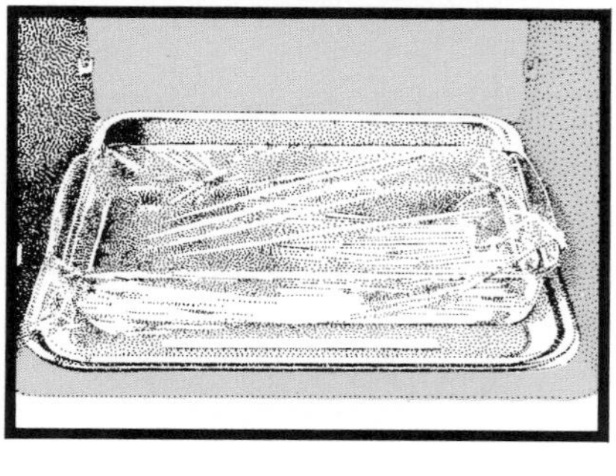

The microwave works wonders with pasta: simply top precooked macaroni or rotini with sauce, tomato slices, and cheese for a dandy lunch (top left). Cook rice in boilable bags on a plate with the bag slit so steam can escape (top right). Spaghetti is cooked in a glass baking dish (above left). Hot cereal is now easy to prepare and serve right in the same dish (above right).

Converting Your Recipes

You will find that your conventional rice or noodle-based casseroles can be easily adjusted to microwave cooking. When you find a similar recipe here, adapt your ingredients to the microwave method, but follow only about three-quarters of the recommended microwave cooking times in the similar preset recipe. Then check, and extend the cooking time at 1-minute intervals until done. Make a note of the final cooking time for a repeat of the dish. By "trial" and trying to avoid "error," you'll soon be able to add to our collection of pasta and rice dishes. Some tips:

- ☐ Casseroles may require occasional stirring to distribute heat.
- ☐ Cooked pasta or rice to be used in a casserole should be slightly firmer than if it is to be eaten at once. Simply cook a bit less.
- ☐ Quick-cooking rice may be substituted in converting from conventional recipes that call for uncooked rice, in order to make sure the rice will cook in the same short time as the rest of the ingredients. Otherwise precook regular rice to a firm stage and add to the casserole.
- ☐ To reheat pasta, rice, and cereals in the microwave without drying out, cover tightly with plastic wrap. Set at 80 for just a few minutes, depending upon amount.
- ☐ Pasta and rice are best when added to other ingredients, as in casseroles. However, the oven can cook them separately. Place spaghetti in 13×9-inch baking dish. Add 2½ cups hot water for 2 ounces of uncooked spaghetti; 4 cups for 4 ounces. Bring water to a boil on HI (6 minutes for 2 ounces; 10 minutes for 4 ounces of spaghetti). Then finish on 50 (6 minutes for 2 ounces; 8 minutes for 4 ounces).
- ☐ For rice, add 2 cups water to 1 cup of uncooked rice. Cook on HI 4 to 5 minutes, or until water comes to a boil. Finish cooking on 50, 13 to 15 minutes. Allow 5 minutes standing time.
- ☐ Cook grits or other hot cereals on HI 6 to 7 minutes for ⅓ cup grits (uncooked). Follow package directions for liquid.

COOKING/DEFROSTING GUIDE — CONVENIENCE RICE AND PASTA

Food	Amount	Cook Control Setting	Time (in minutes)	Special Notes
Rice, cooked refrigerated	1 cup	80 (reheat)	1½-2	Use covered bowl. Let stand 2 minutes, stir.
Cooked, frozen	1 cup 2 cups	80 (reheat) 80 (reheat)	2-3 3-4	
Pouch, frozen	11 oz.	80 (reheat)	6-7	Slit pouch.
Fried rice, frozen	10 oz.	HI (max. power)	5-6	Use covered casserole. Stir twice. Let stand 5 minutes.
Spanish rice, canned	12 oz.	HI (max. power)	4-5	Use covered casserole. Stir twice. Let stand 3 minutes.
Lasagna, frozen	21 oz.	70 (roast)	19-20	Use covered casserole. Let stand, covered, 5 minutes.
Macaroni and beef, frozen	11 oz. package	HI (max. power)	7-9	Use covered casserole. Stir twice.
Macaroni and cheese, frozen	10 oz.	HI (max. power)	7-9	Use covered casserole. Stir twice.
Spaghetti and meatballs, frozen	14 oz.	HI (max. power)	8-10	Use covered casserole. Stir twice.

Su 8/93

1 Cup Rice

$1\frac{3}{4}$ water

30 min @ 80

then let sit 15

min

Recipe No. 173

Artichoke Pilaf

Preset Cooking Time: 7 minutes

- 2 jars (6 ounces each) marinated artichoke hearts, drained, 3 tablespoons liquid reserved
- 1 cup chopped onions
- ½ cup thinly sliced celery
- 1 clove garlic, minced
- 1 cup chicken broth
- 1 cup quick cooking rice
- ⅓ cup minced parsley
- ½ teaspoon salt
- ⅛ teaspoon pepper

Combine reserved artichoke liquid, onions, celery, and garlic in 2-quart microproof casserole. Place in oven. Set recipe number 173. Touch START. *(Oven cooks: HI, 3 minutes.)*

At Pause, add remaining ingredients; blend well. Cover. Touch START. *(Oven cooks: HI, 2 minutes.)*

At Pause, stir. Cover. Touch START. *(Oven cooks: HI, 2 minutes.)*

Remove cover and let stand 5 minutes before serving.

4 to 6 servings

Recipe No. 174

Chinese Fried Rice

Preset Cooking Time: 7 minutes

- 2 tablespoons butter or margarine
- 3 cups cooked rice
- 1½ tablespoons soy sauce
- 3 large eggs
- 1 tablespoon water
- ¼ teaspoon sugar
- ¼ cup thinly sliced green onions

Place butter in 3-quart microproof casserole. Place in oven. Set recipe number 174. Touch START. *(Oven cooks: HI, 1 minute.)*

At Pause, add rice and soy sauce; blend well. Beat eggs, water, and sugar until blended; pour into center of rice. Cover. Touch START. *(Oven cooks:* 70, 3 *minutes.)*

At Pause, stir in green onions. Cover. Touch START. *(Oven cooks:* 70, 3 *minutes.)*

Stir before serving.

4 to 6 servings

Recipe No. 175

All Seasons Rice

Preset Cooking Time: 17 minutes

- 2 cups chicken or beef broth
- 1 cup long grain rice
- ¼ cup minced onion
- 2 tablespoons minced parsley

Combine all ingredients in 3-quart microproof casserole. Cover and place in oven. Set recipe number 175. Touch START. *(Oven cooks: HI, 12 minutes; stands:* 0, 5 *minutes).*

4 servings

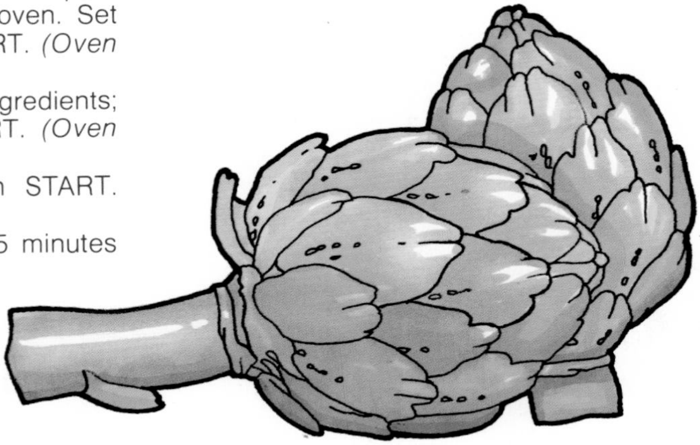

Recipe No. 176 ⊞

Rice Pilaf

Preset Cooking Time: 23 minutes

- 2 cups water
- 1 cup long grain rice
- ¼ cup chopped green pepper
- ¼ cup chopped onion
- ¼ cup instant minced onion
- 2 tablespoons butter or margarine
- 2 teaspoons chicken bouillon granules

Combine all ingredients in 2-quart microproof casserole. Cover and place in oven. Set recipe number 176. Touch START. *(Oven cooks: HI,* 5 *minutes;* 50, 13 *minutes; stands:* 0, 5 *minutes.)*

Stir through before serving.

4 servings

⊞ *Recipe can be increased. See "Quantity", page 12.*

Recipe No. 177

Spanish Rice

Preset Cooking Time: 40 minutes

- 1½ cups water
- 1 can (16 ounces) whole tomatoes, chopped
- 1 can (6 ounces) tomato paste
- ¼ cup finely chopped onion
- ¼ cup chopped celery
- 1 teaspoon sugar
- 1 teaspoon salt
- ½ teaspoon oregano
- 1 clove garlic, minced
- ⅔ cup long grain rice

Combine all ingredients except rice in 2-quart microproof casserole. Cover and place in oven. Set recipe number 177. Touch START. *(Oven cooks: HI, 5 minutes.)*

At Pause, add rice; blend well. Cover. Touch START. *(Oven cooks:* 50, 30 *minutes; stands:* 0, 5 *minutes.)*

6 to 8 servings

Recipe No. 178

Chicken Noodle au Gratin

Preset Cooking Time: 15 minutes

- 1½ cups broken uncooked thin egg noodles
- 1 cup chicken broth
- ½ cup milk
- ½ teaspoon salt
- ⅛ teaspoon pepper
- 2 to 3 cups coarsely chopped cooked chicken or turkey
- 1 cup (4 ounces) shredded Cheddar cheese
- ¼ cup sliced stuffed green olives

Combine noodles, broth, milk, salt, and pepper in 2-quart microproof casserole; stir lightly. Cover and place in oven. Set recipe number 178. Touch START. *(Oven cooks:* 70, 5 *minutes.)*

At Pause, stir in chicken, cheese, and olives. Cover. Touch START. *(Oven cooks:* 70, 5 *minutes.)*

At Pause, stir. Cover. Touch START. *(Oven cooks:* 20, 5 *minutes.)*

4 to 6 servings

Recipe No. 179

Noodles and Cheese

Preset Cooking Time: 7 minutes

- ¼ cup butter or margarine
- ⅓ cup slivered almonds
- 2 cups (8 ounces) shredded Swiss cheese
- ½ cup milk
- 1 large egg, lightly beaten
- 1 teaspoon parsley flakes
- ¼ teaspoon pepper
- ¼ teaspoon nutmeg
- 3 cups cooked wide egg noodles

Place butter and almonds in 1½-quart microproof casserole. Place in oven. Set recipe number 179. Touch START. *(Oven cooks: HI, 1 minute.)*

At Pause, add remaining ingredients except noodles; blend well. Add noodles; toss until separated and evenly coated. Cover. Touch START. *(Oven cooks: HI, 4 minutes; stands:* 0, 2 *minutes.)*

4 to 6 servings

Recipe No. 180

San Francisco Dish

Preset Cooking Time: 17 minutes

- 1 tablespoon beef bouillon granules
- 2½ cups hot water
- 1 medium onion, sliced
- 2 tablespoons butter or margarine
- 1 cup long grain rice
- ½ cup broken uncooked spaghetti (1-inch pieces)

Dissolve bouillon in hot water; set aside. Place onion and butter in 3-quart microproof casserole. Cover and place in oven. Set recipe number 180. Touch START. *(Oven cooks: HI, 2 minutes.)*

At Pause, add rice, spaghetti, and bouillon; stir lightly. Cover. Touch START. *(Oven cooks: HI, 15 minutes.)*

Let stand 5 minutes before serving.

5 servings

All Seasons Rice (page 143) with Shrimp Creole (page 132) →

Recipe No. 181

Casserole Italiano

Preset Cooking Time: 25 minutes

- 1 pound lean ground beef
- 1½ cups spaghetti sauce
- 1½ cups water
- 1 can (16 ounces) green beans, drained
- 1 package (7 ounces) uncooked elbow macaroni
- 2 tablespoons onion flakes
- 1 tablespoon sugar
- 1 teaspoon Italian seasoning
- ½ teaspoon salt
- ⅛ teaspoon pepper
- 1 clove garlic, minced
- 1 cup (4 ounces) shredded mozzarella cheese

Crumble beef into 3-quart microproof casserole. Place in oven. Set recipe number 181. Touch START. *(Oven cooks: HI, 3 minutes.)*

At Pause, remove from oven. Stir to break up beef; drain. Add remaining ingredients except cheese; blend well. Cover and place in oven. Touch START. *(Oven cooks: HI, 12 minutes.)*

At Pause, stir. Cover. Touch START. *(Oven cooks:* 60, 10 *minutes.)*

Sprinkle with cheese. Cover and let stand 10 minutes before serving.

6 to 8 servings

Recipe No. 182

Stroganoff Casserole

Preset Cooking Time: 27 minutes

- 1 pound lean ground beef
- ¼ cup chopped onion
- 2 cloves garlic, minced
- 3 cups (4 ounces) uncooked medium-width egg noodles
- 1 cup sliced mushrooms
- 1 can (13¾ ounces) beef broth
- ⅛ teaspoon pepper
- 1 container (8 ounces) dairy sour cream
- 2 tablespoons chopped parsley

Combine beef, onion, and garlic in 2-quart microproof casserole. Place in oven. Set recipe number 182. Touch START. *(Oven cooks: HI, 3 minutes.)*

At Pause, stir. Touch START. *(Oven cooks: HI, 2 minutes.)*

At Pause, stir in noodles, mushrooms, broth, and pepper. Cover. Touch START. *(Oven cooks:* 50, 11 *minutes.)*

At Pause, stir. Cover. Touch START. *(Oven cooks: 50,* 11 *minutes.)*

Let stand 2 minutes. Blend in sour cream and sprinkle with parsley before serving.

6 servings

Spaghetti Bolognese (page 148) →

Recipe No. 183

Spaghetti Bolognese

Preset Cooking Time: 35 minutes

- 1 pound lean ground beef
- ½ cup chopped onion
- 2 cloves garlic, minced
- 1 can (28 ounces) whole tomatoes, broken up
- 2 cans (6 ounces each) tomato paste
- 2 teaspoons salt
- 2 teaspoons oregano
- ¼ teaspoon basil
- ¼ teaspoon thyme
- ⅛ teaspoon pepper
- Hot cooked spaghetti

Crumble beef into 3-quart microproof casserole. Add onion and garlic. Place in oven. Set recipe number 183. Touch START. *(Oven cooks: HI, 3 minutes.)*

At Pause, remove from oven. Stir to break up beef; drain. Place in oven. Touch START. *(Oven cooks: HI, 2 minutes.)*

At Pause, add remaining ingredients except spaghetti. Cover. Touch START. *(Oven cooks: 50, 30 minutes.)*

Let stand 5 minutes before serving over spaghetti.

10 servings (about 1½ quarts sauce)

Recipe No. 184

Macaroni and Cheese Vegetable Medley

Preset Cooking Time: 25 minutes

- 1½ cups hot water
- 1 cup uncooked elbow macaroni
- 1 package (10 ounces) frozen chopped broccoli
- 1 package (10 ounces) frozen sliced carrots
- 4 tablespoons butter or margarine
- ½ cup milk
- 1 tablespoon cornstarch
- ½ teaspoon salt
- ¼ teaspoon pepper
- ¼ teaspoon garlic powder
- ¼ teaspoon dry mustard
- 2 cups (8 ounces) shredded Cheddar cheese

Combine hot water, macaroni, broccoli, and carrots in 2-quart microproof casserole. Dot with butter. Cover and place in oven. Set recipe number 184. Touch START. *(Oven cooks: 70, 7 minutes.)*

At Pause, stir. Cover. Touch START. *(Oven cooks: 70, 8 minutes.)*

At Pause, combine milk, cornstarch, salt, pepper, garlic powder, and dry mustard in glass measure. Stir until cornstarch is dissolved. Stir into macaroni mixture. Blend in cheese. Cover. Touch START. *(Oven cooks: 70, 5 minutes; stands: 0, 5 minutes.)*

Let stand until all liquid is absorbed.

6 to 8 servings

Complements for Your Meal

Your microwave oven enables you to enter one of the most exciting areas of the culinary arts: The world of succulent crisp-cooked vegetables. Because very little water is used, sometimes none at all, vegetables emerge from the microwave oven with bright, fresh color, full of flavor, tender and nutritious. Even reheated, fresh vegetables retain their original flavor and color. They do not dry out, because the steam that heats them is primarily generated within the vegetables themselves. Canned vegetables heat well too, because they can be drained before cooking so that they retain their full fresh taste after cooking.

You'll truly be amazed at how easy it is to cook whole vegetables, like acorn squash or cauliflower. Try Savory Cauliflower (page 166) for an exciting introduction to microwave vegetable cookery.

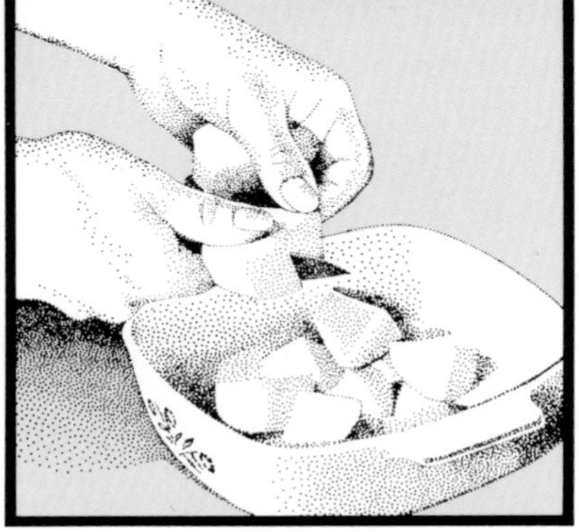

Arrange asparagus with the tender tips overlapped in the center of the dish. Carrots cook a bit more quickly and are more interesting when cut diagonally (above). Corn-on-the-Cob (page 157) cooked right in the husk is just delicious (above right). For best results, when cutting vegetables for cooking, make sizes as uniform as possible (right).

Converting Your Recipes

Vegetables are best when eaten at the crisp stage, tender but resilient to the bite. However, if you prefer a softer texture, increase water and cooking time. To adapt a conventional recipe to the microwave oven, find a similar recipe in the chapter and check the vegetable cooking guides. The following tips will give you additional help in adapting or creating your own recipes:

- ☐ Check doneness after the shortest recommended cooking times. Add more cooking time to suit individual preferences.
- ☐ When using the temperature probe, a small amount of liquid should be added. Insert probe into the center of the vegetable dish and set at 150°F.
- ☐ If necessary, frozen vegetables may be used in recipes calling for fresh vegetables. It is not necessary to thaw frozen vegetables before cooking.
- ☐ Freeze small portions of your favorite vegetable dishes in boilable plastic pouches. If you use metal twist ties, be sure to replace with string or rubber band before cooking. Cut a steam vent in pouch and reheat on microproof plate.
- ☐ To prevent boiling over when preparing vegetable dishes with cream sauces, use a baking dish large enough to allow for bubbling. Use a lower power setting such as 60 or 70.
- ☐ Celery, onions, green peppers, and carrots need to be partially cooked before adding to a casserole. In general, you should partially cook all vegetables before combining with already cooked meats, fish, or poultry.
- ☐ To cook mashed potatoes, cube potatoes. Add a small amount of water. Cook, tightly covered, until soft. Season and mash.
- ☐ To reheat mashed potatoes, set at 80, stirring once during cooking time.
- ☐ Because carrots and beets are dense, they require more water and a longer cooking period to prevent dehydration and toughening during cooking.

Using the Cooking Guide

1. All fresh or frozen vegetables are cooked and reheated on HI.
2. Choose a wide, shallow dish so vegetables can be spread out.
3. Add ¼ cup water for each ½ to 1 pound fresh vegetables. Do not add water for washed spinach, corn on the cob, squash, baking potatoes, or eggplant.
4. Do not salt vegetables until after cooking.
5. Cover all vegetables tightly.
6. Stir vegetables once during cooking time.
7. Pouches of frozen vegetables require steam vents. Slit pouch and cook on microproof dish.
8. Frozen vegetables without sauces can be cooked in their cartons without water. Remove waxed paper wrapping before placing carton in oven. (Remove frozen-in-sauce vegetables if packaged in cartons rather than pouches. Place in 1½-quart microproof casserole. Add liquid before cooking as package directs.)
9. After cooking, allow all vegetables to stand, covered, for 2 to 3 minutes.

COOKING GUIDE — VEGETABLES

Food	Amount	Fresh Vegetable Preparation	Time (in minutes)	Water	Standing Time (in minutes)	Special Notes
Artichokes 3½" in diameter	Fresh: 1 2 4	Wash thoroughly. Cut tops off each leaf.	7-8 11-12	¼ cup ½ cup	2-3 2-3	When done, a leaf peeled from whole comes off easily.
	Frozen: 10 oz.	Slit pouch	5-6			
Asparagus: spears and cut pieces	Fresh: 1 lb.	Wash thoroughly. Snap off tough base and discard.	2-3	¼ cup	None	Stir or rearrange once during cooking time.
	Frozen: 10 oz.		7-8	None	2-3	
Beans: green, wax, French-cut	Fresh: 1 lb.	Remove ends. Wash well. Leave whole or break in pieces.	12-14	¼ cup	2-3	Stir once or rearrange as necessary.
	Frozen: 10 oz.		7-8	None	None	
Beets	4 medium	Scrub beets. Leave 1" of top on beet.	16-18	¼ cup	None	After cooking, peel. Cut or leave whole.
Broccoli	Fresh, whole 1-1½ lbs.	Remove outer leaves. Slit stalks.	9-10	¼ cup	3	Stir or rearrange during cooking time.
	Frozen, whole		8-10	¼ cup	3	
	Fresh, chopped, 1-1½ lbs.		12-14	¼ cup	2	
	Frozen, chopped 10 oz.		8-9	None	2	
Brussels sprouts	Fresh: 1 lb.	Remove outside leaves if wilted. Cut off stems. Wash	8-9	¼ cup	2-3	Stir or rearrange once during cooking time.
	Frozen: 10 oz.		6-7	None	None	
Cabbage	½ medium head, shredded	Remove outside wilted leaves.	5-6	¼ cup	2-3	
	1 medium head, wedges		13-15	¼ cup	2-3	Rearrange wedges after 7 minutes.
Carrots	4: sliced or diced	Peel and cut off tops.	7-9	1 Tb.	2-3	Stir once during cooking time.
	6: sliced or diced	Fresh young carrots cook best.	9-10	2 Tbs.	2-3	
	8: tiny, whole		8-10	2 Tbs.	2-3	
	Frozen: 10 oz.		8-9	None	None	
Cauliflower	1 medium, in flowerets	Cut tough stem. Wash, remove outside leaves.	7-8	¼ cup	2-3	Stir after 5 minutes.
	1 medium, whole	Remove core.	8-9	½ cup	3	Turn over once.
	Frozen: 10 oz.		8-9	¼ cup	3	Stir after 5 minutes.
Celery	2½ cups, 1" slices	Clean stalks thoroughly.	8-9	¼ cup	2	
Corn: kernel	Frozen: 10 oz.		5-6	¼ cup	2	Stir halfway through cooking time.
On the cob	1 ear 2 ears 3 ears 4 ears	Husk, wrap each in waxed paper. Place on glass tray in oven. Cook no more than 4 at a time.	3-4 6-7 9-10 11-12	None None None None	2 2 2 2	Rearrange halfway through cooking time unless cooked on microproof rack.
	Frozen, 2 ears 4 ears	Flat dish, covered.	5½-6 10-11	None None	2	Rearrange halfway through cooking time.
Eggplant	1 medium, sliced	Wash and peel. Cut into slices or cubes.	5-6	2 Tb.	3	
	1 medium, whole	Pierce skin.	6-7			Place on microproof rack.
Greens: collard, kale, etc.	Fresh: 1 lb.	Wash. Remove wilted leaves or tough stem.	6-7	None	2	
	Frozen: 10 oz.		7-8	None	2	

COOKING GUIDE — VEGETABLES

Food	Amount	Fresh Vegetable Preparation	Time (in minutes)	Water	Standing Time (in minutes)	Special Notes
Mushrooms	Fresh: ½ lb., sliced	Add butter or water.	2-4	2 Tbs.		Stir halfway through cooking time.
Okra	Fresh: ½ lb. Frozen: 10 oz.	Wash thoroughly. Leave whole or cut in thick slices.	3-5 7-8	¼ cup None	2 2	
Onions	1 lb., tiny whole 1 lb., medium to large	Peel. Add 1 Tb. butter. Peel and quarter. Add 1 Tb. butter.	6-7 7-9	¼ cup ¼ cup	3 3	Stir once during cooking time.
Parsnips	4 medium, quartered	Peel and cut.	8-9	¼ cup	2	Stir once during cooking time.
Peas: green	Fresh: 1 lb. Fresh: 2 lbs. Frozen 10 oz.	Shell peas. Rinse well.	7-8 8-9 5-6	¼ cup ½ cup None	2 2-3 None	Stir once during cooking time.
Peas and onions	Frozen: 10 oz.		6-8	2 Tbs.	2	
Pea pods	Frozen: 6 oz.		3-4	2 Tbs.	3	
Potatoes, sweet 5-6 oz. ea.	1 2 4 6	Scrub well. Pierce with fork. Place on rack or paper towel in circle, 1" apart.	4-4½ 6-7 8-10 10-11	None None None None	3 3 3 3	
Potatoes, white baking 6-8 oz. ea.	1 2 3 4 5	Wash and scrub well. Pierce with fork. Place on rack or paper towel in circle, 1" apart.	4-6 6-8 8-12 12-16 16-20	None None None None None	3 3 3 3 3	
russet, boiling	3	Peel potatoes, cut in quarters.	12-16	½ cup	None	Stir once during cooking time.
Rutabaga	Fresh: 1 lb. Frozen: 10 oz.	Wash well. Remove tough stems or any wilted leaves.	6-7 7-8	None None	2 2	Stir once during cooking time.
Spinach	Fresh: 1 lb. Frozen: 10 oz.	Wash well. Remove tough stems. Drain.	6-7 7-8	None None	2 2	Stir once during cooking time.
Squash, acorn or butternut	1-1½ lbs. whole	Scrub. Pierce with fork.	10-12	None		Cut and remove seeds to serve.
Spaghetti squash	2-3 lbs.	Scrub, pierce. Place on rack.	6 per lb.	None	5	Serve with butter, Parmesan cheese, or spaghetti sauce.
Turnips	4 cups cubed	Peel, wash.	9-11	¼ cup	3	Stir after 5 minutes.
Zucchini	3 cups sliced	Wash; do not peel.	7-8	¼ cup	2	Stir after 4 minutes.

COOKING GUIDE — CONVENIENCE VEGETABLES

Food	Amount	Cook Control Setting	Time (in minutes)	or	Temperature Probe Setting	Special Notes
Au gratin vegetables, frozen	11½ oz.	70 (roast)	10-12	or	150°	Use glass loaf dish, covered.
Baked beans, frozen	6 oz.	70 (roast)	8-10	or	150°	Use 1½-quart casserole, covered. Stir once.
Corn, scalloped frozen	12 oz.	70 (roast)	7-8	or	150°	Use 1-quart casserole, covered.
Potatoes stuffed, frozen	2	70 (roast)	10-12			Use shallow dish. Cover with waxed paper.
Tots, frozen	16 oz. 32 oz.	80 (reheat) 80 (reheat)	9-10 12-14			Use 2-quart round or oval baking dish. Rearrange once.
Creamed potato mix	4-5 oz.	70 (roast)	20-24	or	150°	
Au gratin, frozen	11½ oz.	70 (roast)	12			Use 1½-quart casserole, covered with waxed paper.
Instant mashed	3½ oz. packet	HI (max. power)	5-6			Use covered casserole. Follow package directions. Reduce liquid by 1 tablespoon.
Peas, pea pods, chestnuts, frozen	10 oz.	HI (max. power)	6-7			Place pouch on plate. Slit pouch. Flex once during cooking time to mix.
Stuffing mix	6 oz.	HI (max. power)	8			Use 1½-quart casserole, covered. Follow package directions.

Note: When cooking vegetables, use temperature probe only after vegetables are thawed.

Using the Blanching Guide

The microwave oven can be a valuable and appreciated aid in preparing fresh vegetables for the freezer. (The oven is *not* recommended for canning.) Some vegetables don't require any water at all and, of course, the less water used the better. You'll have that "fresh picked" color and flavor for your produce. Here are some tips in preparing vegetables for blanching:

- ☐ Choose young, tender vegetables.
- ☐ Clean and prepare for cooking according to Cooking Guide.
- ☐ Measure amounts to be blanched; place by batches, in microproof casserole.
- ☐ Add water according to chart.
- ☐ Cover and cook on HI for time indicated on chart.
- ☐ Stir vegetables halfway through cooking.
- ☐ Let vegetables stand, covered, 1 minute after cooking.
- ☐ Place vegetables in ice water at once to stop cooking. When vegetables feel cool, spread on towel to absorb excess moisture.
- ☐ Package in freezer containers or pouches. Seal, label, date, and freeze quickly.

BLANCHING GUIDE — VEGETABLES

Food	Amount	Water	Approximate Time (in minutes)	Casserole Size
Asparagus (cut in 1-inch pieces)	4 cups	¼ cup	4½	1½ quart
Beans, green or wax (cut in 1-inch pieces)	1 pound	½ cup	5	1½ quart
Broccoli (cut in 1-inch pieces)	1 pound	⅓ cup	6	1½ quart
Carrots (sliced)	1 pound	⅓ cup	6	1½ quart
Cauliflower (cut in flowerets)	1 head	⅓ cup	6	2 quart
Corn (cut from cob)	4 cups	none	4	1½ quart
Corn-on-the-cob (husked)	6 ears	none	5½	1½ quart
Onion (quartered)	4 medium	½ cup	3 - 4½	1 quart
Parsnips (cubed)	1 pound	¼ cup	2½ - 4	1½ quart
Peas (shelled)	4 cups	¼ cup	4½	1½ quart
Snow peas	4 cups	¼ cup	3½	1½ quart
Spinach (washed)	1 pound	none	4	2 quart
Turnips (cubed)	1 pound	¼ cup	3 - 4½	1½ quart
Zucchini (sliced or cubed)	1 pound	¼ cup	4	1½ quart

Recipe No. 185

Cabbage

Preset Cooking Time: 8 minutes

½ medium head cabbage, shredded
¼ cup water

Place cabbage in 1-quart microproof casserole. Add water. Cover and place in oven. Set recipe number 185. Touch START. *(Oven cooks: HI, 4 minutes.)*

At Pause, stir. Cover. Touch START. *(Oven cooks: HI, 2 minutes; stands: 0, 2 minutes.)*

Drain before serving.

4 servings

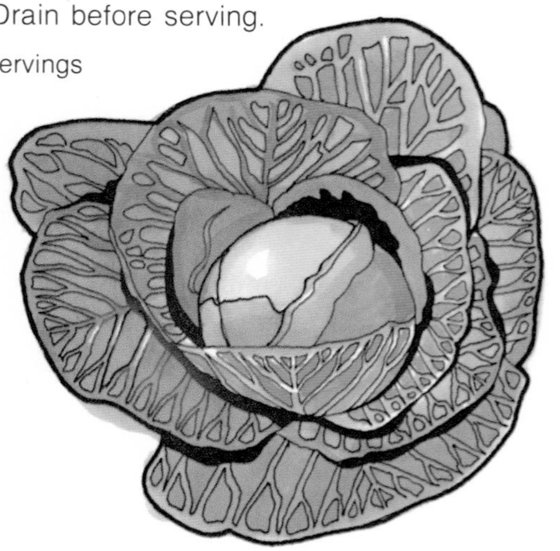

Recipe No. 186 ⊞

Candied Sweet Potatoes

Preset Cooking Time: 22 minutes

5 sweet potatoes (5 to 6 ounces each)
1 cup firmly packed brown sugar
⅓ cup water
2 tablespoons butter or margarine
½ teaspoon salt

Scrub potatoes and pierce at intervals with fork. Place, spoke fashion, 1 inch apart, on microwave roasting rack. Place in oven. Set recipe number 186. Touch START. *(Oven cooks: HI, 10 minutes.)*

At Pause, remove from oven; let stand 3 minutes. Peel and slice. Arrange slices in 2-quart microproof casserole; set aside. Combine brown sugar, water, butter, and salt in 2-cup glass measure. Place in oven. Touch START. *(Oven cooks: 70, 2 minutes.)*

At Pause, stir. Touch START. *(Oven cooks: 70, 2 minutes.)*

At Pause, remove from oven. Pour sauce over potatoes. Cover and place in oven. Touch START. *(Oven cooks: HI, 8 minutes.)*

Spoon sauce over potatoes before serving.

6 servings

Recipe No. 187

Canned Vegetables

Preset Cooking Time: 2 minutes

1 can (8 ounces) canned vegetables, drained

Pour vegetables into 1-quart microproof casserole. Cover and place in oven. Set recipe number 187. Touch START. *(Oven cooks:* 80, 1 *minute.)*

At Pause, stir. Cover. Touch START. *(Oven cooks:* 80, 1 *minute.)*

Let stand 2 to 3 minutes before serving.

2 servings

Recipe No. 188

Carrots

Preset Cooking Time: 10 minutes

1 pound carrots, peeled and thinly sliced
2 tablespoons water

Place carrots in 1-quart microproof casserole. Add water. Cover and place in oven. Set recipe number 188. Touch START. *(Oven cooks: HI, 5 minutes.)*

At Pause, stir. Cover. Touch START. *(Oven cooks: HI, 5 minutes.)*

Let stand 2 to 3 minutes. Drain before serving.

4 servings

Recipe No. 189 ⊞

Cauliflower

Preset Cooking Time: 11 minutes

1 head cauliflower ($1\frac{1}{3}$ pounds)
$\frac{1}{4}$ cup water

Remove stem and outer leaves from cauliflower; discard. Rinse well. Break into florets. Place in $1\frac{1}{2}$- to 2-quart microproof casserole. Add water. Cover and place in oven. Set recipe number 189. Touch START. *(Oven cooks: HI, 5 minutes.)*

At Pause, stir. Cover. Touch START. *(Oven cooks: HI, 3 minutes; stands:* 0, 3 *minutes.)*

Drain before serving.

5 to 6 servings

Recipe No. 190

Carrot-Broccoli Casserole

Preset Cooking Time: $15\frac{3}{4}$ minutes

1 package (10 ounces) frozen broccoli spears
1 can ($10\frac{3}{4}$ ounces) cream of chicken soup, undiluted
1 cup finely shredded carrots
$\frac{1}{2}$ cup dairy sour cream
1 tablespoon all-purpose flour
1 tablespoon minced onion
$\frac{1}{4}$ teaspoon salt
$\frac{1}{8}$ teaspoon pepper
2 tablespoons butter or margarine
$\frac{3}{4}$ cup herb-seasoned stuffing cubes

Place broccoli in package on microproof plate. Place in oven. Set recipe number 190. Touch START. *(Oven cooks: HI, 3 minutes.)*

At Pause, remove from oven; set aside. Combine soup, carrots, sour cream, flour, onion, salt, and pepper in $1\frac{1}{2}$-quart microproof casserole. Cut broccoli into 1-inch pieces; stir into soup mixture. Cover and place in oven. Touch START. *(Oven cooks: HI, 6 minutes.)*

At Pause, remove from oven. Stir; set aside. Place butter in 2-cup glass measure. Place in oven. Touch START. *(Oven cooks: HI, 45 seconds.)*

At Pause, remove from oven. Add stuffing cubes to butter; blend well. Spoon over broccoli mixture. Place in oven. Touch START. *(Oven cooks: HI, 6 minutes.)*

5 to 6 servings

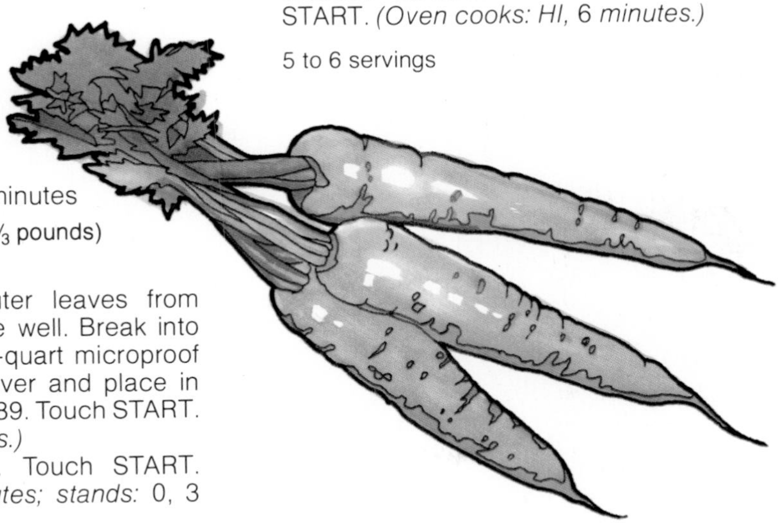

⊞ *Recipe can be increased. See "Quantity", page 12.*

Recipe No. 191 ⊞

Corn-on-the-Cob

Preset Cooking Time: 9 minutes

2 unhusked ears of corn (about 14 ounces each)
Butter or margarine
Salt, to taste

Discard any soiled outer leaves of husks. Soak corn in cold water 5 to 10 minutes to clean and moisten. Drain well; do not dry. Place on microwave roasting rack. Place in oven. Set recipe number 191. Touch START. *(Oven cooks: HI, 7 minutes; stands:* 0, 2 *minutes.)*

Serve with butter and salt.

2 servings

Corn can be husked before cooking. Wrap each ear in waxed paper or plastic wrap. Set recipe number and cook as directed above.

⊞ *Recipe can be increased. See "Quantity", page 12.*

Recipe No. 192

Cranberry Carrots

Preset Cooking Time: 14 minutes

1 pound carrots, thinly sliced
2 tablespoons water
1/4 cup butter or margarine
1/4 cup jellied cranberry sauce
Salt, to taste

Place carrots and water in 1½- to 2-quart microproof casserole. Cover and place in oven. Set recipe number 192. Touch START. *(Oven cooks: HI,* 10 *minutes.)*

At Pause, remove from oven. Remove carrots from casserole; drain water. Set carrots aside. Place butter in casserole. Cover and place in oven. Touch START. *(Oven cooks: HI,* 1 *minute.)*

At Pause, add cranberry sauce; blend well. Cover. Touch START. *(Oven cooks: HI,* 1 *minute.)*

At Pause, stir in carrots. Season with salt. Cover. Touch START. *(Oven cooks: HI,* 2 *minutes.)*

4 servings

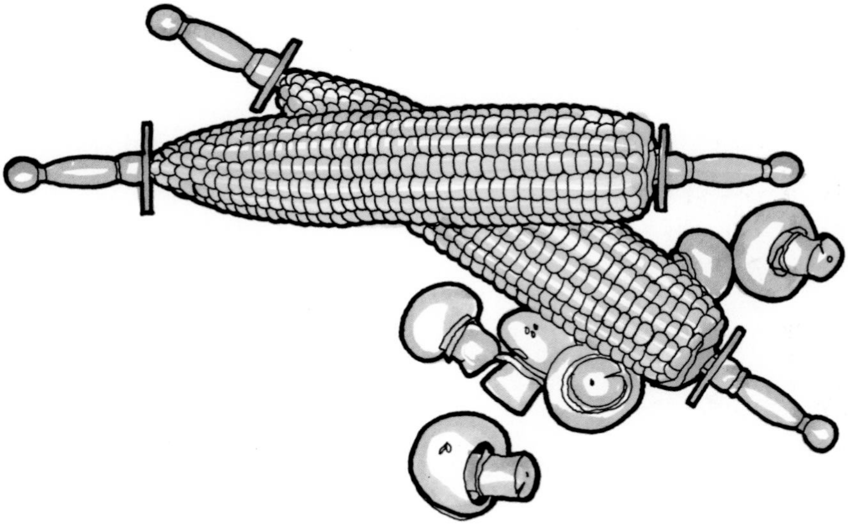

← *Twice-Baked Potatoes (page 168), Green Beans Italiano (page 159), Cranberry Carrots*

Recipe No. 193

Corn-Mushroom Scallop

Preset Cooking Time: 14 minutes

1 can (17 ounces) cream-style corn
¼ pound mushrooms, sliced
1 large egg, lightly beaten
¾ cup soda-cracker crumbs, divided
1 tablespoon chopped chives
¼ teaspoon white pepper
2 tablespoons butter or margarine

Combine corn, mushrooms, and egg in 1-quart microproof casserole; blend well. Stir in ½ cup cracker crumbs, chives, and pepper. Spread evenly in casserole. Sprinkle with remaining ¼ cup cracker crumbs. Dot with butter. Place in oven. Set recipe number 193. Touch START. *(Oven cooks: HI, 9 minutes; stands: 0, 5 minutes.)*

4 servings

Recipe No. 194

Country Style Potatoes

Preset Cooking Time: 21 minutes

5 medium potatoes, peeled and shredded (about 6 cups)
¼ cup water
1½ cups milk
¼ cup chopped chives
¼ cup butter or margarine, cut up
1 teaspoon salt
¼ cup grated Parmesan cheese
Paprika

Place potatoes and water in 2-quart microproof casserole. Cover and place in oven. Set recipe number 194. Touch START. *(Oven cooks: HI, 12 minutes.)*

At Pause, add milk, chives, butter, and salt; stir carefully. Stir in cheese. Sprinkle with paprika. Do not cover. Touch START. *(Oven cooks: 50, 9 minutes.)*

6 servings

Recipe No. 195

Creamed Potato Mix

Preset Cooking Time: 25 to 29 minutes

1 package (5 ounces) creamed potato mix

Prepare potato mix as directed on package in 3-quart round microproof casserole. Place in oven. Insert temperature probe. Cover lightly with waxed paper. Set recipe number 195. Touch START. *(Oven cooks: 70, 20 to 24 minutes to 150°F; stands: 0, 5 minutes.)*

4 servings

Recipe No. 196

Creamy Cabbage

Preset Cooking Time: 10 minutes

1 medium head cabbage, shredded
¼ cup water
1 package (3 ounces) cream cheese, cut into cubes
2 tablespoons milk
½ teaspoon salt
½ teaspoon celery seed
Dash pepper
Chopped parsley

Place cabbage and water in 2-quart microproof casserole. Cover and place in oven. Set recipe number 196. Touch START. *(Oven cooks: HI, 5 minutes.)*

At Pause, stir. Cover. Touch START. *(Oven cooks: HI, 4 minutes.)*

At Pause, add remaining ingredients except parsley. Cover. Touch START. *(Oven cooks: HI, 1 minute.)*

Stir to combine cream cheese and cabbage. Sprinkle with parsley before serving.

5 to 6 servings

Recipe No. 197

Crumb Topped Tomatoes

Preset Cooking Time: 4½ minutes

- 4 medium tomatoes
- 1½ tablespoons butter or margarine, melted
- 1½ tablespoons dry bread crumbs
- 1 tablespoon onion soup mix
- 1 tablespoon chopped parsley
- 1 tablespoon chopped fresh basil, or 1 teaspoon dried basil

Cut slice from top of each tomato; discard. Arrange tomatoes, cut-sides up, in circle on microproof plate. Combine butter, bread crumbs, soup mix, parsley, and basil; blend well. Divide mixture among tomatoes, spreading onto cut surfaces. Place in oven. Set recipe number 197. Touch START. *(Oven cooks: HI, 4½ minutes.)*

4 servings

Recipe No. 198 ⊞

Eggplant

Preset Cooking Time: 7 minutes

- 1 eggplant (1 pound)

Wash eggplant and pierce skin in several places. Place on microwave roasting rack. Place in oven. Set recipe number 198. Touch START. *(Oven cooks: HI, 7 minutes.)*

Let stand 3 minutes before slicing.

4 to 6 servings

⊞ *Recipe can be increased. See "Quantity", page 12.*

Recipe No. 199

Green Beans Amandine

Preset Cooking Time: 9 minutes

- ½ cup sliced almonds
- 2 tablespoons butter or margarine
- 1 package (10 ounces) frozen French cut green beans
- Salt and pepper, to taste

Place almonds and butter in 1-cup glass measure; set aside. Place beans in package on microproof plate. Place in oven. Set recipe number 199. Touch START. *(Oven cooks: HI, 6 minutes.)*

At Pause, remove from oven; set aside. Place almonds and butter in oven. Touch START. *(Oven cooks: HI, 1 minute.)*

At Pause, stir. Touch START. *(Oven cooks: HI, 1 minute.)*

At Pause, remove from oven. Transfer beans to microproof serving dish. Add almonds, salt, and pepper; toss lightly. Place in oven. Touch START. *(Oven cooks: HI, 1 minute.)*

3 to 4 servings

Recipe No. 200

Green Beans Italiano

Preset Cooking Time: 17½ minutes

- 3 slices bacon
- 2 packages (10 ounces each) frozen green beans
- 1 small onion, thickly sliced
- ¾ cup Italian dressing

Arrange bacon on paper towel-lined microproof plate. Place in oven. Cover with paper towel. Set recipe number 200. Touch START. *(Oven cooks: HI, 3½ minutes.)*

At Pause, remove from oven. Crumble bacon; set aside. Place beans in packages on microproof plate. Place in oven. Touch START. *(Oven cooks: HI, 5 minutes.)*

At Pause, turn packages over. Touch START. *(Oven cooks: HI, 5 minutes.)*

At Pause, remove from oven. Transfer beans to 1½-quart microproof casserole. Add onion and dressing; blend well. Cover and place in oven. Touch START. *(Oven cooks: HI, 4 minutes.)*

Sprinkle with crumbled bacon before serving.

6 servings

Recipe No. 201

Harvard Beets

Preset Cooking Time: 6½ minutes

- 1 can (16 ounces) diced or sliced beets
- ¼ cup sugar
- ¼ cup wine vinegar
- 1 tablespoon cornstarch
- ½ teaspoon salt
- ⅛ teaspoon pepper

Drain beet liquid into 1-cup glass measure. Add water to equal 1 cup liquid; set aside. Combine sugar, vinegar, cornstarch, salt, and pepper in 1-quart microproof casserole; stir until cornstarch is dissolved. Stir in beet-water mixture. Place in oven. Set recipe number 201. Touch START. *(Oven cooks: HI, 2 minutes.)*

At Pause, stir. Touch START. *(Oven cooks: HI, 2 minutes.)*

At Pause, add beets; stir to coat. Cover. Touch START. *(Oven cooks: HI, 2½ minutes.)*

4 servings

Recipe No. 202

Mushroom-Pimiento Rice

Preset Cooking Time: 19 minutes

- 12 mushrooms (about ½ pound)
- 6 shallots (about 12 ounces), minced
- 3 tablespoons butter or margarine
- 2½ cups chicken broth
- 1¼ cups long grain rice
- 1 jar (4 ounces) pimientos, drained and diced
- Salt and pepper, to taste

Mince mushroom stems. Cut caps into ⅛-inch thick slices; set aside. Combine minced stems, shallots, and butter in 3-quart microproof casserole. Place in oven. Set recipe number 202. Touch START. *(Oven cooks: 90, 2 minutes.)*

At Pause, stir. Touch START. *(Oven cooks: 90, 2 minutes.)*

At Pause, stir in broth and rice. Cover. Touch START. *(Oven cooks: 90, 10 minutes.)*

At Pause, add mushroom caps. Cover. Touch START. *(Oven cooks: HI, 5 minutes.)*

Add pimientos; blend well. Cover and let stand until all liquid is absorbed. Season with salt and pepper before serving.

6 to 8 servings

Recipe No. 203

Onions

Preset Cooking Time: 12 minutes

- 1 pound onions, peeled and cut into quarters
- ¼ cup water
- 1 tablespoon butter

Place onions, water, and butter in wide, shallow, microproof baking dish. Cover and place in oven. Set recipe number 203. Touch START. *(Oven cooks: HI, 4 minutes.)*

At Pause, stir. Cover. Touch START. *(Oven cooks: HI, 5 minutes; stands: 0, 3 minutes.)*

3 to 4 servings

Harvard Beets →

Recipe No. 204

Pan Baked Potato Halves

Preset Cooking Time: 11¾ minutes

- ¼ cup grated Parmesan cheese
- ½ teaspoon salt
- ¼ teaspoon white pepper
- 2 tablespoons butter or margarine
- 4 medium potatoes (4 to 5 ounces each), cut in half lengthwise
- Paprika

Combine cheese, salt, and pepper; blend well; set aside. Place butter in small microproof bowl. Place in oven. Set recipe number 204. Touch START. *(Oven cooks: HI, 45 seconds.)*

At Pause, remove from oven. Dip cut sides of potatoes in butter, then in cheese mixture. Arrange potatoes, cut-sides up, in circle in shallow microproof baking dish. Touch START. *(Oven cooks: HI, 11 minutes.)*

Let stand 5 minutes. Sprinkle with paprika before serving.

8 servings

Recipe No. 205 ⊞

Parmesan Potatoes

Preset Cooking Time: 9 minutes

- 8 buttery crackers
- ¼ cup grated Parmesan cheese
- 1 teaspoon garlic powder
- ½ teaspoon salt
- ½ teaspoon paprika
- ⅛ teaspoon pepper
- ¼ cup butter or margarine
- 1 pound potatoes, peeled and cut into 1-inch cubes
- 1 tablespoon grated Parmesan cheese
- 3 tablespoons minced parsley

Place crackers, ¼ cup cheese, garlic powder, salt, paprika, and pepper in blender or food processor container; cover and process to make fine crumbs. Transfer crumb mixture to plastic bag; set aside. Place butter in 8-inch round microproof baking dish. Place in oven. Set recipe number 205. Touch START. *(Oven cooks: HI, 1 minute.)*

At Pause, remove from oven. Add potatoes; stir to coat. Drain and reserve any remaining butter.

Add potatoes, in batches, to crumb mixture in plastic bag; shake to coat evenly. Arrange potatoes in single layer in shallow microproof baking dish or pie plate just large enough to accommodate. Cover with plastic wrap and place in oven. Touch START. *(Oven cooks: HI, 5 minutes.)*

At Pause, stir in reserved butter. Do not cover. Touch START. *(Oven cooks: HI, 3 minutes.)*

Sprinkle with remaining 1 tablespoon cheese, and garnish with parsley before serving.

4 servings

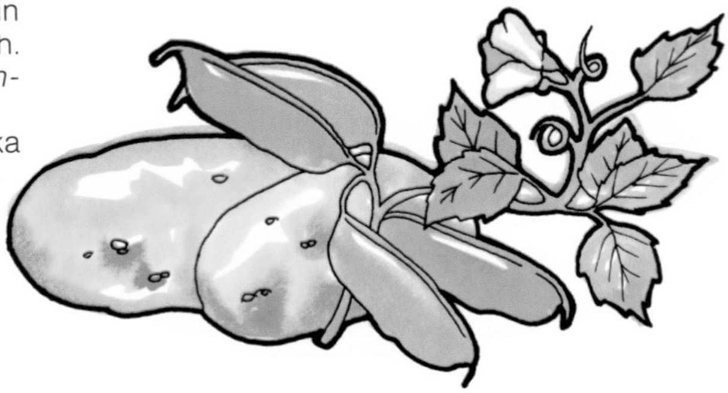

Recipe No. 206 ⊞

Parsley New Potatoes

Preset Cooking Time: 12 minutes

- 12 new potatoes (1 pound)
- ¼ cup water
- 2 tablespoons butter
- 1 tablespoon minced parsley
- Dash salt and pepper

Peel a ½-inch strip around middle of each potato. Place in 2-quart microproof casserole. Add water. Cover and place in oven. Set recipe number 206. Touch START. *(Oven cooks: HI, 6 minutes.)*

At Pause, stir. Cover. Touch START. *(Oven cooks: HI, 6 minutes.)*

Drain. Stir in butter, parsley, salt, and pepper. Serve hot.

4 servings

Recipe No. 207

Peas Francine

Preset Cooking Time: 10 minutes

- 2 cups shelled green peas
- 1/4 cup water
- 1 teaspoon sugar
- 3 or 4 large lettuce leaves
- Dash salt and pepper

Combine peas, water, and sugar in 1½-quart microproof casserole. Cover and place in oven. Set recipe number 207. Touch START. *(Oven cooks: HI, 4 minutes.)*

At Pause, stir. Cover with lettuce, overlapping leaves as necessary. Cover. Touch START. *(Oven cooks: HI, 6 minutes.)*

Discard lettuce leaves. Drain peas; stir in salt and pepper. Cover and let stand 2 to 3 minutes before serving.

4 servings

Recipe No. 208 ⊞

Green Peas

Preset Cooking Time: 10 minutes

- 1 pound peas in shells
- 1/4 cup water

Shell peas; rinse and drain. Place peas and water in wide, shallow, microproof baking dish. Cover and place in oven. Set recipe number 208. Touch START. *(Oven cooks: HI, 4 minutes.)*

At Pause, stir. Cover. Touch START. *(Oven cooks: HI, 4 minutes; stands: 0, 2 minutes.)*

Drain, and serve seasoned with butter and salt, if desired.

2 servings

Recipe No. 209

Corn and Pepper Pudding

Preset Cooking Time: 24 minutes

- 2 tablespoons butter or margarine
- 2 tablespoons chopped green pepper
- 2 tablespoons chopped pimiento
- 2 cans (17 ounces each) cream-style corn
- 2 large eggs, lightly beaten
- 3 tablespoons all-purpose flour
- 1 tablespoon instant minced onion
- 1 teaspoon salt
- 1/4 teaspoon pepper

Combine butter, green pepper, and pimiento in shallow 1½-quart round or oval microproof baking dish. Place in oven. Set recipe number 209. Touch START. *(Oven cooks: 90, 2 minutes.)*

At Pause, stir in remaining ingredients; blend well. Cover. Touch START. *(Oven cooks: 70, 9 minutes.)*

At Pause, stir. Do not cover. Touch START. *(Oven cooks: 70, 8 minutes; stands: 0, 5 minutes.)*

6 servings

Recipe No. 210

Baked Potatoes

Preset Cooking Time: 7 minutes

- 2 potatoes (6 ounces each)

Scrub potatoes and rinse well. Pierce at intervals with fork. Place about 1 inch apart on microwave roasting rack. Place in oven. Set recipe number 210. Touch START. *(Oven cooks: HI, 7 minutes.)*

Let stand 3 minutes before serving.

2 servings

⊞ *Recipe can be increased. See "Quantity", page 12.*

Recipe No. 211

Potato Salad

Preset Cooking Time: 16 minutes

- 2 pounds potatoes, peeled and cut into 1-inch cubes
- ½ cup water
- ¼ teaspoon salt
- ¼ cup Italian dressing
- 6 large hard-cooked eggs, chopped, divided
- ½ cup shopped pimiento, divided
- 1 cup mayonnaise
- 1 cup chopped celery
- ½ cup chopped onion
- Salt and pepper, to taste
- Minced parsley

Place potatoes, water, and salt in 4-quart microproof casserole. Cover and place in oven. Set recipe number 211. Touch START. *(Oven cooks: HI, 8 minutes.)*

At Pause, stir. Cover. Touch START. *(Oven cooks: HI, 8 minutes.)*

At Pause, remove from oven; drain. Pour dressing over potatoes; toss lightly. Set aside ¼ cup egg for garnish; add remaining eggs to potatoes; toss lightly. Set aside 1 tablespoon pimiento for garnish; add remaining pimiento to potato mixture. Blend in mayonnaise, celery, and onion. Season with salt and pepper. Spoon into serving bowl. Garnish with reserved egg, pimiento, and parsley.

6 servings

Recipe No. 212

Ratatouille

Preset Cooking Time: 22 minutes

- 1 eggplant (1 pound)
- ¼ cup olive oil
- 1 medium onion, sliced
- 2 cloves garlic, minced
- 3 medium zucchini, sliced (about 3 cups)
- 1 green pepper, seeded and cut into strips
- 4 firm medium tomatoes, cut into quarters
- ¼ cup minced parsley
- 1 teaspoon basil
- 1 teaspoon salt
- ¼ teaspoon pepper
- Pinch thyme
- 2 tablespoons grated Parmesan cheese

Wash eggplant and pierce skin in several places. Place on microwave roasting rack. Place in oven. Set recipe number 212. Touch START. *(Oven cooks: HI, 7 minutes.)*

At Pause, remove from oven; set aside. Combine olive oil, onion, and garlic in 2½-quart microproof casserole. Cover and place in oven. Touch START. *(Oven cooks: HI, 4 minutes.)*

At Pause, add zucchini and green pepper. Peel eggplant, if desired, and cut into 1½-inch cubes. Add to zucchini mixture; blend well. Cover. Touch START. *(Oven cooks: HI, 5 minutes.)*

At Pause, stir in tomatoes, parsley, basil, salt, pepper, and thyme. Do not cover. Touch START. *(Oven cooks: HI, 6 minutes.)*

Sprinkle with Parmesan cheese before serving.

6 to 8 servings

← *Ratatouille, Veal Cutlets (Guide, page 76)*

Recipe No. 213

Sautéed Mushrooms

Preset Cooking Time: 4 minutes

- ½ pound mushrooms, cleaned and sliced
- ¼ cup butter or margarine
- 1 clove garlic, minced

Combine all ingredients in 8-inch microproof baking dish. Place in oven. Set recipe number 213. Touch START. *(Oven cooks: 90, 2 minutes.)*

At Pause, stir. Touch START. *(Oven cooks: 90, 2 minutes.)*

2 to 4 servings

Serve with roast beef or steak, or as a "surprise" side dish with any meal. Sautéed Mushrooms also make a fine main dish when served on toast and sprinkled with Parmesan cheese.

Recipe No. 214

Savory Cauliflower

Preset Cooking Time: 10½ minutes

- 1 head cauliflower (1⅓ pounds)
- ¼ cup water
- ½ cup mayonnaise
- 1 tablespoon instant minced onion
- ½ teaspoon dry mustard
- ¼ teaspoon salt
- 4 slices Cheddar cheese
- Paprika

Cut cone-shaped wedge from cauliflower core. Place cauliflower, cut-side up, in 1½-quart microproof casserole. Add water. Cover and place in oven. Set recipe number 214. Touch START. *(Oven cooks: HI, 5 minutes.)*

At Pause, turn over. Cover. Touch START. *(Oven cooks: HI, 4 minutes.)*

At Pause, remove from oven; drain. Combine mayonnaise, onion, mustard, and salt; spoon over cauliflower. Lay cheese slices on top. Place in oven. Do not cover. Touch START. *(Oven cooks: 70, 1½ minutes.)*

Sprinkle with paprika. Let stand 2 minutes before serving.

6 servings

Recipe No. 215

Scalloped Potato Mix

Preset Cooking Time: 19 minutes

- 1 package (7 ounces) scalloped potato mix

Prepare scalloped potatoes as directed on package in 3-quart microproof casserole. Cover and place in oven. Set recipe number 215. Touch START. *(Oven cooks: HI, 4 minutes; 50, 10 minutes; stands: 0, 5 minutes.)*

Stir through before serving.

6 servings

Recipe No. 216

Spinach

Preset Cooking Time: 6 minutes

- 1 pound spinach, tough stems removed
- Salt and pepper, to taste

Rinse spinach and drain. Place in wide, shallow, microproof baking dish. Cover and place in oven. Set recipe number 216. Touch START. *(Oven cooks: HI, 6 minutes.)*

Let stand 2 minutes before draining. Season with salt and pepper before serving.

2 servings

Mushroom-Pimiento Rice (page 160), Corn-on-the-Cob (page 157) →

Recipe No. 217

Spinach Oriental

Preset Cooking Time: 5 minutes

- 10 ounces spinach, tough stems removed
- 1 can (8 ounces) sliced water chestnuts, drained
- 4 green onions, sliced
- 2 tablespoons vegetable oil
- 2 tablespoons wine vinegar
- 2 tablespoons soy sauce
- 1 teaspoon sugar

Rinse spinach and drain; tear into bite-size pieces. Combine spinach, water chestnuts, and green onions in 2-quart microproof casserole. Cover and place in oven. Set recipe number 217. Touch START. *(Oven cooks: HI, 4 minutes.)*

At Pause, remove from oven; drain. Stir, cover, and set aside. Combine oil, vinegar, soy sauce, and sugar in 1-cup glass measure; stir until sugar is dissolved. Place in oven. Touch START. *(Oven cooks: HI, 1 minute.)*

Stir and pour over spinach mixture; toss lightly. Serve immediately.

4 servings

Recipe No. 218 ⊞

Sweet Potatoes

Preset Cooking Time: 4½ minutes

- 1 sweet potato (about 5 ounces)

Scrub potato and rinse well. Pierce at intervals with fork. Place on microwave roasting rack. Place in oven. Set recipe number 218. Touch START. *(Oven cooks: HI, 4½ minutes.)*

Let stand 3 minutes before serving.

1 serving

If making more than 2 sweet potatoes, arrange in circle, 1 inch apart, on microwave roasting rack. Cooking time increases about 2 minutes for each additional potato.

⊞ *Recipe can be increased. See "Quantity", page 12.*

Recipe No. 219

Sweet-Sour Red Cabbage

Preset Cooking Time: 23 minutes

- 1 head red cabbage (1½ pounds), shredded
- 1 tart apple, peeled, cored, and diced
- 5 tablespoons wine vinegar
- 1 tablespoon butter or margarine
- 3 tablespoons sugar
- 1 teaspoon salt

Combine cabbage, apple, vinegar, and butter in 3-quart microproof casserole; blend well. Cover and place in oven. Set recipe number 219. Touch START. *(Oven cooks: HI, 6 minutes.)*

At Pause, stir. Cover. Touch START. *(Oven cooks: HI, 6 minutes.)*

At Pause, stir. Cover. Touch START. *(Oven cooks: HI, 6 minutes.)*

At Pause, add sugar and salt; blend well. Cover. Touch START. *(Oven cooks: HI, 5 minutes.)*

6 servings

Recipe No. 220

Twice-Baked Potatoes

Preset Cooking Time: 23 minutes

- 4 potatoes (6 ounces each)
- ½ cup butter or margarine, cut up
- ½ cup dairy sour cream
- ½ teaspoon salt
- Dash pepper
- Paprika

Scrub potatoes and rinse well. Pierce at intervals with fork. Arrange in circle, 1 inch apart, on microwave roasting rack. Place in oven. Set recipe number 220. Touch START. *(Oven cooks: HI, 16 minutes; stands: 0, 3 minutes.)*

At Pause, remove from oven. Remove ¼-inch horizontal slice from top of each potato. Using teaspoon, carefully remove pulp; place in mixing bowl. Set shells aside. Add butter, sour cream, salt, and pepper to pulp; beat with electric mixer until smooth. Divide mixture evenly and spoon into shells. Place in circle on microwave roasting rack. Place in oven. Touch START. *(Oven cooks: HI, 4 minutes.)*

Sprinkle with paprika before serving.

4 servings

Pour on the Praise

Sauces are a cinch in your Kenmore Spacemaster Auto Recipe 300 Microwave Oven. They are definitely a microwave success story. For those of us who have slaved over a hot stove with whisk in hand and double boiler at full speed, those days are gone forever. Sauces simply do not stick or scorch as they do when prepared on the stove top. They heat evenly and require less time and attention. You don't have to stir constantly and can simply retire that double boiler. Usually, just an occasional stirring is all that is required to prevent lumping. Sometimes, a quick beating after cooking can be added to make a sauce velvety-smooth. You can measure, mix, and cook all in the same cup, or in the serving pitcher itself! Choose Tarragon Sauce (page 179) or Bearnaise Sauce (page 172) to perk up meat or vegetables, others for desserts. Just try making a sauce the microwave way and you'll turn an ordinary food into an elegant treat.

Basic White Sauce (page 179) is typical of the preparation ease the microwave method provides. The simple steps are illustrated (right and above right). The addition of herbs or spices turns Basic White Sauce into something new each time you use it (above).

Converting Your Recipes

All those sauces generally considered too difficult for the average cook are easy in the microwave oven. When looking for a sauce recipe similar to the conventional one you want to convert, find a recipe with a similar quantity of liquid and similar main thickening ingredient such as cornstarch, flour, egg, cheese, or jelly. Read the directions carefully to determine procedure, timing, and cook control setting. Then, when you stir, notice the progress of the sauce, and remove when the right consistency or doneness is reached. Keep notes to help you the next time. The following tips will help:

- ☐ Use a microproof container about twice the volume of ingredients to safeguard against the sauce boiling over — so easy with milk- and cream-based sauces.
- ☐ Sauces and salad dressings with ingredients not sensitive to high heat should be cooked on HI. Basic White Sauce is an example.
- ☐ Bring cornstarch-thickened mixtures to a boil and remove as soon as thickened. Remember, overcooking will destroy the thickening agent.
- ☐ You will notice that more flour or cornstarch is required in microwave cooking than in conventional cooking to thicken sauces and gravies, since they will not be reduced by evaporation.
- ☐ Stirring quickly two or three times during cooking is sufficient to ensure even cooking. Too many stirrings may slow cooking.
- ☐ To reheat sauces: Dessert sauces to 125°F with temperature probe. Main dish sauces, such as gravy or canned spaghetti sauce, to 150°F.
- ☐ When sauces require time to develop flavor or if they contain eggs, which might curdle, they should be cooked slowly, on 50 or even 30. Don't allow delicate egg yolk sauces to boil.

Recipe No. 221 ⊞

Apricot Dessert Sauce

Preset Cooking Time: 4 minutes

1 cup apricot nectar
1/4 cup sugar
1 tablespoon cornstarch
1 teaspoon grated lemon peel
3 tablespoons apricot-flavored brandy

Combine apricot nectar, sugar, cornstarch, and lemon peel in 2-cup glass measure; stir until sugar and cornstarch are dissolved. Place in oven. Set recipe number 221. Touch START. *(Oven cooks: HI, 1 1/2 minutes.)*

At Pause, stir. Touch START. *(Oven cooks: HI, 1 1/2 minutes.)*

At Pause, add brandy; blend well. Touch START. *(Oven cooks: HI, 1 minute.)*

Stir through several times. Serve warm or chilled over ice cream, rice pudding, tapioca, or pound cake.

1 1/3 cups

To make a Lemon Dessert Sauce, substitute 1/2 cup water for the 1 cup apricot nectar, lemon juice for the brandy, and add 1 egg yolk and 1 tablespoon butter.

⊞ *Recipe can be increased. See "Quantity", page 12.*

Apricot Dessert Sauce with Fluffy Tapioca (page 192), Lemon Dessert Sauce variation on pound cake →

Recipe No. 222 ⊞

Béarnaise Sauce

Preset Cooking Time: 1 minute

- 4 egg yolks
- 2 teaspoons tarragon vinegar
- 1 teaspoon instant minced onion
- ½ teaspoon chervil
- Dash white pepper
- ½ cup butter or margarine
- 1 teaspoon minced parsley

Combine egg yolks, vinegar, onion, chervil, and pepper in blender or food processor container; set aside. Place butter in 1-cup glass measure. Place in oven. Set recipe number 222. Touch START. *(Oven cooks: HI, 1 minute 10 seconds.)*

With blender at high speed, gradually add melted butter through cover opening; process until thick and creamy. Stir in parsley. Serve warm over broiled steak, green vegetables, poached eggs, or fish.

½ cup

Recipe No. 223

Best Ever French Dressing

Preset Cooking Time: 9 minutes

- ½ cup lemon juice
- ¼ cup wine vinegar
- 1 small onion, sliced
- 1 clove garlic, cut in half
- ¾ cup sugar
- ½ cup water
- 2 tablespoons corn syrup
- 1 cup vegetable oil
- ½ cup catsup
- 1 teaspoon salt
- 1 teaspoon paprika
- 1 teaspoon celery salt
- 1 teaspoon dry mustard

Combine lemon juice, vinegar, onion, and garlic; set aside. Combine sugar, water, and corn syrup in 4-cup glass measure. Place in oven. Set recipe number 223. Touch START. *(Oven cooks: HI, 9 minutes.)*

Remove from oven; let stand until cool. Strain lemon-vinegar mixture, discarding onion and garlic. Add to syrup along with remaining ingredients. Beat with electric mixer until thick.

Serve chilled over salad or your favorite combination of raw or blanched vegetables.

2½ cups

Recipe No. 224

Butterscotch Sauce

Preset Cooking Time: 5 minutes

- 1¼ cups firmly packed brown sugar
- 1½ tablespoons cornstarch
- ½ cup light cream
- ¼ cup butter
- 2 tablespoons corn syrup
- ⅛ teaspoon salt
- 1 teaspoon vanilla

Combine brown sugar and cornstarch in 1½-quart microproof casserole. Add cream, butter, corn syrup, and salt; stir until cornstarch and brown sugar are dissolved. Place in oven. Set recipe number 224. Touch START. *(Oven cooks: HI, 2 minutes.)*

At Pause, stir. Touch START. *(Oven cooks: HI, 3 minutes.)*

Stir through. Stir in vanilla. Serve hot or chilled over ice cream or cake.

1½ cups

Recipe No. 225 ⊞

Clarified Butter

Preset Cooking Time: 2½ minutes

- 1 cup butter

Place butter in 2-cup glass measure. Place in oven. Set recipe number 225. Touch START. *(Oven cooks: 20, 2½ minutes.)*

Let stand 3 to 4 minutes. Skim foam from top. Slowly pour off yellow oil. This is the clarified butter. Discard the leftover impurities. Serve as dipping sauce for steamed clams, crab legs, or shrimp.

⅓ cup

Recipe No. 226 ⊞

Choco-Peanut Butter Sauce

Preset Cooking Time: 3½ minutes

- ¼ cup milk
- 1 square (1 ounce) unsweetened chocolate
- 1 cup sugar
- 1 tablespoon light corn syrup
- ⅓ cup peanut butter
- ¼ teaspoon vanilla

Place milk and chocolate in 4-cup glass measure. Place in oven. Set recipe number 226. Touch START. *(Oven cooks: HI, 1½ minutes.)*

At Pause, stir until chocolate is melted. Add sugar and corn syrup; blend well. Touch START. *(Oven cooks: HI, 2 minutes.)*

Add peanut butter and vanilla; blend well. Serve hot or chilled over ice cream, cake, or sliced bananas.

1 cup

Recipe No. 227 ⊞

Cranberry Sauce

Preset Cooking Time: 7 minutes

- 3 cups (1 pound) cranberries
- ½ cup sugar
- ⅓ cup water

Combine all ingredients in 2-quart microproof casserole. Cover and place in oven. Set recipe number 227. Touch START. *(Oven cooks: HI, 7 minutes.)*

Remove from oven; stir through several times. Let stand until cool. Cover and chill before serving.

2 cups

For a festive touch, cut 4 oranges in half, scoop out orange and membranes, and cut shells in a zig-zag pattern. Fill with Cranberry Sauce. Sprinkle with chopped pecans or walnuts.

⊞ *Recipe can be increased. See "Quantity", page 12.*

Recipe No. 228

Easy Gravy

Preset Cooking Time: 4 minutes

- ¼ cup fat-free meat or poultry drippings
- ¼ cup all-purpose flour
- 2 cups warm broth, water, or pan drippings
- Salt and pepper, to taste

Pour drippings into 2-quart glass measure. Add flour; stir until smooth. Pour in broth; stir briskly with wire whisk until blended. Place in oven. Set recipe number 228. Touch START. *(Oven cooks: HI, 2 minutes.)*

At Pause, stir. Touch START. *(Oven cooks: HI, 1 minute.)*

At Pause, stir. Touch START. *(Oven cooks: HI, 1 minute.)*

Season with salt and pepper; blend until smooth. Serve hot with meat, potatoes, or dressing.

2½ cups

Recipe No. 229 ⊞

Hollandaise Sauce

Preset Cooking Time: 2 minutes

- ¼ cup butter
- ¼ cup light cream
- 2 egg yolks, well beaten
- 1 tablespoon lemon juice
- ½ teaspoon dry mustard
- ¼ teaspoon salt

Place butter in 4-cup glass measure. Place in oven. Set recipe number 229. Touch START. *(Oven cooks: HI, 1 minute.)*

At Pause, remove from oven. Add remaining ingredients. Beat with electric mixer or wire whisk until smooth. Place in oven. Touch START. *(Oven cooks: 70, 30 seconds.)*

At Pause, beat until blended. Touch START. *(Oven cooks: 70, 15 seconds.)*

At Pause, stir. Touch START. *(Oven cooks: 70, 15 seconds.)*

Beat until smooth. Serve immediately over cooked asparagus or broccoli.

¾ cup

If sauce curdles, beat in 1 teaspoon hot water, and continue beating until smooth.

To reheat Hollandaise Sauce, cook on 20 for 15 to 30 seconds. Stir; let stand 1 minute. Repeat until hot.

Recipe No. 230 ⊞

Hot Fudge Sauce

Preset Cooking Time: 5 minutes

- 1 cup sugar
- 2 squares (1 ounce each) unsweetened chocolate
- ⅓ cup milk
- 3 tablespoons light corn syrup
- 1 large egg, well beaten
- 1 teaspoon vanilla

Combine all ingredients except vanilla in 4-cup glass measure; blend well. Place in oven. Set recipe number 230. Touch START. *(Oven cooks: HI, 2 minutes.)*

At Pause, stir until blended. Touch START. *(Oven cooks:* 50, 1½ *minutes.)*

At Pause, stir. Touch START. *(Oven cooks:* 50, 1½ *minutes.)*

Blend in vanilla. Briskly stir with wire whisk until clear and shiny. Refrigerate until cool; sauce will thicken as it stands. Serve over ice cream, chocolate cake, fresh fruit, or as a fondue for dipping pound cake or fresh berries.

1 cup

Recipe No. 231 ⊞

Hot Lemony Dill Sauce

Preset Cooking Time: 5 minutes

- ½ cup butter or margarine
- 2 tablespoons all-purpose flour
- 1 teaspoon chicken bouillon granules
- ½ teaspoon dillweed
- ½ teaspoon salt
- 1 cup chicken broth
- 2 tablespoons lemon juice

Place butter in 2-cup glass measure. Place in oven. Set recipe number 231. Touch START. *(Oven cooks: HI,* 1½ *minutes.)*

At Pause, add flour, bouillon, dillweed, and salt; blend well. Briskly stir in broth. Touch START. *(Oven cooks: HI,* 1½ *minutes.)*

At Pause, stir. Touch START. *(Oven cooks: HI,* 1 *minute.)*

At Pause, stir. Touch START. *(Oven cooks: HI,* 1 *minute.)*

Blend in lemon juice. Serve with broiled or Poached Salmon, or Simple Salmon Ring (page 129).

1½ cups

⊞ *Recipe can be increased. See "Quantity", page 12.*

← *Rum Custard Sauce (page 176), Hot Fudge Sauce*

Recipe No. 232 ⊞

Lemon Butter Sauce

Preset Cooking Time: $1\frac{1}{2}$ minutes

- $\frac{1}{2}$ cup butter
- 2 tablespoons lemon juice
- $\frac{1}{8}$ teaspoon salt
- $\frac{1}{8}$ teaspoon white pepper

Combine all ingredients in 2-cup glass measure. Place in oven. Set recipe number 232. Touch START. *(Oven cooks: HI, $1\frac{1}{2}$ minutes.)*

Stir sauce. Serve immediately with seafood, hot green vegetables, or Simple Salmon Ring (page 129).

$\frac{2}{3}$ cup

Recipe No. 233 ⊞

Orange Sauce

Preset Cooking Time: 3 minutes

- $\frac{2}{3}$ cup orange juice
- 3 tablespoons fat-free duckling drippings
- 2 tablespoons brown sugar
- 1 tablespoon cornstarch
- 2 teaspoons grated orange peel
- 2 tablespoons orange-flavored liqueur

Combine all ingredients except liqueur in 2-cup glass measure; stir until brown sugar and cornstarch are dissolved. Place in oven. Set recipe number 233. Touch START. *(Oven cooks: HI, $1\frac{1}{2}$ minutes.)*

At Pause, stir. Touch START. *(Oven cooks: HI, $1\frac{1}{2}$ minutes.)*

Stir in liqueur. Serve hot with Duckling (page 112).

$1\frac{1}{4}$ cups

Not having duckling? Any poultry drippings will do. Or, simply increase orange juice by 3 tablespoons, and use as a dessert sauce.

Recipe No. 234 ⊞

Rum Custard Sauce

Preset Cooking Time: 11 minutes

- $1\frac{1}{2}$ cups milk
- $\frac{1}{2}$ cup light cream
- $\frac{1}{3}$ cup sugar
- $\frac{1}{8}$ teaspoon salt
- 3 large eggs, lightly beaten
- 3 tablespoons rum

Combine milk, cream, sugar, and salt in 2-quart glass measure. Place in oven. Set recipe number 234. Touch START. *(Oven cooks: 70, 4 minutes.)*

At Pause, stir $\frac{1}{2}$ cup milk mixture into eggs; gradually stir eggs into milk mixture. Touch START. *(Oven cooks: 50, 2 minutes.)*

At Pause, stir. Touch START. *(Oven cooks: 30, $2\frac{1}{2}$ minutes.)*

At Pause, stir. Touch START. *(Oven cooks: 30, $2\frac{1}{2}$ minutes.)*

Let stand until cooled to room temperature. Stir in rum. Serve over bread pudding, banana pudding, or poached peaches.

$2\frac{1}{2}$ cups

⊞ *Recipe can be increased. See "Quantity", page 12.*

Hollandaise Sauce (page 173), → Raisin Brandy Sauce (page 179)

Recipe No. 235 ⊞

Raspberry Sauce

Preset Cooking Time: 6 minutes

1 package (10 ounces) frozen raspberries
1 teaspoon cornstarch
1 tablespoon water

Place raspberries in $1\frac{1}{2}$-quart microproof bowl. Place in oven. Set recipe number 235. Touch START. *(Oven cooks: HI, 3 minutes.)*

At Pause, remove from oven. Break up raspberries with wooden spoon. Press through sieve, discarding seeds, if desired. Return to bowl. Dissolve cornstarch in water; stir into berries. Place in oven. Touch START. *(Oven cooks: HI, 3 minutes.)*

Stir through several times. Serve over angel food cake or ice cream.

$1\frac{1}{2}$ cups

Recipe No. 236 ⊞

Spicy Barbecue Sauce

Preset Cooking Time: 10 minutes

1 can (8 ounces) tomato sauce
$\frac{1}{4}$ cup wine vinegar
2 tablespoons brown sugar
2 tablespoons prepared mustard
1 tablespoon instant minced onion
1 tablespoon Worcestershire sauce
1 teaspoon celery seed
$\frac{1}{4}$ teaspoon salt
1 clove garlic, minced (optional)
Dash hot pepper sauce

Combine all ingredients in 4-cup glass measure; blend well. Cover with plastic wrap and place in oven. Set recipe number 236. Touch START. *(Oven cooks: HI, $2\frac{1}{2}$ minutes.)*

At Pause, stir. Cover. Touch START. *(Oven cooks: HI, $2\frac{1}{2}$ minutes; stands: 0, 5 minutes.)*

Stir through before serving with Country Style Ribs (page 99), chicken, or pork chops.

$1\frac{1}{3}$ cups

This sauce can also be used as a marinade before cooking to enhance the flavor of spareribs, pork, chicken, or lamb. Refrigerate meat in sauce from 2 to 24 hours.

Recipe No. 237 ⊞

Strawberry Sauce

Preset Cooking Time: 4 minutes

1 pint strawberries, hulled
1 cup water
$\frac{1}{2}$ cup sugar
2 tablespoons cornstarch
2 tablespoons butter
$\frac{1}{2}$ cup lemon juice

Set aside a few of the best strawberries for garnish. Force remaining strawberries through food mill, or purée with blender or food processor. Strain to remove seeds; set purée aside. Combine water, sugar, and cornstarch in 4-cup glass measure; stir until sugar and cornstarch are dissolved. Place in oven. Set recipe number 237. Touch START. *(Oven cooks: HI, 2 minutes.)*

At Pause, stir. Cover. Touch START. *(Oven cooks: HI, 1 minute.)*

At Pause, stir. Cover. Touch START. *(Oven cooks: HI, 1 minute.)*

Add butter; stir until melted. Stir in lemon juice and strawberry purée; blend well. Serve chilled over pound cake, vanilla pudding, custard, or as a parfait sauce.

$2\frac{1}{2}$ cups

Recipe No. 238 ⊞

Tarragon Sauce

Preset Cooking Time: 3 minutes

- ½ cup unsalted butter
- ⅓ cup dry white wine
- 2 tablespoons minced fresh tarragon or 2 teaspoons dried tarragon
- 1 tablespoon chopped chives
- 1 tablespoon tarragon vinegar
- ½ teaspoon salt
- ¼ teaspoon pepper
- 3 egg yolks, beaten

Place all ingredients except egg yolks in 4-cup glass measure. Place in oven. Set recipe number 238. Touch START. *(Oven cooks: HI, 2 minutes.)*

At Pause, remove from oven. Stir small amount butter mixture into egg yolks; gradually stir yolk mixture into butter mixture. Place in oven. Touch START. *(Oven cooks:* 50, 1 *minute.)*

Beat with wire whisk until smooth. Serve immediately with poached eggs, broiled meat, cooked cauliflower or carrots.

1½ cups

Recipe No. 239 ⊞

Basic White Sauce

Preset Cooking Time: 6¾ minutes

- 1 cup milk
- 2 tablespoons butter
- 2 tablespoons all-purpose flour
- Dash white pepper
- Dash nutmeg

Pour milk into 4-cup glass measure. Place in oven. Set recipe number 239. Touch START. *(Oven cooks:* 70, 2 *minutes.)*

At Pause, remove from oven; set aside. Place butter in 2-cup glass measure. Place in oven. Touch START. *(Oven cooks: HI,* 45 *seconds.)*

At Pause, stir flour into butter until smooth. Touch START. *(Oven cooks: HI,* 1 *minute.)*

At Pause, briskly stir in warm milk, pepper, and nutmeg with wire whisk. Touch START. *(Oven cooks: HI, 3 minutes.)*

Serve over cooked broccoli or cauliflower, or use as base for other sauces.

1 cup

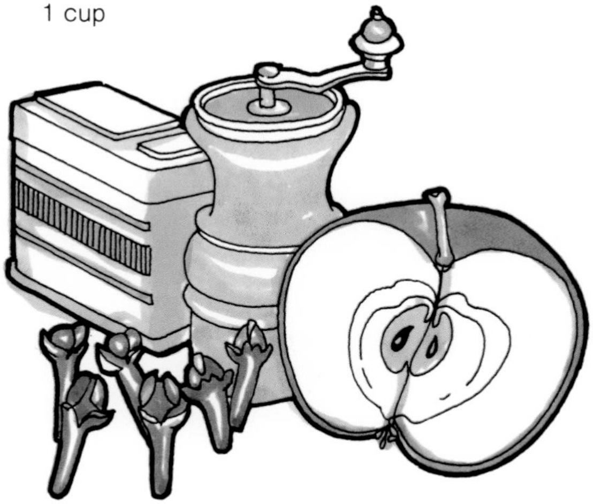

Recipe No. 240 ⊞

Raisin Brandy Sauce

Preset Cooking Time: 10 minutes

- ½ cup raisins
- ¼ cup apple brandy
- 3 tablespoons brown sugar
- 1 tablespoon cornstarch
- 1 cup apple juice
- 2 tablespoons lemon juice
- ⅛ teaspoon ground cloves
- ⅛ teaspoon nutmeg

Combine raisins and brandy in small microproof bowl. Place in oven. Set recipe number 240. Touch START. *(Oven cooks: HI,* 1 *minute.)*

At Pause, remove from oven; set aside. Combine brown sugar and cornstarch in 2-cup glass measure. Briskly stir in juices until well blended. Place in oven. Touch START. *(Oven cooks: HI, 3 minutes.)*

At Pause, stir in cloves, nutmeg, and raisin-brandy mixture. Touch START. *(Oven cooks: HI,* 1 *minute; stands:* 0, 5 *minutes.)*

Serve warm with ham, beef tongue, baked squash, gingerbread, or baked apples.

1½ cups

⊞ *Recipe can be increased. See "Quantity", page 12.*

How Sweet It Is!

Desserts can transform a simple meal into a delectable feast. From baked fresh fruit to fudgy chocolate cake, they make the perfect ending to any meal. Here are some traditional family favorites, glamorous party desserts, and spur-of-the-moment treats. All are quick and easy with your microwave oven. In no time at all, cakes will rise before your eyes, custards will become thick and creamy, and pie fillings will bubble and thicken. Brownies and bar cookies are delicious, fast and fun to make, and if you've never tried home-made candies, now is the time! It's impossible to fail when you make candy the microwave way.

Yellow food coloring added to Homemade Pie Shell (page 192) will enhance the appearance. Chocolate wafer or graham cracker Crumb Crust (page 190) is a quick dessert when filled with pudding (top left). Rich Chocolate Fudge (page 196) is easy. A candy thermometer can be used to check the soft ball stage (234°F) on the thermometer) when making candy (top right). Other ingredients are added after cooking (above left). Microwave cakes rise higher than conventional. Fill cake pans only half-full (above right).

← *Devil's Food Cake (page 191) with Snow White Frosting (page 198), Coconut Squares (page 190), Date Oatmeal Bars (page 190)*

Converting Your Recipes

How easy it is! Puddings and custards can be baked without the usual water bath, and they need only occasional stirring. Fruits retain their bright color and fresh-picked flavor. Cakes cook so quickly; yet they are superior in texture, taste, and height. When you discover how effortless it is to make candy, you'll be trying all those recipes you've been longing to do. Because cakes and pie crusts cook so fast, they do not brown. If you like a browned surface, there are many ways to give desserts a browned look. So try adapting your dessert recipes following the guidance of a similar recipe here and these tips:

- ☐ You can enhance your light batter cookies and cakes with cinnamon, nutmeg, brown sugar, coffee, nuts, toppings, frostings, glazes, food coloring, etc.
- ☐ Small drop cookies and slice 'n bake cookies don't do as well as the larger bar cookies. Drop cookies must be cooked in small batches; they tend to cook unevenly, and need to be removed individually from the oven when finished.
- ☐ A serviceable cookie sheet can be made by covering cardboard with waxed paper.
- ☐ Layer cakes are generally baked one layer at a time. Baking is usually begun on 50 or 60 for the first 7 minutes, then finished on HI. If cake appears to be rising unevenly, rotate the dish one-quarter turn as necessary. Denser batters, such as fruit cakes and carrot cakes, require slower, gentler cooking. Set at 30 for good results.
- ☐ A pie shell is cooked when very slight browning occurs on top, and surface appears opaque and dry.
- ☐ For even cooking, select fruit of uniform size to be cooked whole, as in baked apples, or to be cooked in pieces, as in apple pie.
- ☐ Remove baked custards from oven when centers are nearly firm. They will continue to cook and set after removal.
- ☐ To avoid lumping, puddings should be stirred once or twice during the second half of cooking.

COOKING GUIDE — PUDDING AND PIE FILLING MIX

Food	Amount	Time (in minutes)	Cook Control Setting	Special Notes
Pudding and pie filling mix	3¼ ounces 5½ ounces	6½ - 7 8 - 10	HI (max. power) HI (max. power)	Follow package directions. Stir every 3 minutes. Use 4-cup glass measure.
Egg custard	3 ounces	8 - 10	70 (roast)	Follow package directions. Stir every 3 minutes. Use 4-cup glass measure.
Tapioca	3¼ ounces	6 - 7	HI (max. power)	Follow package directions. Stir every 3 minutes. Use 4-cup glass measure.

COOKING/DEFROSTING GUIDE — CONVENIENCE DESSERTS

Food	Amount	Cook Control Setting	Time	Special Notes
Brownies, other bars, frozen	12-13 oz.	30 (defrost)	2-3 minutes	In original ¾" foil tray, lid removed. Let stand 5 minutes.
Cookies, frozen	6	30 (defrost)	50-60 seconds	Place on paper plate or towels.
Pineapple upside-down cake mix	21½ oz.	50 (simmer) HI (max. power)	3 minutes 4 minutes	Use 9" round glass dish. Remove enough batter for 2 cupcakes, bake separately. Rotate if rising unevenly.
Cupcakes or crumb cakes, frozen	1 or 2	30 (defrost)	½-1 minute	Place on shallow plate.
Cheesecake, frozen	17-19 oz.	30 (defrost)	4-5 minutes	Remove from foil pan to plate. Let stand 1 minute.
Pound cake, frozen	10¾ oz.	30 (defrost)	2 minutes	Remove from foil pan to plate. Rotate once. Let stand 5 minutes.
Cake, frozen 2- or 3-layer	17 oz.	30 (defrost)	2½-3 minutes	Remove from foil pan to plate. Watch carefully, frosting melts fast. Let stand 5 minutes.
Custard pie, frozen	9" pie	70 (roast)	4-5½ minutes	Remove from foil pan to plate. Center should be nearly set.
Fruit pie, frozen, unbaked, 2 crusts	9" pie	HI (max. power)	13-15 minutes	On glass pie plate. Brown, if desired, in preheated 425° conventional oven 8-10 minutes.
Frozen fruit	10 oz. 16 oz.	HI (max. power) HI (max. power)	5-5½ minutes 7-9 minutes	On microproof plate. Slit pouch. Flex halfway through cooking time to mix. Remove from bag. Place in glass casserole, cover. Stir halfway through cooking time.

Recipe No. 241

Almond Bark

Preset Cooking Time: 7½ minutes

1 cup whole blanched almonds
1 teaspoon butter or margarine
1 pound white chocolate

Line large baking sheet with waxed paper; set aside. Place almonds and butter in 9-inch glass pie plate. Place in oven. Set recipe number 241. Touch START. *(Oven cooks: HI, 2½ minutes.)*

At Pause, stir. Touch START. *(Oven cooks: HI, 2 minutes.)*

At Pause, remove from oven; set aside. Place chocolate in large microproof bowl. Place in oven. Touch START. *(Oven cooks: HI, 3 minutes.)*

Stir almonds into chocolate. Pour onto prepared baking sheet. Spread to desired thickness. Refrigerate until set. Break into pieces, and store in airtight container.

1½ pounds

Recipe No. 242

Applesauce

Preset Cooking Time: 12 minutes

6 cups sliced peeled cooking apples
½ cup water
1 tablespoon lemon juice
¼ cup sugar
½ teaspoon cinnamon or nutmeg

Place apples, water, and lemon juice in 2-quart microproof casserole. Cover and place in oven. Set recipe number 242. Touch START. *(Oven cooks: HI, 6 minutes.)*

At Pause, stir. Touch START. *(Oven cooks: HI, 6 minutes.)*

Stir in sugar and cinnamon. Serve warm or chilled with pork or as a light dessert.

4 to 6 servings

Recipe No. 243 ⊞

Baked Apples

Preset Cooking Time: 8 minutes

- 2 baking apples (1 pound)
  Lemon juice
- 2 teaspoons slivered almonds
- 2 teaspoons raisins
- 2 teaspoons brown sugar
- 1/4 teaspoon cinnamon
- 4 tablespoons water
- 2 teaspoons butter or margarine

Core apples, starting from tops, without cutting all the way through. Remove a thin circle of peel around tops. Sprinkle with lemon juice. Combine almonds, raisins, brown sugar, and cinnamon; mix lightly. Fill apples with mixture. Place each apple in microproof custard cup. Add 2 tablespoons water to each cup. Dot each apple with 1 teaspoon butter. Place in oven. Cover with waxed paper. Set recipe number 243. Touch START. *(Oven cooks: HI, 5 minutes; stands: 0, 3 minutes.)*

2 servings

Recipe No. 244

Baked Maple Bananas

Preset Cooking Time: 3 minutes

- 2 tablespoons butter or margarine
- 3 tablespoons maple syrup
- 4 bananas, cut in half crosswise and then lengthwise
- 1 tablespoon lemon juice
- 1/4 teaspoon cinnamon (optional)

Place butter in shallow microproof baking dish. Place in oven. Set recipe number 244. Touch START. *(Oven cooks: HI, 30 seconds.)*

At Pause, add maple syrup; blend well. Add bananas. Spoon butter mixture over bananas. Touch START. *(Oven cooks: HI, 1 minute.)*

At Pause, turn bananas over. Touch START. *(Oven cooks: HI, 1 1/2 minutes.)*

Sprinkle with lemon juice and cinnamon. Serve warm.

4 servings

You can also cook whole bananas and cut into serving portions at the table.

⊞ *Recipe can be increased. See "Quantity", page 12.*

Lemon Pineapple Creme (page 193), Baked Maple Bananas →

Recipe No. 245

Chocolate-Raisin Nut Clusters

Preset Cooking Time: 2½ minutes

1 pound semisweet chocolate
1 cup cashews
½ cup plump raisins

Place chocolate in 2-quart glass measure. Place in oven. Set recipe number 245. Touch START. *(Oven cooks: HI, 2½ minutes.)*

Add cashews and raisins; stir until blended. Drop mixture by teaspoonfuls onto waxed paper. Let stand until firm. If mixture in bowl becomes too firm, reheat on 30 for 1 to 2 minutes.

1½ pounds

Recipe No. 247

Chocolate Nut Brownies

Preset Cooking Time: 8 minutes

2 squares (1 ounce each) unsweetened chocolate
½ cup unsalted butter
2 large eggs
¾ cup sugar
½ cup all-purpose flour
1 tablespoon vanilla
1 teaspoon baking powder
¼ teaspoon salt
1 cup coarsely chopped walnuts
1 cup semisweet chocolate pieces
Confectioners sugar

Place chocolate squares and butter in 4-cup glass measure. Place in oven. Set recipe number 247. Touch START. *(Oven cooks: HI, 2 minutes.)*

At Pause, remove from oven. Stir; set aside. Break eggs into large bowl; beat with fork until blended. Add chocolate mixture, sugar, flour, vanilla, baking powder, and salt; blend well. Stir in walnuts and chocolate pieces. Pour into 9-inch microproof deep-dish pie plate or quiche dish. Place in oven. Touch START. *(Oven cooks: HI, 6 minutes.)*

Cool completely before sprinkling with confectioners sugar. Cut into wedges.

10 brownies

Recipe No. 246 ⊞

Brownie Mix

Preset Cooking Time: 9 minutes

1 package (16 ounces) brownie mix
1 tablespoon confectioners sugar

Butter 8-inch round microproof pie plate; set aside. Prepare brownie batter as directed on package. Pour into prepared pie plate. Place in oven. Set recipe number 246. Touch START. *(Oven cooks: 50, 7 minutes; HI, 2 minutes.)* Rotate dish if rising unevenly.

Let stand until cooled. Sprinkle with confectioners sugar, and cut into wedges or squares.

16 brownies

⊞ *Recipe can be increased. See "Quantity", page 12.*

Recipe No. 248

Cake Mix

Preset Cooking Time: 8 minutes

1 package (9 ounces) single-layer cake mix

Line bottom of 9-inch round microproof baking dish with waxed paper; set aside. Prepare cake batter as directed on package. Pour into prepared dish. Place straight-sided, 2-inch diameter glass, open end up, in center of dish. Place in oven. Set recipe number 248. Touch START. *(Oven cooks:* 60, 7 *minutes; HI,* 1 *minute.)*

Let cool in pan 3 to 5 minutes. Gently twist glass to remove before inverting cake onto serving plate. Remove waxed paper.

1 layer

A 6-cup microproof Bundt-type pan or ring mold can be substituted for baking dish with glass.

Recipe No. 249

Caramel Nut Candy

Preset Cooking Time: 3 minutes

1 pound light caramels
2 tablespoons water
2 cups (12 ounces) mixed nuts

Lightly butter 8-inch square baking pan; set aside. Place caramels and water in 2-quart glass measure. Place in oven. Set recipe number 249. Touch START. *(Oven cooks: HI,* 3 *minutes.)*

Stir with wooden spoon until caramels are completely melted. Blend in nuts. Pour into prepared pan and refrigerate until firm. Cut into 1-inch squares. Wrap each piece in plastic wrap before storing.

64 pieces

Recipe No. 250

Chocolate Chip Bars

Preset Cooking Time: 7 minutes

½ cup butter or margarine
¾ cup firmly packed brown sugar
2 large eggs, lightly beaten
1 teaspoon vanilla
1 cup chopped nuts
1 cup semisweet chocolate pieces
½ cup all-purpose flour
1 teaspoon baking powder
Confectioners sugar or instant cocoa drink mix

Place butter in 2-quart glass measure. Place in oven. Set recipe number 250. Touch START. *(Oven cooks: HI,* 1 *minute.)*

At Pause, remove from oven. Add brown sugar, eggs, and vanilla; blend well. Stir in nuts, chocolate, flour, and baking powder. Spread in 9-inch round microproof baking dish. Place in oven. Touch START. *(Oven cooks: HI,* 6 *minutes.)* If bars are rising unevenly, touch STOP, and rotate dish one-quarter turn. Touch START.

Let stand in pan until cool. Sprinkle with confectioners sugar, and cut into bars or wedges.

24 bars

Recipe No. 251

Chocolate Fudge Frosting

Preset Cooking Time: 3 minutes

1 square (1 ounce) unsweetened chocolate
1 cup sugar
⅓ cup milk
¼ cup butter or margarine
⅛ teaspoon salt
1 teaspoon vanilla
¼ cup chopped nuts

Combine chocolate, sugar, milk, butter, and salt in 4-cup glass measure. Place in oven. Set recipe number 251. Touch START. *(Oven cooks: HI,* 1½ *minutes.)*

At Pause, stir. Touch START. *(Oven cooks: HI,* 1½ *minutes.)*

Add vanilla; beat with electric mixer until almost cool. Add nuts; beat until mixture is spreading consistency.

1 cup

Recipe No. 252

Chocolate Pudding Cake

Preset Cooking Time: 16¾ minutes

- 1 cup all-purpose flour
- ¾ cup sugar
- 2 tablespoons unsweetened cocoa powder
- 2 teaspoons baking powder
- ½ teaspoon salt
- 2 tablespoons butter
- ½ cup milk
- ½ cup chopped nuts
- 1 teaspoon vanilla
- 1¼ cups water
- ¾ cup firmly packed brown sugar
- ¼ cup unsweetened cocoa powder
- Whipped cream

Sift flour, granulated sugar, 2 tablespoons cocoa, baking powder, and salt into bowl; set aside. Place butter in 1-cup glass measure. Place in oven. Set recipe number 252. Touch START. *(Oven cooks: HI, 45 seconds.)*

At Pause, remove from oven. Add butter, milk, nuts, and vanilla to flour mixture; blend well. Pour into 8-inch round microproof baking dish. Combine water, brown sugar, and ¼ cup cocoa; pour evenly over batter; do not stir. Place in oven. Cover with paper towel. Touch START. *(Oven cooks: HI, 11 minutes; stands:* 0, 5 *minutes.)*

Cake will be soft and uneven in appearance. Spoon into individual serving dishes. Serve topped with whipped cream.

9 servings

Recipe No. 253

Cherry Crunch

Preset Cooking Time: 20 minutes

- 1 package (9 ounces) single-layer white or yellow cake mix
- ¼ cup chopped nuts
- 2 tablespoons brown sugar
- 2 teaspoons cinnamon
- 1 can (21 ounces) cherry pie filling
- ½ cup butter or margarine
- Whipped cream or vanilla ice cream

Combine cake mix, nuts, brown sugar, and cinnamon. Spoon pie filling evenly into 8-inch round microproof baking dish; sprinkle evenly with cake mix mixture; set aside. Place butter in 1-cup glass measure. Place in oven. Set recipe number 253. Touch START. *(Oven cooks: HI,* 1 *minute.)*

At Pause, remove from oven. Drizzle over cake mix mixture. Place baking dish in oven. Touch START. *(Oven cooks: HI, 7 minutes.)*

At Pause, rotate dish one-quarter turn. Touch START. *(Oven cooks: HI, 7 minutes; stands:* 0, 5 *minutes.)*

Serve warm, topped with whipped cream.

6 to 8 servings

Recipe No. 254

Chewy Coconut Bars

Preset Cooking Time: 7 minutes

- ½ cup butter or margarine
- 2 large eggs
- ¾ cup firmly packed brown sugar
- ½ cup all-purpose flour
- 1 teaspoon baking powder
- 1 teaspoon vanilla
- 1 cup chopped nuts
- 1 cup flaked coconut
- Confectioners sugar

Place butter in 1-cup glass measure. Place in oven. Set recipe number 254. Touch START. *(Oven cooks: HI,* 1 *minute.)*

At Pause, remove from oven; set aside. Break eggs into mixing bowl. Beat with electric mixer until lemon-colored. Add butter, brown sugar, flour, baking powder, and vanilla; blend well. Stir in nuts and coconut. Pour into 8-inch round microproof baking dish. Place in oven. Touch START. *(Oven cooks: HI, 6 minutes.)*

Sprinkle with confectioners sugar. Cool completely before cutting into bars or wedges.

18 to 20 bars

Chocolate Nut Brownies (page 186), Chewy Coconut Bars, Chocolate Chip Bars (page 187), Date Oatmeal Bars (page 190) →

Recipe No. 255

Cranapple Jelly

Preset Cooking Time: 24 minutes

- 4 cups cranapple juice
- 1 package ($1\frac{3}{4}$ ounces) powdered fruit pectin
- 4 cups sugar

Combine juice and pectin in 4-quart microproof casserole. Cover and place in oven. Set recipe number 255. Touch START. *(Oven cooks: HI, 7 minutes.)*

At Pause, stir. Cover. Touch START. *(Oven cooks: HI, 5 minutes.)*

At Pause, add sugar; blend well. Do not cover. Touch START. *(Oven cooks: HI, 6 minutes.)*

At Pause, stir. Touch START. *(Oven cooks: HI, 6 minutes.)*

Skim foam with metal spoon. Pour into hot sterilized jars, and seal.

6 cups

Recipe No. 256

Coconut Squares

Preset Cooking Time: 8 minutes

- $\frac{1}{4}$ cup butter or margarine
- 1 cup graham-cracker crumbs
- 1 teaspoon sugar
- 1 cup flaked coconut
- $\frac{2}{3}$ cup sweetened condensed milk
- $\frac{1}{2}$ cup chopped nuts
- 1 cup semisweet chocolate pieces

Place butter in 9-inch round microproof baking dish. Place in oven. Set recipe number 256. Touch START. *(Oven cooks: HI, 1 minute.)*

At Pause, add cracker crumbs and sugar; blend well. Pat mixture firmly into bottom of dish. Touch START. *(Oven cooks: HI, 2 minutes.)*

At Pause, remove from oven; let stand until partially cooled. Combine coconut, milk, and nuts; spoon carefully over crust. Place in oven. Touch START. *(Oven cooks: HI, 4 minutes.)*

At Pause, sprinkle with chocolate. Touch START. *(Oven cooks: HI, 1 minute.)*

Spread melted chocolate evenly over crust. Cool before cutting into squares or wedges.

16 to 20 squares

Recipe No. 257

Crumb Crust

Preset Cooking Time: 3 minutes

- 5 tablespoons butter or margarine
- $1\frac{1}{4}$ cups fine graham-cracker crumbs
- 1 tablespoon sugar

Place butter in 9-inch microproof pie plate. Place in oven. Set recipe number 257. Touch START. *(Oven cooks: HI, $1\frac{1}{2}$ minutes.)*

At Pause, blend in cracker crumbs and sugar. If desired, set aside 2 tablespoons crumb mixture to sprinkle over top of pie. Press remaining crumb mixture firmly into bottom and sides of plate. Touch START. *(Oven cooks: HI, $1\frac{1}{2}$ minutes.)*

Cool completely before filling.

One 9-inch pie shell

Vanilla wafers, gingersnaps, or chocolate wafers also make delicious crumb crusts.

Recipe No. 258

Date Oatmeal Bars

Preset Cooking Time: 12 minutes

- 1 cup chopped dates
- $\frac{1}{2}$ cup raisins
- $\frac{1}{2}$ cup water
- 2 tablespoons sugar
- 1 tablespoon all-purpose flour
- $\frac{1}{2}$ cup chopped nuts
- $\frac{1}{2}$ cup butter or margarine
- $\frac{1}{4}$ teaspoon baking soda
- 1 tablespoon water
- 1 cup firmly packed brown sugar
- 1 cup all-purpose flour
- 1 cup rolled oats
- $\frac{1}{4}$ teaspoon salt
- 1 teaspoon cinnamon

Grease 9-inch round microproof baking dish; set aside. Combine dates, raisins, $\frac{1}{2}$ cup water, sugar, and 1 tablespoon flour in microproof bowl. Place in oven. Set recipe number 258. Touch START. *(Oven cooks: HI, 2 minutes.)*

At Pause, stir. Cover. Touch START. *(Oven cooks: HI, 1 minute.)*

At Pause, remove from oven. Stir in nuts; set aside. Place butter in large microproof bowl. Place in oven. Touch START. *(Oven cooks: HI, 1 minute.)*

At Pause, remove from oven. Dissolve baking soda in remaining 1 tablespoon water. Add to butter; add brown sugar, remaining 1 cup flour, oats, and salt. Firmly pat two thirds of the mixture into prepared baking dish. Spread with date mixture. Stir cinnamon into remaining oat mixture; crumble over date mixture. Place in oven. Touch START. *(Oven cooks: HI, 8 minutes.)*

Cover with aluminum foil, and let stand until cool. Cut into bars or wedges.

24 bars

Recipe No. 259

Devil's Food Cake

Preset Cooking Time: 18 minutes

- 2 cups sifted all-purpose flour
- 1 1/4 teaspoons baking soda
- 1/4 teaspoon salt
- 2 cups sugar
- 1/2 cup shortening
- 1/2 cup unsweetened cocoa powder
- 1 teaspoon vanilla
- 1 cup boiling water
- 1/2 cup buttermilk
- 2 large eggs, beaten

Grease bottoms of two 8-inch round microproof baking dishes. Line bottoms with waxed paper; set aside. Sift together flour, baking soda, and salt; set aside. Cream sugar, shortening, cocoa, and vanilla in large mixing bowl with electric mixer until light and fluffy. Stir in boiling water, buttermilk, and eggs; blend well. Gradually beat in flour mixture until smooth. Divide mixture between prepared pans. Place 1 pan in oven. Set recipe number 259. Touch START. *(Oven cooks: 50, 8 minutes.)*

At Pause, rotate pan one-quarter turn. Touch START. *(Oven cooks: HI, 1 minute.)*

At Pause, remove from oven. Place second pan in oven. Touch START. *(Oven cooks: 50, 8 minutes.)*

While second layer is cooking, let first layer stand 5 minutes before inverting onto wire rack.

At Pause, rotate pan one-quarter turn. Touch START. *(Oven cooks: HI, 1 minute.)*

Remove from oven. Let stand 5 minutes before inverting onto wire rack. Remove waxed paper, and cool completely before frosting.

8 to 10 servings

To frost and fill, try Chocolate Fudge Frosting (page 187) or Snow White Frosting (page 198).

Recipe No. 260

Danish Apple Pie

Preset Cooking Time: 12 minutes

- 7 cooking apples, peeled, cored, and sliced (about 6 cups)
- 3/4 cup sugar
- 2 tablespoons all-purpose flour
- 1 teaspoon cinnamon
- 1/8 teaspoon salt
- 1 baked 9-inch Homemade Pie Shell (page 192)
- 1/4 cup all-purpose flour
- 1/4 cup firmly packed brown sugar
- 2 tablespoons butter or margarine

Place apples in large bowl. Combine granulated sugar, 2 tablespoons flour, cinnamon, and salt; sprinkle over apples; toss lightly to coat. Arrange apples evenly in pie shell. Combine 1/4 cup flour and brown sugar; cut in butter with pastry blender or 2 knives. Sprinkle evenly over apples. Place in oven. Set recipe number 260. Touch START. *(Oven cooks: HI, 12 minutes.)*

Cool before serving.

6 to 8 servings

If you are in a hurry and use a ready-made pie shell, be sure to place it in a microproof pie plate before filling.

Recipe No. 261

Fluffy Tapioca

Preset Cooking Time: 16 minutes

- 2 cups milk
- 3 tablespoons quick-cooking tapioca
- 5 tablespoons sugar, divided
- 1 large egg, separated
- 1/8 teaspoon salt
- 1 teaspoon vanilla
- Apricot Dessert Sauce (page 170)

Combine milk, tapioca, 3 tablespoons sugar, egg yolk, and salt in 2-quart microproof casserole; blend well. Place in oven. Set recipe number 261. Touch START. *(Oven stands:* 0, 5 *minutes; cooks: HI,* 6 *minutes.)*

At Pause, beat with wire whisk until well blended. Touch START. *(Oven cooks:* 70, 5 *minutes.)*

Meanwhile, beat egg white in small mixing bowl with electric mixer until foamy. Gradually beat in remaining 2 tablespoons sugar until soft peaks form.

Stir vanilla into tapioca. Fold egg whites into tapioca a little at a time until just blended. Serve topped with Apricot Dessert Sauce.

5 servings

Recipe No. 262

Fresh Strawberry Jam

Preset Cooking Time: 23 minutes

- 5 cups crushed hulled strawberries
- 2 teaspoons lemon juice
- 1 package (1 3/4 ounces) powdered fruit pectin
- 7 cups sugar

Combine strawberries, lemon juice, and pectin in 6-quart microproof casserole. Place in oven. Set recipe number 262. Touch START. *(Oven cooks: HI,* 5 *minutes.)*

At Pause, stir. Touch START. *(Oven cooks: HI,* 6 *minutes.)*

At Pause, add sugar; blend well. Touch START. *(Oven cooks: HI,* 6 *minutes.)*

At Pause, stir. Touch START. *(Oven cooks: HI,* 6 *minutes.)*

Skim foam with metal spoon. Pour into hot sterilized jars, and seal.

2 quarts

Recipe No. 263

Golden Apple Chunks

Preset Cooking Time: 8 minutes

- 4 medium cooking apples, peeled, cored, and cut into quarters
- 1/4 cup firmly packed brown sugar
- 1 teaspoon cinnamon
- 2 tablespoons butter or margarine

Place apples in 1-quart microproof casserole. Combine brown sugar and cinnamon; sprinkle over apples. Dot with butter. Cover and place in oven. Set recipe number 263. Touch START. *(Oven cooks: HI,* 4 *minutes.)*

At Pause, stir. Touch START. *(Oven cooks: HI,* 4 *minutes.)*

4 servings

Recipe No. 264

Homemade Pie Shell

Preset Cooking Time: 6 minutes

- 1 cup all-purpose flour
- 1 teaspoon salt
- 6 tablespoons shortening
- 2 tablespoons ice water
- 1 large egg, lightly beaten

Combine flour and salt. Cut in shortening with pastry blender or 2 knives until mixture is consistency of small peas. Sprinkle with ice water. Stir with fork until mixture holds together. Gather into a ball. Roll out on floured pastry cloth to 12-inch circle. Fit into 9-inch microproof pie plate. Trim and flute edge. Prick at intervals with fork. Brush with egg. Place in oven. Set recipe number 264. Touch START. *(Oven cooks: HI,* 6 *minutes.)*

Cool completely before filling.

One 9-inch pie shell

Recipe No. 265

Lemon Pineapple Crème

Preset Cooking Time: 6 minutes

- 1 can (8 ounces) crushed pineapple
- 3/4 cup sugar, divided
- 2/3 cup water
- 3 tablespoons cornstarch
- 2 large eggs, separated
- 1 package (3 ounces) cream cheese, cut into cubes
- 2 tablespoons lemon juice
- 1 teaspoon grated lemon peel

Combine pineapple, 1/2 cup sugar, water, and cornstarch in 4-cup glass measure; stir until cornstarch is dissolved. Place in oven. Set recipe number 265. Touch START. *(Oven cooks: HI, 2 1/2 minutes.)*

At Pause, stir. Touch START. *(Oven cooks: HI, 2 1/2 minutes.)*

At Pause, beat egg yolks in small mixing bowl with electric mixer until lemon-colored. Stir into pineapple mixture; stir in cream cheese, lemon juice, and lemon peel. Touch START. *(Oven cooks:* 80, 1 *minute.)*

Beat with electric mixer until blended. Let stand until cool. Beat egg whites in small bowl until frothy. Gradually beat in remaining 1/4 cup sugar until soft peaks form. Fold into pudding. Spoon into individual dessert dishes, and chill before serving.

5 to 6 servings

Recipe No. 266

Mints

Preset Cooking Time: 6 minutes

- 2 cups sugar
- 1/4 cup light corn syrup
- 1/4 cup milk
- 1/4 teaspoon cream of tartar
- 8 to 10 drops peppermint extract, to taste
- Red or green food coloring

Combine sugar, corn syrup, milk, and cream of tartar in 2-quart glass measure. Place in oven. Set recipe number 266. Touch START. *(Oven cooks: HI, 6 minutes.)*

Let stand 3 minutes, or until slightly cooled. Beat with electric mixer until creamy, flavoring with peppermint extract and tinting with food coloring. Drop by teaspoonfuls onto aluminum foil. Let stand until cool. Store in airtight container.

36 mints

Recipe No. 267

Peanut Brittle

Preset Cooking Time: 9 minutes

- 1 cup sugar
- 1/2 cup corn syrup
- 1 3/4 to 2 cups unsalted dry-roasted peanuts
- 1 teaspoon butter or margarine
- 1 teaspoon vanilla
- 1 teaspoon baking soda

Generously grease large baking sheet; set aside. Combine sugar and corn syrup in 2-quart glass measure. Place in oven. Set recipe number 267. Touch START. *(Oven cooks: HI, 4 minutes.)*

At Pause, stir in peanuts with wooden spoon. Touch START. *(Oven cooks: HI, 3 minutes.)*

At Pause, stir in butter and vanilla. Touch START. *(Oven cooks: HI, 2 minutes.)*

Add baking soda; stir until light and foamy. Pour onto prepared baking sheet; spread quickly to edges using back of wooden spoon. As candy cools, stretch into thin sheet using palms of hands. Cool completely before breaking into pieces. Store in airtight container in cool place.

1 pound

Recipe No. 268

Peanut Crispy Bars

Preset Cooking Time: 3½ minutes

- ¼ cup butter or margarine
- 5 cups miniature or 40 regular marshmallows
- ⅓ cup peanut butter
- 5 cups crispy rice cereal
- 1 cup unsalted dry-roasted peanuts, chopped

Lightly grease 12 × 7-inch baking dish; set aside. Place butter in 3-quart microproof bowl. Place in oven. Set recipe number 268. Touch START. *(Oven cooks: HI, 1 minute.)*

At Pause, add marshmallows. Cover. Touch START. *(Oven cooks: HI, 2½ minutes.)*

Add peanut butter; stir until smooth. Stir in cereal and peanuts. Press warm mixture into prepared baking dish. Cool before cutting into bars.

36 bars

Recipe No. 269

Pecan Pie

Preset Cooking Time: 13 minutes

- ¼ cup butter or margarine
- 1¼ cups pecan halves
- 1 cup sugar
- ½ cup dark corn syrup
- 3 large eggs, lightly beaten
- 1 teaspoon vanilla
- ⅛ teaspoon salt
- 1 baked 9-inch Homemade Pie Shell (page 192)

Place butter in microproof bowl. Place in oven. Set recipe number 269. Touch START. *(Oven cooks: HI, 1 minute.)*

At Pause, add remaining ingredients except pie shell; blend well. Pour into pie shell. Place in oven. Touch START. *(Oven cooks: 70, 12 minutes.)*

Cool to room temperature or chill before serving.

8 servings

If you are in a hurry and use a ready-made pie shell, be sure to place it in a microproof pie plate before filling.

Recipe No. 270

Fresh Peaches in Raspberry Liqueur

Preset Cooking Time: 7½ minutes

- 3 tablespoons raspberry liqueur
- 2 large peaches, halved, peeled and pitted

Place liqueur in small glass bowl. Place in oven. Set recipe number 270. Touch START. *(Oven cooks: HI, 30 seconds.)*

At Pause, add peaches; stir to coat. Touch START. *(Oven cooks: 50, 5 minutes; stands: 0, 2 minutes.)*

Gently stir peaches to coat with liqueur. Serve hot over ice cream. For a special occasion, divide between 2 wine glasses and fill glasses with champagne.

2 servings

Recipe No. 271 ⊞

Pudding Mix

Preset Cooking Time: 7 minutes

- 1 package (3¼ ounces) pudding and pie filling mix
- 2 cups milk

Place pudding mix in 2-quart microproof bowl. Stir in milk. Place in oven. Set recipe number 271. Touch START. *(Oven cooks: HI, 4 minutes.)*

At Pause, stir. Touch START. *(Oven cooks: HI, 3 minutes.)*

Pour into individual dessert dishes, and chill before serving.

4 servings

⊞ *Recipe can be increased. See "Quantity", page 12.*

Recipe No. 272

Pumpkin Cupcakes

Preset Cooking Time: 12 minutes

- 1/2 cup firmly packed brown sugar
- 1/4 cup sugar
- 1 large egg
- 6 tablespoons vegetable oil
- 1/2 cup canned or mashed cooked pumpkin
- 1/2 teaspoon vanilla
- 1 cup all-purpose flour
- 2 tablespoons milk
- 1/2 teaspoon cinnamon
- 1/2 teaspoon salt
- 1/4 teaspoon baking powder
- 1/4 teaspoon baking soda
- 1/8 teaspoon ginger

Combine sugars, egg, and oil; beat until smooth. Blend in pumpkin and vanilla. Add remaining ingredients; blend until smooth. Spoon batter into 6 paper-lined microproof custard or muffin cups, filling cups half full. Place in oven. If using custard cups, arrange in circle. Set recipe number 272. Touch START. *(Oven cooks:* 30, 6 *minutes.)* If cupcakes are rising unevenly, touch STOP, and rotate cups one-quarter turn. Touch START.

At Pause, remove from oven. Pour remaining batter into cups as above. Place in oven. Touch START. *(Oven cooks:* 30, 6 *minutes.)*

Cool completely before frosting with your favorite cream cheese frosting.

12 cupcakes

Recipe No. 273

Raisin Bread Pudding

Preset Cooking Time: 18 1/2 minutes

- 4 slices raisin bread, cut into cubes (about 4 cups)
- 1/4 cup raisins
- 3 large eggs
- 1/2 cup firmly packed brown sugar
- 1 teaspoon vanilla
- Dash salt
- 2 cups milk
- 2 tablespoons butter or margarine
- Cinnamon or nutmeg

Combine bread and raisins in 2-quart round microproof baking dish; set aside. Combine eggs, brown sugar, vanilla, and salt; beat until well blended; set aside. Combine milk and butter in 2-quart glass measure. Place in oven. Set recipe number 273. Touch START. *(Oven cooks: HI, 4 1/2 minutes.)*

At Pause, remove from oven. Gradually stir egg mixture into milk mixture. Pour over bread and raisins. Sprinkle with cinnamon. Place in oven. Cover with waxed paper. Touch START. *(Oven cooks:* 50, 14 *minutes.)*

Center may be slightly soft but will set as pudding cools. Serve warm or chilled.

6 servings

Recipe No. 274

Rich Chocolate Fudge

Preset Cooking Time: 20 minutes

- 4 cups sugar
- 1 can (13 ounces) evaporated milk, undiluted
- 1 cup butter or margarine
- 1 package (12 ounces) semisweet chocolate pieces
- 1 jar (7 ounces) marshmallow creme
- 1 cup chopped nuts
- 1 teaspoon vanilla

Butter 9-inch square or 12×7-inch baking dish; set aside. Combine sugar, milk, and butter in 4-quart microproof bowl. Place in oven. Set recipe number 274. Touch START. *(Oven cooks: HI, 10 minutes.)*

At Pause, stir. Touch START. *(Oven cooks: HI, 10 minutes.)*

Stir in chocolate and marshmallow creme; blend well. Stir in nuts and vanilla. Pour into prepared dish. Cool before cutting into squares.

48 squares

Recipe No. 275

Rocky Road Candy

Preset Cooking Time: 5 minutes

- 1 package (12 ounces) semisweet chocolate pieces
- 1 package (12 ounces) butterscotch pieces
- ½ cup butter
- 1 package (10½ ounces) miniature marshmallows
- 1 cup chopped nuts

Butter 13×9-inch baking dish; set aside. Combine chocolate, butterscotch, and butter in 4-quart microproof bowl. Place in oven. Set recipe number 275. Touch START. *(Oven cooks: 70, 5 minutes.)*

Stir until blended. Stir in marshmallows and nuts. Pour into prepared dish and spread evenly. Refrigerate 2 hours, or until set before cutting into squares.

45 squares

Try these variations: Substitute ½ cup chopped nuts plus ½ cup chopped dried fruit, or 1 cup chopped dried fruit for the cup chopped nuts. Dried apricots, pitted prunes, or candied fruit would be delicious.

Rocky Road Candy, Almond Bark (page 183), Mints (page 193) →

Recipe No. 276

Scotch Nut Oatmeal Cake

Preset Cooking Time: 15¼ minutes

- 2 tablespoons butter or margarine
- ¾ cup firmly packed brown sugar, divided
- ¼ cup butterscotch pieces
- ¼ cup chopped walnuts
- ¾ cup water
- ½ cup rolled oats
- ¼ cup butter or margarine, cut up
- ½ cup sugar
- 1 large egg
- ¾ cup all-purpose flour
- ½ teaspoon baking soda
- ½ teaspoon salt
- ½ teaspoon cinnamon
- ½ teaspoon nutmeg

Place 2 tablespoons butter in 8-inch round microproof baking dish. Place in oven. Set recipe number 276. Touch START. *(Oven cooks: HI, 45 seconds.)*

At Pause, remove from oven. Combine ¼ cup brown sugar, butterscotch pieces, and walnuts; mix lightly. Spread evenly over butter in bottom of baking dish. Place straight-sided, 2-inch diameter glass, open end up, in center of baking dish; set aside. Pour water into microproof bowl. Place in oven. Touch START. *(Oven cooks: HI, 2 minutes.)*

At Pause, stir oats and ¼ cup butter into water. Let stand until butter is softened. Add sugar, remaining ½ cup brown sugar, and egg; blend well. Add remaining ingredients; stir just until blended. Pour over nut mixture in baking dish. Place in oven. Touch START. *(Oven cooks: HI, 7½ minutes; stands:* 0, 5 *minutes.)*

Gently twist glass to remove. Invert cake onto serving plate. Serve warm or chilled.

8 servings

A 6-cup microproof Bundt-type pan or ring mold can be substituted for baking dish with glass. After melting butter in pan, spread over sides with pastry brush.

Recipe No. 277

Snow White Frosting

Preset Cooking Time: 4 to 5 minutes

- 1 cup sugar
- ½ cup water
- ¼ teaspoon cream of tartar
- Dash salt
- 2 egg whites
- 1 teaspoon vanilla

Combine sugar, water, cream of tartar, and salt in 2-cup glass measure. Place in oven. Insert temperature probe. Set recipe number 277. Touch START. *(Oven cooks:* 70, 4 *to* 5 *minutes to* 200°F; *holds warm:* 10.)

Beat egg whites in small mixing bowl with electric mixer until soft peaks form. Gradually beat hot syrup into egg whites. Beat in vanilla. Beat 5 minutes, or until thick and fluffy.

1½ to 2 cups

Recipe No. 278

Yogurt Pumpkin Pie

Preset Cooking Time: 3 minutes

- 1 cup canned or cooked mashed pumpkin
- ¼ cup firmly packed brown sugar
- 1 teaspoon cinnamon
- ½ teaspoon nutmeg
- ¼ teaspoon ginger
- ¼ teaspoon salt
- 1 container (9 ounces) frozen whipped topping
- 1 container (8 ounces) vanilla yogurt
- 1 9-inch Crumb Crust Pie Shell (page 190)

Combine pumpkin, brown sugar, cinnamon, nutmeg, ginger, and salt in 3-quart microproof bowl. Place in oven. Set recipe number 278. Touch START. *(Oven cooks: HI, 2 minutes.)*

At Pause, remove from oven and let stand 10 minutes. Remove cover from whipped topping. Place in oven. Touch START. *(Oven cooks:* 30, 1 *minute.)*

Stir topping carefully. Fold topping and yogurt into cooled pumpkin mixture. Spoon into pie shell. Refrigerate about 4 hours, or until set.

6 servings

From Freezer to Table — Fast!

One of the great attractions of the microwave oven is its ability to defrost raw food or heat frozen cooked food. Detailed Defrosting Guides are provided at the beginning of the recipe chapters, in general, to aid your preparation of the food included in those recipes. Here, as a special convenience, many common and frequently used items that have been included among the 300 preset recipes are presented for you. We've also included some basic information about microwave defrosting. You'll also want to spend more time studying the special Programmed Defrost method and instructions on using the temperature probe spacer in your Use & Care Manual. Many of the same principles and techniques that apply to microwave cooking also apply to microwave defrosting and heating. Microwaves are attracted to water or moisture molecules. As soon as microwaves have thawed a portion of the item, they are more attracted to the thawed portion. The frozen portion continues to thaw, but

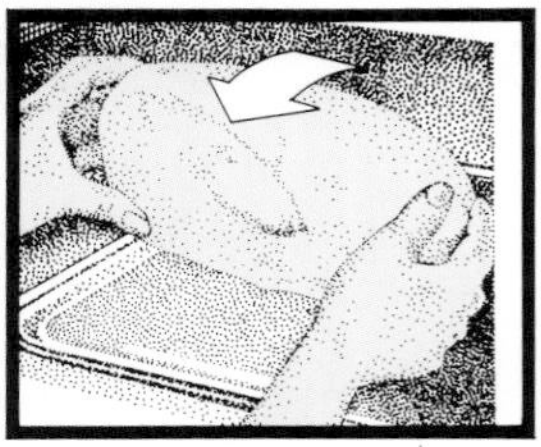

Defrost most food in its original wrapper (above left). Thawed portions of ground beef (above) are removed from the oven so cooking does not start. Fish fillets (far left) are separated as soon as possible. Many foods are turned over during defrosting (left).

this is due to the warmth produced in the thawed portion. Special techniques, such as shielding and rotating, are helpful to be sure the thawed portion does not cook before the rest defrosts. It is often necessary to turn, stir, and separate to assist the defrosting process. Defrosting requires standing time to complete. Because food differs in size, weight, and density, recommended defrosting times can only be approximate. Additional standing time may be necessary to defrost completely. Read the Defrosting Guides throughout the book for times, temperature, and special instructions about defrosting specific foods. Here are some tips to aid you toward fast and easy defrosting.

- ☐ Poultry, seafood, fish, meat, and most vegetables may be defrosted in their original closed package. You may leave metal clips in poultry during defrosting, but you should remove them as soon as possible before cooking. Replace metal twists on bags with string or rubber bands before defrosting.
- ☐ Plastic-wrapped packages from the supermarket meat department may not be wrapped with a plastic wrap recommended for microwave use. If in doubt, unwrap package and place food on a microproof plate.
- ☐ Poultry wings, legs, and the small or bony ends of meat or fish may need to be covered with pieces of aluminum foil for part of the thawing time to prevent cooking while the remainder thaws.
- ☐ Large items should be turned and rotated halfway through defrosting time to provide more even thawing.
- ☐ Food textures influence thawing time. Because of air space, porous foods like cake and bread defrost more quickly than a solid mass, such as a sauce, or roast.
- ☐ Do not thaw food wrapped in aluminum or in foil dishes except as approved, page 17.
- ☐ The edges will begin cooking if meat, fish, and seafood are completely thawed in the microwave oven. Therefore, food should still be icy in the center when removed from oven. It will finish thawing while standing.
- ☐ Remove portions of ground meat as soon as thawed, returning frozen portions to the oven.
- ☐ To thaw half of a frozen vegetable package, wrap half the package with aluminum foil. When unwrapped side is thawed, separate and return balance to freezer.
- ☐ Thin or sliced items, such as fish fillets, meat patties, etc., should be separated as soon as possible. Remove thawed pieces and allow others to continue thawing.
- ☐ Casseroles, saucy foods, vegetables, and soups should be stirred once or twice during defrosting to redistribute heat.
- ☐ Frozen fried foods may be defrosted but will not be crisp when heated in the microwave oven.
- ☐ Freezing tips: It is helpful to freeze in small quantities rather than in one large piece. When freezing casseroles, it's a good idea to insert an empty paper cup in the center so no food is present there. This speeds thawing. Depressing the center of ground meat when freezing also hastens thawing later. Take care to wrap and package food well to retain its original quality. The wrapped food should be air-free, with air-tight seals. Store at 0°F. or less for no longer than the times recommended for freezing.

Recipe No. 279

Ground Beef

Preset Defrost Time: 11 minutes

1 pound frozen lean ground beef

Remove any metal rings, wire twist ties, or foil wrapping from package. Place beef in package in microproof baking dish. Place in oven. Set recipe number 279. Touch START. *(Oven defrosts:* 30, 3 *minutes.)*

At Pause, turn meat over. Remove thawed portions from oven. Touch START. *(Oven defrosts:* 30, 3 *minutes; stands:* 0, 5 *minutes.)*

Recipe No. 280 ⊞

Rolled Rib Roast

Preset Defrost Time: 28 minutes

1 frozen rolled rib roast (3 pounds)

Remove any metal rings, wire twist ties, or foil wrapping from package. Place roast in package in microproof baking dish. Place in oven. Set recipe number 280. Touch START. *(Oven defrosts:* 30, 10 *minutes.)*

At Pause, turn over. Touch START. *(Oven defrosts:* 30, 8 *minutes; stands:* 0, 10 *minutes.)*

It may be necessary to let roast stand additional time if still slightly frozen in center.

Recipe No. 281 ⊞

Steaks

Preset Defrost Time: 18 minutes

1 frozen steak (2 pounds)

Remove any metal rings, wire twist ties, or foil wrapping from package. Place steak in package in microproof baking dish. Place in oven. Set recipe number 281. Touch START. *(Oven defrosts:* 30, 4 *minutes.)*

At Pause, turn over. Touch START. *(Oven defrosts:* 30, 4 *minutes; stands:* 0, 10 *minutes.)*

Recipe No. 282 ⊞

Stew Beef

Preset Defrost Time: 16 minutes

2 pounds frozen beef for stew

Remove any metal rings, wire twist ties, or foil wrapping from package. Place beef in package in microproof baking dish. Place in oven. Set recipe number 282. Touch START. *(Oven defrosts:* 30, 3 *minutes.)*

At Pause, turn beef over and separate into pieces. Touch START. *(Oven defrosts:* 30, 3 *minutes; stands:* 0, 10 *minutes.)*

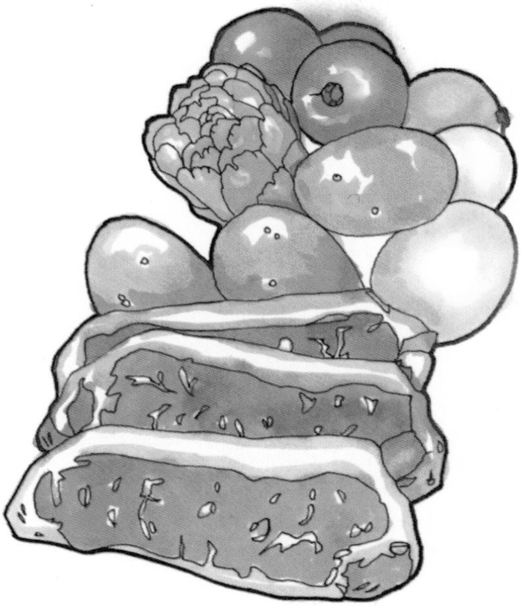

Recipe No. 283

Pork Chops

Preset Defrost Time: 14 minutes

1 pound frozen pork chops, ½ inch thick

Remove any metal rings, wire twist ties, or foil wrapping from package. Place chops in package in microproof baking dish. Place in oven. Set recipe number 283. Touch START. *(Oven defrosts:* 30, 2 *minutes.)*

At Pause, turn chops over and separate. Touch START. *(Oven defrosts:* 30, 2 *minutes; stands:* 0, 10 *minutes.)*

⊞ *Recipe can be increased. See "Quantity", page 12.*

Recipe No. 284

Cut Up Chicken

Preset Defrost Time: 22 minutes

2 pounds frozen chicken parts

Remove any metal rings, wire twist ties, or foil wrapping from package. Place chicken in package in microproof baking dish. Place in oven. Set recipe number 284. Touch START. *(Oven defrosts:* 30, 7 *minutes.)*

At Pause, turn parts over and separate. If wing and leg tips begin to cook before centers are thoroughly defrosted, cover with small strips of aluminum foil, keeping foil at least 1 inch away from oven walls. Touch START. *(Oven defrosts:* 30, 5 *minutes; stands:* 0, 10 *minutes.)*

Recipe No. 285

Whole Chicken

Preset Defrost Time: 24 minutes

1 frozen whole chicken (3 pounds)

Remove any metal rings, wire twist ties, or foil wrapping from package. Place chicken in package in microproof baking dish. Place in oven. Set recipe number 285. Touch START. *(Oven defrosts:* 30, 7 *minutes.)*

At Pause, turn chicken over. Touch START. *(Oven defrosts:* 30, 7 *minutes, stands:* 0, 10 *minutes.)*

Recipe No. 286 ⊞

Fish Fillets

Preset Defrost Time: 11 minutes

1 pound frozen fish fillets

Remove any metal rings, wire twist ties, or foil wrapping from package. Place fillets in package in microproof baking dish. Place in oven. Set recipe number 286. Touch START. *(Oven defrosts:* 30, 4 *minutes.)*

At Pause, turn fillets over and separate. Touch START. *(Oven defrosts:* 30, 2 *minutes; stands:* 0, 5 *minutes.)*

Recipe No. 287 ⊞

Whole Fish

Preset Defrost Time: 11 minutes

1 frozen fish (10 ounces)

Remove any metal rings, wire twist ties, or foil wrapping from package. Place fish in package in shallow microproof baking dish. Place in oven. Cover head with aluminum foil. Set recipe number 287. Touch START. *(Oven defrosts:* 30, 4 *minutes.)*

At Pause, turn over. Touch START. *(Oven defrosts:* 30, 2 *minutes; stands:* 0, 5 *minutes.)*

⊞ *Recipe can be increased. See "Quantity", page 12.*

Frozen vegetables (page 204) can be thawed and cooked right in the package. Many other frozen foods can be placed right on a serving plate and thawed and cooked. →

Recipe No. 288 ⊞

Crab Meat

Preset Defrost Time: 7 minutes

1 package (6 ounces) frozen crab meat

Remove any metal rings, wire twist ties, or foil wrapping from package. Place crab meat in package in microproof baking dish. Place in oven. Set recipe number 288. Touch START. *(Oven defrosts:* 30, 1 *minute.)*

At Pause, turn crab meat over and separate. Touch START. *(Oven defrosts:* 30, 1 *minute; stands:* 0, 5 *minutes.)*

Recipe No. 289 ⊞

Shrimp

Preset Defrost Time: 9 minutes

1 package (1 pound) frozen shrimp

Remove shrimp from package and spread in shallow microproof baking dish. Place in oven. Set recipe number 289. Touch START. *(Oven defrosts:* 30, 2 *minutes.)*

At Pause, rearrange the shrimp. Touch START. *(Oven defrosts:* 30, 2 *minutes; stands:* 0, 5 *minutes.)*

Recipe No. 290 ⊞

Bread, Rolls

Preset Defrost Time: 2 minutes

1 loaf (1 pound) frozen bread, or 1 pound frozen rolls

Remove any metal rings, wire twist ties, or foil wrapping from package. Place bread in package in oven. Set recipe number 290. Touch START. *(Oven defrosts:* 30, 1 *minute.)*

At Pause, turn over. Touch START. *(Oven defrosts:* 30, 1 *minute.)*

Recipe No. 291 ⊞

Vegetables in Sauce

Preset Defrost/Cooking Time: 10 minutes

1 package (10 ounces) frozen vegetables in sauce

Slit pouch and place on microproof plate. Place in oven. Set recipe number 291. Touch START. *(Oven defrosts:* 70, 5 *minutes.)*

At Pause, turn over. Touch START. *(Oven cooks:* 70, 5 *minutes.)*

Pour into serving bowl, and stir before serving.

Recipe No. 292 ⊞

Broccoli, Carrots, Cauliflower

Preset Defrost/Cooking Time: 8 minutes

1 package (10 ounces) frozen broccoli, carrots, or cauliflower

Place vegetables in package on microproof plate. Place in oven. Set recipe number 292. Touch START. *(Oven defrosts/cooks: HI,* 8 *minutes.)*

Pour into serving bowl, and stir before serving.

Recipe No. 293 ⊞

Green Peas

Preset Defrost/Cooking Time: 6 minutes

1 package (10 ounces) frozen green peas

Place peas in package on microproof plate. Place in oven. Set recipe number 293. Touch START. *(Oven defrosts/cooks: HI,* 6 *minutes.)*

Pour into serving bowl, and stir before serving.

⊞ *Recipe can be increased. See "Quantity", page 12.*

Recipe No. 294 ⊞

Spinach

Preset Defrost/Cooking Time: 7 minutes

1 package (10 ounces) frozen spinach

Place spinach in package on microproof plate. Place in oven. Set recipe number 294. Touch START. *(Oven defrosts/cooks: HI, 7 minutes.)*

Let stand 2 minutes before serving.

Recipe No. 295 ⊞

Brownies and other frozen bar cookies

Preset Defrost/Cooking Time: 2 minutes

1 package (12 ounces) frozen brownies or other bar cookies

Remove lid from tray and place in oven. Set recipe number 295. Touch START. *(Oven defrosts: 30, 2 minutes.)*

Let stand 5 minutes before serving.

REMINDER

Additional defrosting information is provided in the Use & Care Manual and in the following Guides:

- ☐ Convenience Breads — Page 74
- ☐ Defrosting Guide - Meat — Pages 77-78
- ☐ Cooking/Defrosting Guide - Convenience Beef — Page 83
- ☐ Defrosting Guide - Poultry — Page 107
- ☐ Defrosting Guide - Seafood — Page 123
- ☐ Cooking/Defrosting Guide - Convenience Seafood — Page 123
- ☐ Cooking/Defrosting Guide - Convenience Rice and Pasta — Page 142
- ☐ Cooking/Defrosting Guide - Convenience Desserts — Page 183

Dinner's in the Oven

Dinner's in the oven! Who doesn't look forward to hearing this familiar saying as mealtime approaches? You'll find that just as in conventional cooking you can prepare a whole two- or three-dish meal at the same time in your microwave oven. For the most successful whole meal, it is important to consider the placement of dishes in the oven, the size and shape of the microproof containers, the kinds of food you select, the timing, and the sequence of cooking. This chapter provides you with all the necessary information and step-by-step instructions for organizing your own whole meals, as well as seven different whole meals that have been preset in the computer memory for you. Start by reading the following basic tips on how to approach whole meal planning:

- ☐ Since microwaves enter from the top of the oven, they are primarily attracted to food placed on the middle metal rack; a smaller amount reaches the bottom tray. It is logical then to place delicate, quick-cooking food on the bottom glass tray and longer-cooking food on the middle metal rack.
- ☐ Whenever the metal middle rack is not being used, remove it from oven.
- ☐ When using a browning dish, place it on the bottom glass tray. Do not cook other foods on the bottom glass tray at the same time.
- ☐ An ideal procedure for whole-meal cooking is to place two foods with similar cooking times on the middle metal rack and one shorter-cooking food on the bottom tray.
- ☐ If all foods require the same cooking time, reverse the location of dishes in the oven halfway through cooking tim.
- ☐ Take advantage of the full shelf area. If a glass baking dish is set on the middle metal rack dishes on the glass tray should be offset for maximum microwave coverage. They are not placed directly under the dish or dishes on the middle metal rack, for example.
- ☐ Check your cooking dishes to be sure they will fit on the same shelf before filling with food.
- ☐ Often covers with knobs are too high to fit easily when the middle metal rack is used. Use plastic wrap instead of casserole lids when necessary.
- ☐ All whole-meal cooking is done on HI.

IMPORTANT GUIDELINES FOR TIMING AND PLANNING

- ☐ If all foods take less than 15 minutes individually, add cooking times together and cook the menu for the total time.
- ☐ If all foods take 15 to 35 minutes individually, add cooking times together and subtract about 5 minutes.
- ☐ If any one food takes over 35 minutes, all the food can be cooked in the time suggested for food taking the longest time.

← *Seasoned Pork Chops, Parsley Potatoes, and Mixed Vegetables cooked all at once in the oven (page 216).*

In order to make the timing and planning easier, we have divided the menus into two types: one-stage and two-stage. For one-stage menus, all the dishes are cooked for the same length of time. The two-stage menus require partial cooking of one main dish and then the addition of other dishes to the oven.

Tips to remember in planning a one- or two-stage menu:

1. Choose a menu from the chart.
2. Review the individual recipe. Occasionally you will find that an ingredient should be prepared ahead; for example, the green pepper and pimiento need to be sautéed before adding the remaining ingredients to Corn and Pepper Pudding (page 163).
3. Check microproof dishes to be sure they fit in the oven together. Change dish sizes if necessary.
4. Place dishes in oven with food from column "A" on the middle metal rack; "B" and "C" are placed on the bottom glass tray.
5. Apply the rules in "Important Guidelines for Timing and Planning." Cooking time for each recipe follows the recipe title in the menu charts. We have not included standing time.
6. Most recipes in whole-meal cooking benefit from stirring, rearranging, or turning about halfway through cooking time.

ONE-STAGE MENUS

Pick one dish from each column in any combination.

A	B	C
All-American Meatballs (15) (page 82)	Corn-Mushroom Scallop (9) (page 158)	Crumb Topped Tomatoes ($4\frac{1}{2}$) (page 159)
Favorite Meatloaf (12) (page 86)	Parsley New Potatoes (12) (page 162)	Frozen Fruit 10 oz. (5) (page 183)
Simple Salmon Ring (35) (page 129)	Broccoli Spears 10 oz. Frozen (8) (page 151)	Lemon Butter Sauce ($1\frac{1}{2}$) (page 176)
Pot Roast in Sherry (70) (page 93)	Corn and Pepper Pudding (19) (page 163)	Cherry Crunch (15) (page 188)
Orange Ginger Pork Chops (22) (page 101)	Pan Baked Potato Halves ($12\frac{3}{4}$) (page 162)	Carrots 10 oz. Frozen (8) (page 151)
Barbecued Chicken (25) (page 109)	Stuffing Mix 6-oz. pkg. (8) (page 153)	Broccoli 10 oz. Frozen (8) (page 151)

To demonstrate one-stage menu planning we have chosen:

(A) All-American Meatballs
page 82 .... 15 min.
(B) Corn-Mushroom Scallop
page 158 .... 9 min.
(C) Crumb Topped Tomatoes
page 159 .... $4\frac{1}{2}$ min.

Note that each individual cooking time takes less than 15 minutes. Using the "Guidelines" (page 207), this one-stage meal will cook in $28\frac{1}{2}$ minutes.

Let's take it step by step:

1. Prepare the All-American Meatballs according to the recipe, omitting the cornstarch and water at this time. Cover with plastic wrap, set aside.
2. Prepare Corn-Mushroom Scallop in $1\frac{1}{2}$-quart casserole. Omit topping of $\frac{1}{4}$ cup of crumbs and butter at this time. Cover with plastic wrap, set aside.
3. Prepare Crumb Topped Tomatoes on 9-inch pie plate.

4. Place middle metal rack in oven. Place meatballs on rack. Place corn dish and tomato dish on bottom glass tray. Cook on HI, 10 minutes.
5. Stir cornstarch and water into meatballs and cover. Stir scalloped corn and cover. Cook on HI, 18½ mintues.
6. Remove from oven and top corn with ¼ cup of crumbs dotted with butter. Let all dishes stand, covered, on heat-resistant surface for 5 minutes before serving.

TWO-STAGE MENUS

Pick one dish from each column in any combination.

A	B	C
Tomato Swiss Steak (63) (page 91)	Parsley New Potatoes (12) (page 162)	Honey Corn Bread Ring (8) (page 68)
Lamb Ragout (40) (page 97)	Pineapple-Zucchini Bread (14½) (page 72)	Frozen Fruit 16 oz. (5) (page 183)
Baked Ham with Pineapple (27) (page 98)	Acorn Squash (11) (page 152)	Golden Apple Chunks (8) (page 192)
Chicken and Vegetables (20) (page 110)	Baked Apples (5) (page 184)	Hard Roll, heat - last 3 min.

Standing time is especially important in whole meal cooking. The Swiss Steak whole meal (above) finishes cooking during standing time (left).

The two-stage procedure is designed to give one recipe a longer time to cook. To demonstrate this we have chosen:

(A) Tomato Swiss Steak
page 91 . . . 1 hour 3 min.
(B) Parsley New Potatoes
page 162 . . . . 12 min.
(C) Honey Corn Bread Ring
page 68 . . . . 8 min.

Using the "Guidelines" (page 207), all foods will be cooked in the time it takes Tomato Swiss Steak, 1 hour 3 minutes.

Let's take it step by step:

1. Prepare Tomato Swiss Steak. Place on bottom glass tray and cook, covered, on HI, 3 minutes.
2. Meanwhile, prepare Parsley New Potatoes. Place in 8×4-inch loaf pan, covered with plastic wrap, and set aside.
3. Prepare Honey Corn Bread Ring.
4. Place middle metal rack in oven. Place steak on middle rack, potatoes and cake on bottom glass tray.
5. Cook on HI, 35 minutes. Rearrange steak, cover. Stir potatoes, cover. If cake is rising unevenly, rotate dish.
6. Cook on HI, 25 minutes, or until steak is cooked. Remove from oven. Drain potatoes, stir in butter, parsley, salt, and pepper. Let all dishes stand 5 minutes before serving.

TEMPERATURE PROBE MENU

Another whole meal method is the use of the temperature probe. All the food will be finished when the meat is ready. HI power is used, even though individual recipes may call for lower power settings. Here is a typical whole meal temperature probe dinner.

Beef Roast Supreme

1 4-pound beef eye-of-round roast
Pan Baked Potato Halves (page 162)
Green Beans Italiano (page 159)

Prepare Pan Baked Potato Halves for cooking as recipe directs in suitable microproof casserole or glass baking dish. Prepare Green Beans Italiano as recipe directs in suitable microproof cookware, but do not cook. Place beef on microproof roasting rack in glass baking dish or other microproof platter. Position middle metal rack in oven. Place beef on middle rack. Insert temperature probe into middle of roast, keeping as near horizontal as possible. Plug temperature probe into oven cavity. Place potato and bean dishes on bottom glass tray. Set temperature probe at 130°F and cook on HI. When temperature probe reaches 95°F, stir vegetables and turn beef roast over, using mitts. Use care not to disturb temperature probe. Continue to cook until done to the preset 130°F internal temperature.

It is sometimes necessary to protect the top of meat with a narrow strip of foil if it shows signs of becoming overdone in that area. Cover dishes as required in individual recipes.

Many meat and vegetable combinations can be used with the temperature probe method. The key to success is to remember that you never want to use temperature probe settings that vary from the proper internal temperature necessary for the meat to be done. Use this recipe as a guide in converting your own whole meal dinners to the temperature probe method.

With practice and imagination you will enjoy trying different combinations. For example, here is a special menu method that puts the meat on the bottom glass tray for the second stage to give it a simmer effect, while the microwave energy is concentrated on the vegetables.

Country Style Ribs
page 99 ...... 1 hour 5 min.
4 Corn-on-the-Cob
page 151 .... 12 min.
4 Baked Potatoes (6 oz. each)
page 152 .... 12 min.

Let's take it step by step:

1. Prepare Country Style Ribs. Cook on 50, 35 minutes; drain.
2. Meanwhile, remove husks and silk from each ear of corn. Wrap each ear individually in waxed paper.

3. Wash and remove any blemishes from potatoes; pierce. Brush both sides of ribs with sauce; cover with plastic wrap.
4. Place middle metal rack in oven. Place ribs on bottom glass tray. Place corn, spoke-fashion, on middle rack; place one potato between each ear of corn. Cook on HI, 30 minutes, or until cooked. Turn vegetables over after 15 minutes.
5. Let stand, covered, 5 minutes before serving.

Now you know the basics for preparing your own whole meals. The following pages give you seven wonderful whole meals included among the 300 preset recipes of your Kenmore Spacemanster Auto Recipe 300 Microwave Oven. Be sure to observe the recommended dish placement.

Recipe No. 296

Scrambled Eggs, Bacon, and Sweet Rolls

Preset Cooking Time: 12 minutes

6 large eggs
⅓ cup milk
2 tablespoons butter, melted
6 slices bacon
6 sweet rolls

Position metal rack in oven. Combine eggs, milk, and butter in 1-quart microproof casserole; beat with fork until blended. Cover; set aside. Arrange bacon on paper towel-lined microproof plate. Cover with paper towel; set aside. Arrange rolls on microproof plate; set aside. Arrange egg mixture and bacon in oven as shown in "A." Set recipe number 296. Touch START. *(Oven cooks: HI, 4 minutes.)*

At Pause, stir eggs. Cover. Touch START. *(Oven cooks: HI, 3 minutes.)*

At Pause, stir eggs. Cover. Place rolls in oven as shown in "B." Touch START. *(Oven cooks: HI, 2 minutes; stands: 0, 3 minutes.)*

Stir eggs before serving

4 to 6 servings

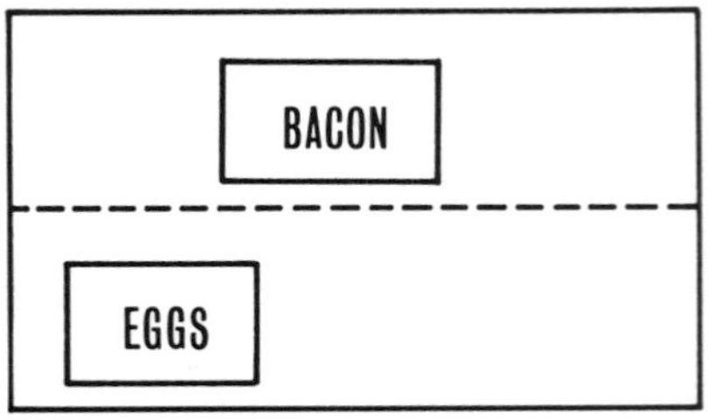

A

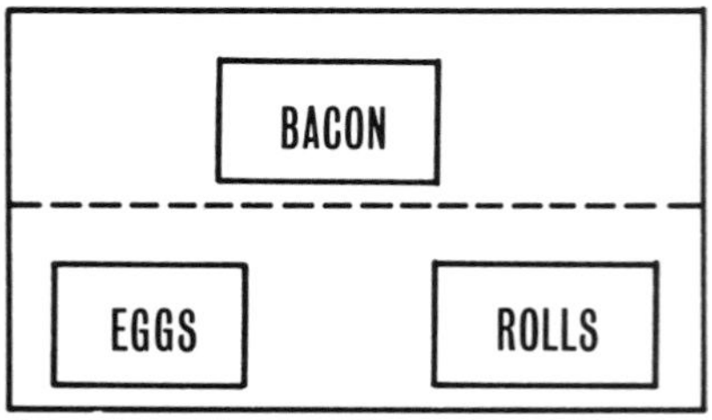

B

Recipe No. 297

Beef Stew, Garlic Bread, and Pudding

Preset Cooking Time: 13 minutes

- 1 can (24 ounces) beef stew
- 1/4 cup butter, melted
- 1/2 teaspoon garlic powder
- 1/2 pound French bread, cut into 1-inch thick slices
- 1 package (3 1/8 ounces) pudding mix
- 2 cups milk

Position metal rack in oven. Pour stew into 1-quart microproof casserole. Cover; set aside. Combine butter and garlic powder. Brush both sides of bread slices with butter mixture. Reshape into loaf and wrap in paper towels. Place on microproof plate; set aside. Place pudding mix in 1-quart microproof casserole. Stir in milk; set aside. Arrange stew and pudding mixture in oven as shown in "A." Set recipe number 297. Touch START. *(Oven cooks: HI, 5 minutes.)*

At Pause, stir stew and pudding. Cover stew. Touch START. *(Oven cooks: HI, 3 1/2 minutes.)*

At Pause, stir stew and pudding. Change position as shown in "B". Place bread in oven as shown in "B." Touch START. *(Oven cooks: HI, 4 1/2 minutes.)*

3 servings

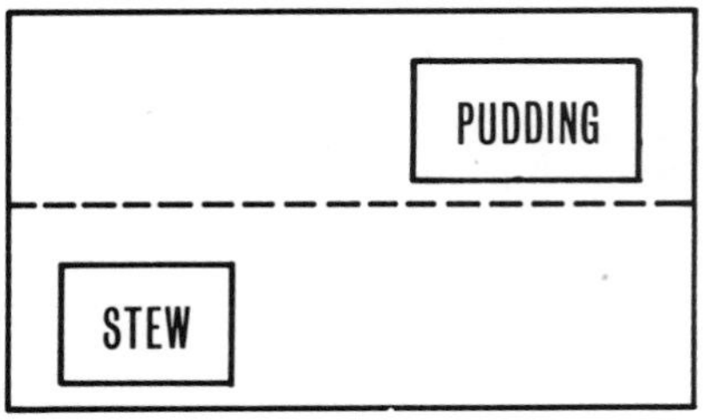

A

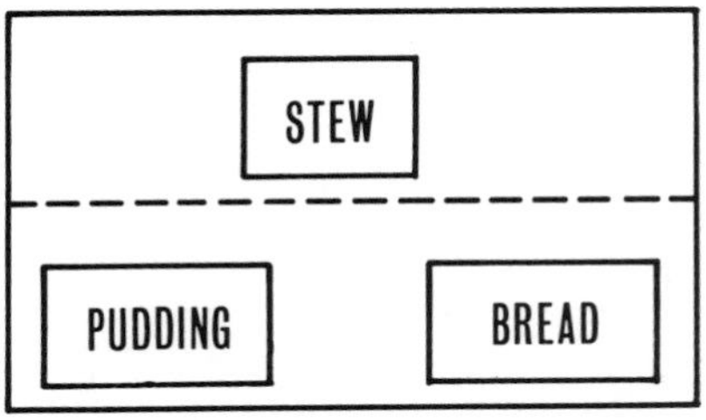

B

Recipe No. 297 Alternate

Chili, Corn Muffins, and Apple Crisp

Preset Cooking Time: 13 minutes

1 can (25 ounces) chili
3 corn muffins
1 recipe Apple Crisp (below)

Position metal rack in oven. Pour chili into 1½-quart microproof casserole. Cover; set aside. Wrap corn muffins in paper towels; set aside. Prepare Apple Crisp batter as directed below. Cover with waxed paper. Arrange chili and Apple Crisp in oven as shown in "A." Set recipe number 297. Touch START. *(Oven cooks: HI, 5 minutes.)*

At Pause, stir chili. Cover. Rotate dishes and change position as shown in "B." Touch START. *(Oven cooks: HI, 3½ minutes.)*

At Pause, stir chili. Cover. Place muffins in oven as shown in "C." Touch START. *(Oven cooks: HI, 4½ minutes.)*

Let Apple Crisp stand 3 minutes before serving.

3 servings

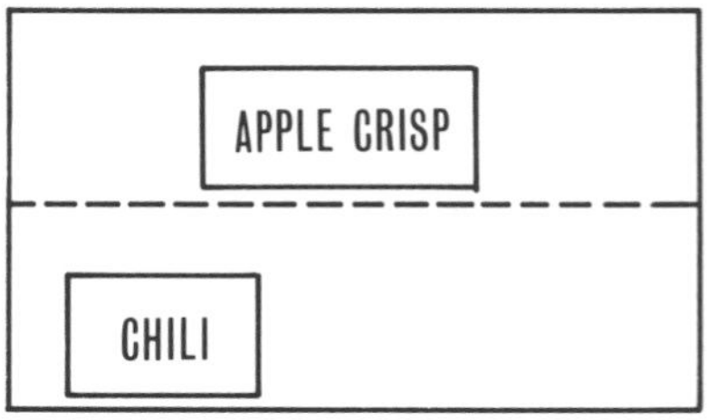

A

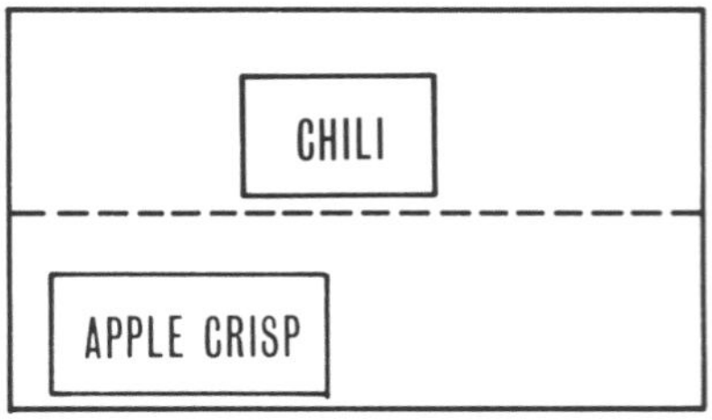

B

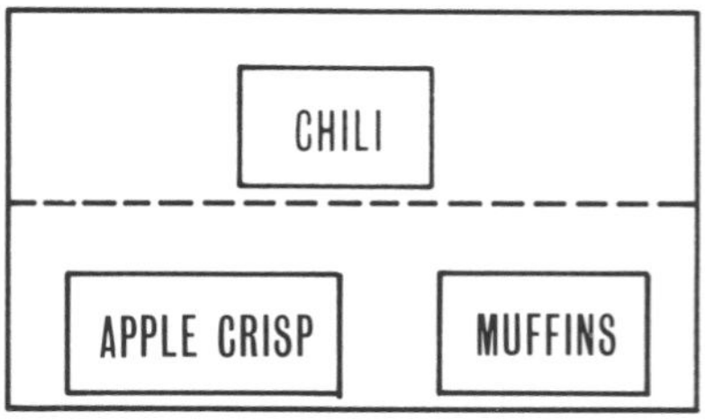

C

Apple Crisp

4 cups sliced tart apples, peeled
½ cup rolled oats
¼ cup butter or margarine
¼ cup all-purpose flour
¼ cup firmly packed brown sugar
1 teaspoon lemon juice
½ teaspoon cinnamon
⅛ teaspoon nutmeg

Arrange apple slices in 8-inch square microproof baking dish. Combine remaining ingredients; blend well. Crumble over apples.

Recipe No. 298

Baked Chicken, Rice, and Asparagus

Preset Cooking Time: 26 minutes

- 3/4 cup corn-flake crumbs
- 1/3 cup grated Parmesan cheese
- 1 broiler-fryer chicken (2 1/2 to 3 pounds), quartered
- 1/4 cup butter, melted
- 1 package (11 ounces) frozen rice in pouch
- 2 cans (14 1/2 ounces each) asparagus spears, drained

Position metal rack in oven. Combine corn-flake crumbs and cheese. Brush chicken lightly with butter; coat with crumb mixture. Arrange chicken in large microproof baking dish, skin-side up, with thickest parts toward outside of dish. Cover with waxed paper; set aside. Place rice in pouch on small microproof plate; slit pouch; set aside. Place asparagus in 8×4-inch microproof loaf pan. Cover with plastic wrap. Arrange all 3 dishes in oven as shown in "A." Set recipe number 298. Touch START. *(Oven cooks: HI, 10 minutes.)*

At Pause, rotate chicken. Touch START. *(Oven cooks: HI 10 minutes.)*

At Pause, rotate rice one-quarter turn. Touch START. *(Oven cooks: HI, 4 minutes.)*

At Pause, remove chicken and asparagus from oven. Rotate rice as shown in "B." Touch START. *(Oven cooks: HI, 2 minutes.)*

3 to 4 servings

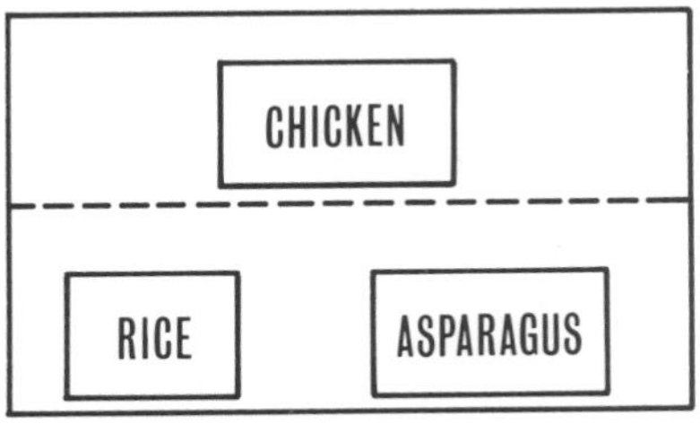

A

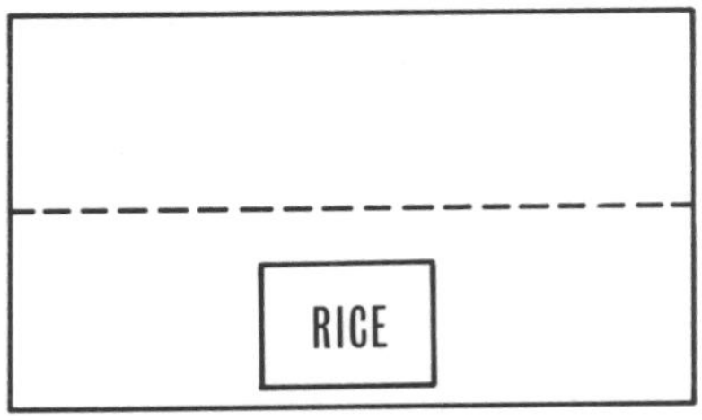

B

Recipe No. 298 Alternate

Seasoned Pork Chops, Parsley Potatoes, and Mixed Vegetables

Preset Cooking Time: 26 minutes

- 1 envelope ($2\frac{1}{4}$ ounces) seasoned coating mix for pork
- 4 pork chops ($1\frac{1}{4}$ pounds)
- 3 potatoes (5 ounces each), peeled and cut into $\frac{3}{4}$-inch cubes
- $\frac{1}{4}$ cup water
- 1 can (16 ounces) mixed vegetables, drained
- Butter or margarine
- 1 tablespoon chopped parsley

Position metal rack in oven. Empty coating mix into plastic bag. Shake pork chops, 1 at a time, in coating mix. Place chops in 12×7-inch microproof baking dish. Cover with waxed paper; set aside. Place potatoes and water in 8×4-inch microproof loaf pan. Cover with plastic wrap; set aside. Place mixed vegetables in 1-quart microproof casserole. Arrange all 3 dishes in oven as shown in "A." Set recipe number 298. Touch START. *(Oven cooks: HI, 10 minutes.)*

At Pause, turn chops over. Cover. Touch START. *(Oven cooks: HI 10 minutes.)*

At Pause, stir potatoes. Cover. Touch START. *(Oven cooks: HI, 4 minutes.)*

At Pause, check pork chops. If done, remove from oven. Touch START. *(Oven cooks: HI, 2 minutes.)*

Remove all dishes from oven. Stir vegetables. Dot potatoes with butter, and sprinkle with parsley before serving.

3 to 4 servings

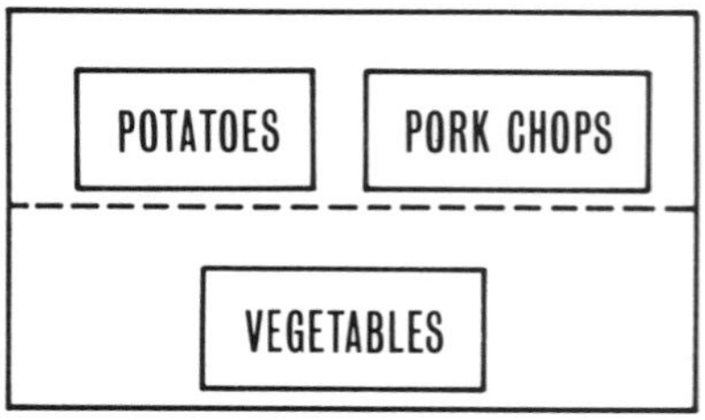

A

Recipe No. 299

Beef & Spaghetti Casserole, Green Peas, and Baked Apple Chunks

Preset Cooking Time: 28 minutes

- 1 package (7½ ounces) spaghetti meat-noodle main dish mix
- 1 pound lean ground beef
- 4 cups hot water
- 1 package (10 ounces) frozen green peas
- 1 recipe Baked Apple Chunks (below)

Position metal rack in oven. Prepare meat-noodle mix, adding beef and hot water as directed on package. Place in 2-quart microproof casserole. Cover; set aside. Place peas in 1-quart microproof casserole. Cover; set aside. Prepare Baked Apple Chunks as directed below. Cover with plastic wrap. Arrange beef mixture and Baked Apple Chunks in oven as shown in "A." Set recipe number 299. Touch START. *(Oven cooks: HI, 20 minutes.)*

At Pause, stir beef mixture and Baked Apple Chunks. Cover both casseroles. Arrange peas in oven as shown in "B." Touch START. *(Oven cooks: HI, 5 minutes.)*

At Pause, remove casserole. Stir apples. Leave dishes as shown in "C". Touch START. *(Oven cooks: HI 3 minutes.)*

4 servings

Baked Apple Chunks

- 4 tart medium cooking apples, peeled, cored, and cut into quarters
- ¼ cup firmly packed brown sugar
- 1 teaspoon cinnamon
- 2 tablespoons butter or margarine

Place apples in 8 × 4-inch microproof loaf pan. Combine brown sugar and cinnamon; blend well. Crumble over apples. Dot with butter.

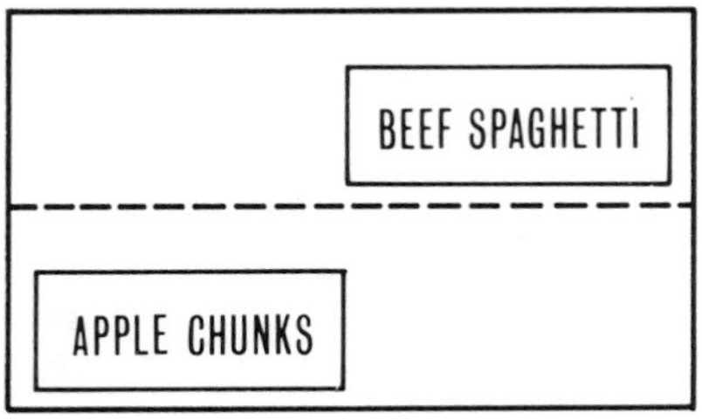

A

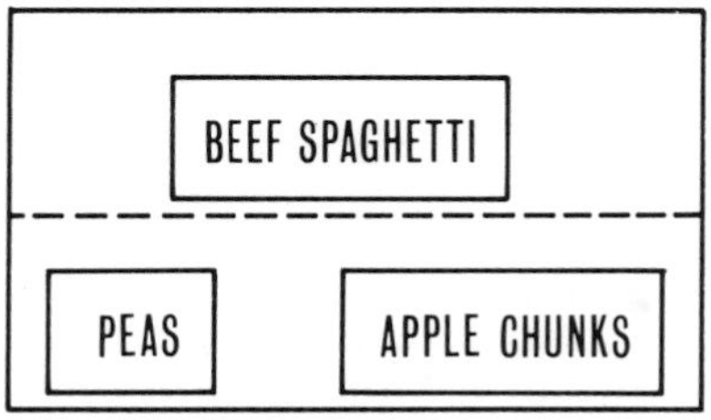

B

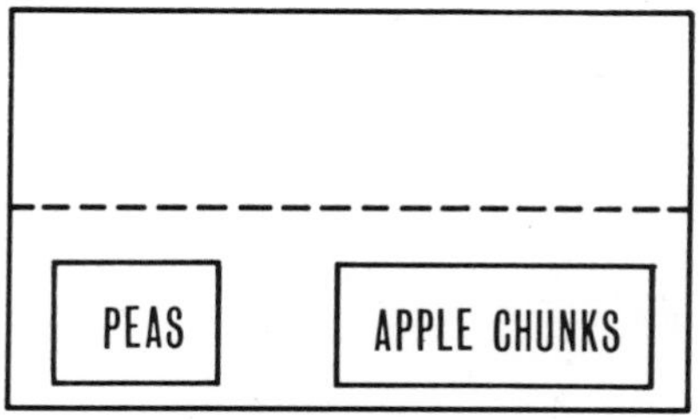

C

Recipe No. 300

Meatloaf, Yellow Squash, and Chocolate Fudge Layer Cake

Preset Cooking Time: 23 minutes

- 1 recipe Meatloaf (below)
- 1 recipe Chocolate Fudge Layer Cake (below)
- 1 medium yellow squash, peeled and thinly sliced
- 1 tablespoon butter
- ¼ teaspoon salt
- Whipped cream

Position metal rack in oven. Prepare Meatloaf and Chocolate Fudge Layer Cake as directed below; set aside. Place squash in 8×4-inch microproof loaf pan. Cover with plastic wrap. Arrange all 3 dishes in oven as shown in "A." Set recipe number 300. Touch START. *(Oven cooks: HI, 15 minutes.)*

At Pause, rotate meatloaf and cake dishes one-half turn. Stir squash; cover. Touch START. *(Oven cooks: HI, 7 minutes.)*

At Pause, remove meatloaf. Touch START. *(Oven cooks: HI, 1 minute.)*

Stir butter and salt into squash. Let cake stand 3 to 5 minutes. Gently twist glass to remove. Invert cake onto serving plate. Remove waxed paper. Slice and serve topped with whipped cream.

6 servings

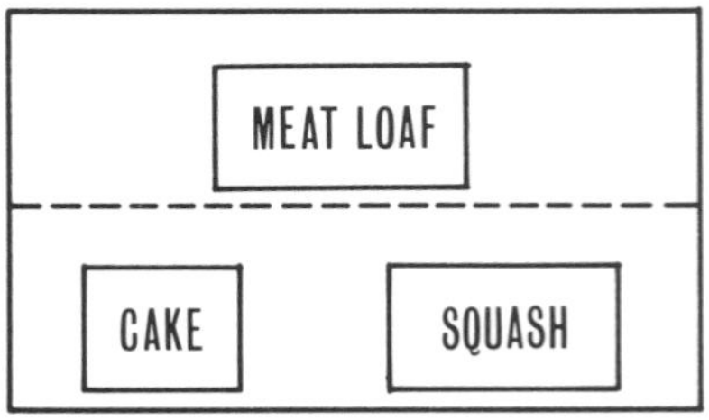

A

Meatloaf

- 1½ pounds lean ground beef
- 2 cups soft bread crumbs
- 1 can (8 ounces) tomato sauce, divided
- ½ cup finely chopped onion
- ¼ cup finely chopped green pepper
- 1 large egg
- 1½ teaspoons salt

Combine beef, bread crumbs, ½ cup tomato sauce, onion, green pepper, egg, and salt; blend well. Pack into 8-inch round microproof baking dish. Insert straight-sided, 2-inch diameter glass, open end up, into center of dish. Pour remaining sauce over beef mixture.

Chocolate Fudge Layer Cake

- 1 package (15 ounces) snacking chocolate fudge cake mix

Prepare cake batter as directed on package. Line bottom of 9-inch round microproof baking dish with waxed paper. Place custard cup, open end up, in center of dish. Pour batter into dish.

A 6-cup microproof Bundt-type pan or ring mold can be substituted for baking dish with glass.

Index

D